Dinah

STUMBLING ON N

CW00468495

BY THE SAME AUTHOR

ABOUT THE SUSSEX SNOWDROP TRUST

The Trust (registered charity 1096622) was set up to provide help for families in Sussex with children suffering from life-threatening or life-limiting illnesses, giving financial assistance to affected families, providing practical care and compassionate support, and supplying specialist equipment to meet the day-to-day needs of the children. Many thanks for supporting the Trust by buying this book.

STUMBLING ON MOUNTAINS

BY DAVID BATHURST

[signature]

with very best
wishes

December 2015

First published in 2015 by

Walk & Write Publications
41 Park Road
Yapton
Arundel
West Sussex BN18 0JE

© David Bathurst 2015

All rights reserved

No part of this book may be reproduced by any means,
nor transmitted into a machine language, without the
written permission of the publisher.

The right of David Bathurst to be identified as the author
of this work has been asserted by him in accordance
with the Copyright, Designs and Patents Act 1988.

Cover and typesetting by the Better Book Company,
5 Lime Close, Chichester PO19 6SW

Printed in the UK by Imprint Digital, Seychelles Farm,
Upton Pyne, Devon EX5 5HY

British Library Cataloguing-in-Publication Data.
A catalogue record for this book is available from the
British Library.

ISBN 978-0-9933241-0-9

The Author is indebted to Terence Whitlock for the
cover illustration

The Author also acknowledges the kind assistance of
Michael and Phil in preparing the script for publication,
and wishes to thank Lorena, Laura and Debbie for their
suggestions and encouragement, and Susan and Jenny
for their love and support.

1

Perranuthnoe(n) – discovery, on consulting your map in driving rain and force 8 winds to check the route you're walking, that the map is double sided and the section you need is on the reverse side requiring entire map to be refolded inside out

I've never understood why on holiday we do things we would never think worthwhile doing at home. Maybe because there's nothing else to do. Spend eight or nine hours getting from home to our cottage, drive out in the evening to try and find a Sainsbury's within twenty miles, come back to the cottage, attempt unsuccessfully to work the remote, go to bed, wake up on Sunday, how on earth are we going to fill the next fifteen hours. Oh look, a pile of leaflets on the sitting room table. A Paper Clip Museum with souvenir shop and café (no hot food served after 2pm). Woodland Paradise with rides on Thomas the Tank Engine and the opportunity to visit Henry the Clown and his friend Ollie the Owl(supplement payable, booking advisable in high season). Antique Pottery and Sheep-Shearing Centre, ring to confirm opening times, no dogs please. And when we've exhausted these and in the process blown our entertainment budget for the week by Thursday lunchtime, it's on with the wellies and the pacamacs because surprise surprise it will always be raining by now, and we'll be walking. For fun.

Walking. I've never got it. I accept the need to walk when I have to. When I was fourteen my humanities teacher persuaded me to spend a day in a wheelchair and then do a piece in the school magazine about what it was like. I spent the day in the wheelchair but never got round to writing the article. It would have been a waste of time anyway because a few weeks later a guy in the year above had an accident and was able to write a piece in the school magazine about what it was like to be in a wheelchair for life. It all taught me never to take my mobility for granted. But it didn't teach me to devote my precious annual leave to fiddling with gaiters, trotting over bogs, pricking blisters or dodging bullocks. My views haven't changed. If I want to admire the scenery I've a good hundred million screensaver choices the press of my laptop button away. Getting from A to B, if B is so great, why not start and finish there. As for circular walks, if you were going to finish at the same point that you started why bother to start at all.

Here we are in Norfolk and it's our last full day, and Louise has downloaded a coastal wildlife walk. Most of our walks on holiday are short enough to ensure we're back at our cottage in time to stick *Countdown* on Channel 4. But with this one we'll be lucky if we catch the late-night nude wrestling on Challenge.

I'd suggested to Louise we just had a lazy day and enjoyed our immediate surroundings. But she said we needed some exercise after yesterday. I'd loved yesterday – well, almost all of yesterday. Louise managed to sort out the fuses first thing which meant I got the full English breakfast she'd promised. We found a town where there were shops on the high street that still sold fresh fish and bathroom accessories and CD's, and the money we paid was going back to local people and the local economy and not multi-billionaires or monster retail conglomerates. Louise and Katie went off and shopped for dinner and Louise bought Katie a swimming costume and bucket and spade. Meanwhile I found a bookshop where I got a newly-published football annual, and a clothes shop where I got Louise a leather jacket and deep purple top and knee-length denim skirt. Then we came home and she got the washing machine to work and cooked us fish and chips. I said a takeaway would be easier but she said she didn't mind the extra washing up, home-cooked was much better. Between them they got the DVD player to work after it had broken down the night before, and we watched a film and Katie went to bed. Then Louise unwrapped the stuff I'd bought her. At once her lift button lit up and her face descended three floors. And I've only gone and lost the wretched receipt.

The walk Louise has planned is a section of the north Norfolk coast. Looking out of the window from the breakfast table I see that weatherwise it's neither one thing nor the other. There's not the plip-plip-plop of little April showers but no April sunshine either. Just a uniform layer of obstinate low cloud. And as I gaze and think of the two hundred and eighty-four things I'd rather be doing with a morning off work, I realise that Louise is talking to me.

'Michael, darling.'

'Mmmm?'

'Is there anyone there?'

'Mmm hmm.'

'Have you done the one thing I asked you to do this morning?'

'Er ... I ...'

'Do you want to phone a friend or ask the audience?' She rises from the table. 'I'll give you a clue, shall I. The upstairs cupboard. That's the ... altogether now, from the top, on the count of three ... the upstairs cupboard. Now, Houston, are you receiving me?'

'Find Katie's coat.'

'Which coat, dearest?'

'Her green one.'

'Wrong, Michael.' There's no mistaking the glee in her eyes. 'It would have been the green one if you hadn't ruined the green one. The correct answer is the red one. With white dots. Which she's getting too big for. Not that you'll have noticed.' She takes my empty cereal bowl, begins to fill the sink with water, squirts in some washing-up liquid, and points to the teacloth hanging on the radiator. 'Any chance of ...'

'Actually, I ...'

'Forget it.' She hurls the dirty plates into the bowl. 'I can always tell when you're in Arsenalworld.'

'I wasn't. Not then.'

'Not that you seem to know what to do with all that rubbish you're carrying around.' Two cereal bowls come spinning out of the water. 'I mean, what happened to that *Mastermind* application I downloaded for you?' She clears her throat. 'Mike Partridge, you have two minutes on Arsenal Football Club, 300 BC to the present.'

'You're forgetting one thing.'

'What?'

'You need general knowledge,' I tell her. 'I can see it now. "Who did Arsenal beat on New Year's Day 1980. Southampton away, one-nil, Willie Young. Who was brought on as Arsenal's sub in the 1979 FA Cup Final. Steve Walford, nearly lost them the match. What was the currency in Hitler's Germany ... the Primark, wasn't it? And at the end of that general knowledge round, Mike Partridge, your score has gone up by precisely zero."'

'Okay, fine.' Amidst an avalanche of creamy white suds she begins to whip the freshly-washed cutlery from the sink and fling it onto the draining board. 'Just try and enjoy being a dad, then, Mike. Enjoy today. Enjoy your daughter for once. Talk to her for once.'

'I always talk to her.'

A spoon with a death wish leaps from the soapy depths and throws itself onto the floor with a clatter. I watch while she picks it up and hurls it back into the sink. 'You know what I mean. Why not start now. While I'm finishing this. Have a game with her maybe.'

'Good idea. What about a netball match.'

'I'm not laughing, Michael. It's not funny any more.'

*

As we drive the nine miles to the start of the walk at Burnham Overy Staithe I'm thinking, I've never seen so much sky, and all of it is a single shade of unappetising light grey. With flat fields to the right and left of us – Norfolk doesn't do hills – and the open sea ahead, the grey just never seems to stop. We park up and spend fifteen minutes getting changed and ready then set off. Katie's not keen and her mum has to coax her. 'I used to love walking at your age,' Louise says. I can tell by looking at Katie that she doesn't believe it any more than I do. Louise directs us eastwards, aiming for Wells-next-the-Sea via Holkham Nature Reserve and Holkham village. It's bearable to begin with, the way through the marsh made easy for us by a wooden boardwalk, but then the boardwalk peters out and we're trudging through sand. Not firm sand, sandcastle-building sand, but dune sand, where each step sees the shoe or boot descending what feels like a hundred feet below sea level and you feel as though you need specialist lifting equipment to yank it out again. Repeat at least ten thousand times, add salt and pepper to taste, and I reckon that'll have got us about a quarter of the way there. I'm looking for some scenic payback but I can't see any. There's initially just farmland and then trees to the right, and we've enough of that in Sussex, and sea across the marsh to the left, and we've a bit of that off Sussex as well. Plus all that sky, too much sky. Louise reminds us that the highlight of this walk is supposed to be the bird life. She announces that if we look carefully we may see curlew, dunlin, finch, skylark, little tern, common tern, ringed plover, wryneck, fieldfare, teal, wigeon and all stations to Southend Central. Her ornithological knowledge might have impressed me more had she not been reading direct from the guidebook. Or if she was able to spot a single real feathered specimen during however long we're picking our way across the sands. It seems like days. I guess that to boast of having witnessed the flight of a marsh harrier or red-throated diver might, just might, have persuaded me that this whole exercise was worthwhile. But all I've managed to identify so far is one great tit and that was only as a result of seeing my reflection in a glass-fronted information board. We could have gone to Dorset. Louise wanted Dorset. Half the driving, and scenery that must be better than this. But oh no, Mike, you had to go for Norfolk because the cottage in Norfolk had all the sports and movie channels and the one in Dorset didn't.

Louise and Katie aren't finding the going any easier or more rewarding so we give up. We turn round and wade our way back to the boardwalk and the village where we started. We all agree that if we never see another grain of sand again it'll be a hundred years too soon. We come across a green and Louise produces two bats and a ball, originally intended for the beach. And while she and Katie begin a game which seems to combine tennis and keepy-uppy I withdraw to a bench and continue checking the football annual for errors about Arsenal. I've found three and we're only on page xvii. Katie is giggling. Her giggle never fails to make other people giggle. She's twice today said I'm the best dad in the world. She's confirmed it in writing on the inside page of my football annual using one of her new Sharpie pens. She's always saying thank you for what we do for her, never takes us for granted. I watch as she hits the ball high into the air and as it descends Louise misses it by a mile. A moment later my daughter's turning round and leaping towards me. 'I won, I won Daddy,' she shrills, and puts her arms round me.

Her smile could light up the whole of New York. There's a warm ebullience in her bluey-grey eyes and ripples of ginger hair, and that hair clothes a head that bubbles with compassion and an amazing degree of empathy and insight for a child of ten years. With her every look, her every word, her every smile, she is the daughter any dad-to-be always longed and prayed for.

But I just can't love her. However much I want to, I can't.

*

I fancy a coffee and bacon sandwich after our walk. But even though we're not due to vacate our cottage for another twenty hours or so, Louise is desperate to start packing within the next two. She suggests she leaves Katie and me in Cromer; she can then drive straight back to the cottage from there while Katie and I follow on by train. Some father-daughter time and the chance for me, as she says, to stuff another hundredweight of grease and carbohydrate down my gob. We agree I'll call her when we get to the station and she'll pick us up from there.

We get to Cromer and it doesn't take us long to find an ideal eating place, neither your greasy spoon nor one that's going to make significant further inroads into holiday money that ceased to exist when, having explored a windmill yesterday afternoon, we paid 50p for a souvenir guide pamphlet. Louise, who's been going on about my excess baggage for some weeks now, suggested I go for a crab and salad platter, more nutritious, fewer calories and a local speciality that's unlikely to be on offer at home. But if it's on the menu it's too far down, and hasn't even made the play-off places; it's the Triple Decker All-Day Breakfast Buster that's got in first, and no others need apply. Meanwhile, Katie opts for a child's portion of chicken nuggets and chips which she downs in two mouthfuls. Then we adjourn to the station. Our train's on time but the previous one was cancelled and there's a large crowd on the platform. As we're waiting for the train to arrive, Katie says she's still hungry. There's a convenience store just next to the station and we've enough time to go in. Louise would have sought out the fruit and vegetables and insisted Katie filled her still rumbling stomach with those, but the clock's ticking and the loose bananas department is out of view. However the 20 per cent-extra-added bags of Walkers are no more than three yards away, and within similar radius is a queue-less checkout. Five minutes later, the train is moving off, it's standing room only, and Katie's downed the last crisp in the packet.

Crisp. It makes my heart jump. Not Walkers Crisp. George Crisp. Death by dangerous driving and taking without consent, in court on Tuesday, and I'm prosecuting it. The family of the deceased are furious that he wasn't charged with manslaughter. They've not only been bothering us on a virtually hourly basis but have been in regular contact with their MP, the Director of Public Prosecutions and Buckingham Palace, and there's talk that they're now lobbying the United Nations. Consequently we're under immense pressure to get it home.

I enjoy my work. I just don't particularly enjoy my boss Howard. His emails are all the same: no message, just a title. It's usually PLEASE RING ME NOW, only without the please. So I'll ring him and he'll demand "What's going on" or if I've delayed more than three minutes since he sent the email, "What the hell is going on." He knows his boundaries in that regard, just, but in frightening the proverbial out of his staff he knows no boundaries. He's four years younger than I am, has a First from Oxford, has moved up the Crown Prosecution Service tree faster than it takes me to change a vest at Marks & Spencer, and just the sound of his voice turns strong men and women to milky yellow blancmange. He does have his good points. In some ways, I wish he didn't. Someone could then have pulled the plug on him long before. But he has his human side and that is his salvation. Like me, he knows his footie and loves his footie. He has a season ticket at Crystal Palace and follows them everywhere. And every time he summons me to his office I'm wishing he was off following them to a Europa League group stage match somewhere in the former Yugoslavia. Because I know he's going to pick my latest piece of advocacy or file reviewing to bits.

I suppose I could have appealed my final warning. An oversight in page two of an email from the police. His words are still ringing in my ear. "A burglar gets off scot free, and all because you don't do page twos." There was a lot more to it than that but the investigating officer didn't want to know and Howard didn't want to know. Now he's got me doing this Crisp matter. Not complex at all, but a test case. A test for me that is. To understand how decisions we make impact on the community. If I mess this up, I can kiss goodbye to my career, my mortgage payments and my Thursday jam sponge and custard at Mrs Peggotty's in Longhill Street. And now the trial is just two working days away and although the file was allocated to me a week before I went on leave, well, never mind my not doing page twos, I've not made it to page one yet.

And the next thing I know the train is slowing down and the conductor's announcing our stop. I get straight on the phone to Louise to tell her we're nearly there, and the moment I've hung up I realise the train is stationary and we are there. I yell to Katie to get up and move herself and we're charging down the aisle to the lobby area by the doors, and already people are getting on and I'm in their way and they're in mine. The "doors closing" beeps begin and I grab Katie's hand and pull her off the train and immediately the doors slide shut and the train moves away. Hand in hand we hurry off the platform. As we reach the ticket barrier I turn to my right to encourage Katie forward and I look at her and it isn't Katie.

2

Ruthwaite(n) – dutiful expression of thanks offered to an elderly relative for her Christmas gift of a triple pack of inferior-make walking socks

She's just the same height, and has the same hair colour, and even the same coat. I'm close, very close, but the Havanas are out of reach, because it's not our daughter.

I reassure myself that any second now I'll wake up in my bed and come to my senses then get back to sleep again and before I know it Katie'll be running into our room at quarter to eight as normal and using Louise's face as a trampoline. Then the reality hits and I'm paralysed. I'm just stood there looking at this total stranger and I'm still holding her hand. And while she in turn stares at me in bewilderment, I'm starting to quiver and I'm starting to hyperventilate.

The girl doesn't cry or say anything. Her expression hasn't changed at all. It's a study in numbness and shock. It's scarier than crying; it's the face of someone whose new situation has robbed her of the ability to be who she is. I realise I'm still holding her hand but I don't dare let it go.

What to do. What the hell to do. There are no railway staff in sight and anyway I'm not sure what they could do or say. I think about going out to meet Louise and asking her advice but think better of it within the millisecond. Then comes a welcome shaft of lucidity and rationality among the swirling mist of fear. Katie and this child's parent or guardian will have got off the train at the next stop and will be waiting on the platform. Louise need never know. I check the timetable and a glance at the departure board shows there's another train to that stop leaving in twenty minutes.

'Where's Mummy?'

She hasn't just spoken. She's shrilled. She's hollered. For a minute I think the roof of the station has blown off. The words echo and bounce round the station buildings and set my head on fire. People look round. People on my platform. People on the opposite platform. And, I would guess, people on every station platform within a radius of five miles. I don't think they're worried for her. Every child cries for their mum at some stage. They're looks of sympathy, of understanding, bringing back memories of those times in their own lives when only mum, nobody else, will do.

I just pray she won't start crying for her dad.

'I know, sweetheart, I know. We'll find her in just a minute or two. Was she on that train?'

She nods and now bursts into tears.

The next train comes in. I point to it. 'We'll be on this train and back with your mummy in no time.'

'I want Mummy.' This time it isn't that loud; it's not Rolling Stones or T Rex loud. But I'm convinced it's going to rip my ears off and propel them into the next county.

We get in and move off. I ring Louise and tell her there's been a bit of a hold-up then turn to the girl again.

'What's your name?'

'Ellie.'

'Where do you live, Ellie?'

She mumbles something.

'Sorry, what was that?'

Again she offers a mumble. I hear with my little ear something beginning with B: Bog or Bod something, I think. It could be Bodmin, it could be Bogota, it could be Bognor. It's not important, not yet, and anyway we're slowing down. The train draws up in the station and the doors slide open and we step onto the platform.

There's nobody there.

I drag Ellie to the ticket office, and now she's howling. The ticket office is open but the grey-shirted clerk behind the window seems to be the only station staff member about. There's a man buying a ticket from him: it's not just a quick single ticket to the next station down the line, but a return to Glasgow, travelling there via Sheffield and Leeds, coming back via Manchester, Bristol, Plymouth and Tierra del Fuego, and using compensation vouchers from a previous journey in part-payment. After three minutes or so, as they go into the relative merits of an additional change at Todmorden, for which there will apparently be a substantial fare increase but with the benefit of being able to leave Peterborough forty-eight minutes later, I push him out of the way. And I screech. 'This is an emergency.' It all comes out in a rush. I've the wrong child, it's my stupid mistake, has it been reported, please, you've got to help. I try to describe Katie but even though I've seen her pretty much every day since she came into our lives I can't even tell the man what colour her eyes are. I plead. I beg. I implore. And as I plead, and beg, and implore, spasms are breaking out all over me and beads of sweat are dripping off my chin and my earlobes and other parts of the body I never knew sweat could reach.

'Wait a sec,' he grunts. He disappears. And the Glasgow-bound traveller's looking at me as though far from simply delaying the finalisation of the arrangements for his Homeric odyssey I've just murdered his wife and ripped the testicles off his schnauzer.

Grey shirt comes back. 'Colleague of mine says small child of your description, with adult female, have just got on a train going back the other way, couple of minutes ago.'

'When's the next one?'

'Seventeen minutes.'

It's not long in the context of the lifetime of planet Earth but it's still at least seventeen decades longer than I can stand. I think about grabbing something from the café just outside the station but one look at the food being dispensed is enough. I don't want the provision of sandwiches made from foam rubber to be added to the child abduction indictment.

The train comes in and we board and take our seats. The howls die down. As soon as we move, I get on the phone to Louise again. She answers almost straight away.

'Just on the way home now.'

'Had a good afternoon together?'

'Er … yeah. Great.'

'All well?'

'Fine.'

'You scum. You lying scum.'

'Sorry?'

'You're telling me you'll be sorry.'

I hang up and the train begins to slow down. The automated tannoy is announcing our imminent arrival. I don't want to be imminently arriving at all. I don't want to be imminently arriving anywhere. I want to be staying on board, wherever the train happens to take me. Wherever there's nobody who knows what a lying scum I am.

'Soon be with your mummy and daddy, Ellie.'

'I haven't got a daddy.'

And then the floodgates burst open once more. I remember that I've a pack of tissues in one of the pockets of my rucksack. I pull it out and I can't open the thing. I hand the whole packet to her and she doesn't try to open it, but just hugs the cellophane wrapping to her sodden cheeks, while I feel slivers of ice coursing through every one of my veins.

Then we draw up at the platform and the train stops. I take Ellie's hand and drag her to one of the sets of sliding doors.

The welcoming committee is waiting on the platform, directly in front of us. There's Louise and Katie holding hands; even through the glass I notice Louise's expression, and her face is a study of motherly relief and wifely rage, motherly joy and wifely fury. And immediately adjacent to them stands a woman wiping her eyes in which there's not so much anger as pure hatred.

The doors slide open. Ellie tears her hand from mine and with a scream of anguished joy she flings herself into the woman's embrace.

'An innocent mistake.' I don't know what else I dare to say.

I expect the woman to make some ill-chosen comments about my parentage but she says nothing, just shakes her head. Then she seizes Ellie's hand, and a moment later they've disappeared.

I move towards Katie and stretch out my hand to her but she turns away and retreats into Louise's arms. I'm used to her doing it in fun. Usually it's when I've had a go at her for disrupting my weekly runthrough of Arsenal's League Cup results, and I'm able to laugh it off and go back to my work. But the fact that now she's doing it for real turns my knees to water.

*

The car journey back to the cottage doesn't pass in complete silence. Katie's now asking her mum what she can watch when we get home and Louise says it's getting late, and why doesn't she just have something to eat then play with her Lego instead. However traumatic the experience has been for her, her appetite at any rate seems unaffected. On arrival back at the cottage she scoffs not only a tuna sandwich but also a portion of fresh fruit salad and natural yogurt with separate helping of chocolate pieces. I go up to say good night, just as I always do at home, and she thanks me for a lovely day and gives me a kiss. Then I come down and Louise goes up to see her, just as she always does at home. Normal service would seem to have been resumed.

But I'm not fooled and it doesn't take more than three seconds after Louise has rejoined me in the lounge for the lights to dim and the main feature to start.

'I don't believe you, Michael! I just don't flaming believe you!'

'It was easily done. More easily done than you might think.'

'You only had to look at the girl, for heaven's sake.' She collapses onto the settee. She's panting, clasping her forehead with her left hand, staring down at the floor. 'We might never have seen her again. I can't bear to think about it.' I try and sit down on the space that's left. She pushes me away. 'And do you know what really pees me off more than anything? That you were prepared to lie about it. Tell me everything was okay. I mean, what yarn would you have spun me when you got back and Katie hadn't been there with me? Eh? That other mum, she was all for getting the police involved. I had to talk her out of it. How could you. How could you. Mm?'

I retreat to one of the other chairs in the sitting room. 'I'm sorry,' I mumble.

'Yes, you are. You are sorry. Sad, sorry, pathetic. I know you've given up on the dad part. But why the hell can't you just try to make an effort once in your sad stupid life. Just the once. I leave her with you a few hours. Just a few hours. And look what happens. I've tried, God knows I've tried. But you've left me no choice. Not this time. I can't forget it. Can't forgive it.'

'What are you saying?'

'I'm leaving you, Mike. Soon as we get home. We're leaving you.'

'You don't mean that.'

'Watch my lips. Leaving you. You've never loved Katie. Now I know you don't love me.' She gets up from the settee. 'I'm sorry. I've got to …'

She walks from the room and goes upstairs but I can still hear her sobs.

*

Once there was so much love.

I met her through work. Before joining the CPS I'd worked as a defence advocate in Chichester. My firm had an office in Brighton and on one occasion I was working there she happened to be temping for us. On her last day with us I asked her out for a drink and we'd fallen in love over the first round of Old Speckled Hen and Hula Hoops. She was living in Falmer, near the university, and as neither of us drove at that time, we'd travel to Brighton by train and meet mid-morning at the station. I'd look out for her opposite the end of platform 8. She was the tall one with the brown eyes and curly brown hair and brown spot on the end of her nose, in the matching brown tracksuit and white Reeboks. She never did glamour, has never done glamour, but at that time I didn't want glamour. I wanted her. We'd abandon the main streets and squares of bland multiple chain stores, cloud-busting office blocks, and the mobile stalls and their smell of festering burgers. Instead we'd head for the little quirky independent shops and businesses tucked away down side streets that seemed to fan out to eternity from the main square and seafront, shops called Malarkey and Attitude and Blue Dog. At some stage we'd adjourn to our favourite tearoom anywhere in the world, offering doughnuts coated with layer on layer of sugar and where one bite anywhere into the interior would send a cascade of runny strawberry jam into the waiting mouth, or scones that came with vats of clotted cream and lemon curd, or brick-sized slabs of tangy, sticky grapefruit cake. Then we'd wander to the seafront and follow the seaside promenade, the Easter-tide air crackling with the fizz of fresh sherbet and the crisp clear early spring sunshine sending a thousand sparks across the still blue waters. My feelings for her just grew and grew from those early days and my longing for her when we were apart was unbearable.

There was one night on our honeymoon, when we were lying in bed in our hotel overlooking the Mediterranean. There was a stillness that could be felt, and through the open window you could almost stroke the cicadas and taste the olives as they clung to the trees outside our window. I turned to her and said "This is too perfect. I'm afraid of when it isn't." She smiled and wiped her forehead and said "It's up to us to ensure there isn't an isn't." It was so easy, too easy then, to believe that there never would be an isn't.

We moved to 87 Park Drive in Chichester while Louise was expecting. There was a loft which was doing nothing. I converted it. I couldn't do the complicated stuff, certainly not the fiddly stuff, but got the help as I needed it and created a new room, a play area for our child with a window providing the best view in our street, perhaps one of the best in the city. Louise looked on and she may not have showered me with praise or taken me out for my favourite Chinese but just said 'I married the right guy.' And at the time that was all I needed or wanted from her.

From the moment Isabel was born, I think I surprised Louise. I think she felt that I wasn't ready to do the dad bit; no, that I'd never be ready to do the dad bit. But I embraced it. On the odd occasion, as I grappled with a soiled nappy or a more than usually obstinate ring-pull on top of a tin of Heinz apricots and rice I caught her eye and I saw a kind of reluctant admiration pass across her face. An "I never expected you to pass the test but you have done" look. Just occasionally Louise let her guard down. On Father's Day when Isabel was one year old I got a card addressed to "the greatest daddy in the universe." Of course I knew that every daughter regards her dad like this but to see it in black and white, or rather gold and blue and pink and grey and purple with glitter round the edge, was what made me almost believe it. My love for Louise, and hers for me, strengthened with the passing days. I found motherhood made Louise sexier than ever. We found a taste of heaven in the high chair and the night feed, bliss among the rompers and sleepsuits, the Pampers and the wet wipes. I never begrudged a second. Isabel was everything to us both. We'd only ever wanted the one child and the fact that she was so perfect seemed to confirm rather than question our views. I wasted little time in ensuring we couldn't have any more. We both thought, we have one in a billion.

She's all we could ever want, all we could ever have hoped for. We didn't dare think we might ever lose her.

If one thing was going to let me down it was what Louise always called Arsenalworld. I think it had started with the *Grandstand* teleprinter when I was about eight or nine, and the presenter mentioning that Arsenal's 1-0 defeat at home to Sunderland was their first home League reverse for five months. And he followed that with gems of wisdom on every other result. Altrincham's sixth scoreless away draw in succession. Forest Green Rovers' ninth match of the season where they'd thrown away a two-goal advantage. I wanted a piece of it. I didn't stop to think that someone, either then or later in life, might actually regard this as an indecent obsession. At the time it seemed as good a diversion as any from the tedium of maths with Mr McKay or physical jerks with Mr Rogerson. The trouble was, by the age of sixteen it had become a kind of diversion from life. And having missed out on so many of the things normal kids did, like the teen disco, and June evening French cricket in St Richards Park, and snogging outside the Haven Street burger bar with Debbie Prichard, and realising what I'd sacrificed, I couldn't bear to think the investment of time and brainpower might be wasted. So I'd redoubled my efforts. In the days before the Internet it meant collecting every last book, every last magazine or newspaper article, visiting the ground to look at archive material, joining the supporters' club. The technology that became available made it easier but I seemed to spend just as much time on it as I had in my childhood. And there I was rolling this ever-increasing snowball along the street of my life, unable and unwilling to leave it behind, fearful of leaving it to melt, resentful of what obstructions might come in its path. And terrified of having to justify what it was all for.

For some reason, when Louise accused me of inhabiting this parallel universe, she always cited Arsenal's Cup run in 1948. That was easy enough. They crashed out to Second Division Bradford at home in the Third Round. But it was her stock example of what I must have been thinking of when I should have been applying my mind to something else. My computer leads trailing across the lounge which accounted for so many cracked plates and smashed cups. Or the vagaries of our lawnmower which if I was distracted for one second would make short work of the tulips and daffodils. And I was banned from even entering the pre-qualifying stage of our local boozer's Jenga championship for fear of precipitating an earthquake that would destroy large parts of Central America. I always feared that a moment's thoughtlessness might prove fatal to our daughter Isabel.

And it did. It started with a low wall. A perfect spot to sit and enjoy a picnic on a scorching cloudless July day. Isabel had this habit of rocking backwards and forwards as she sat. Which was fine if she had something to fall back on, either a chairback or a restraining hand. This time there was neither. Rather, there was a thirty-foot drop into a boulder-strewn river. She rocked back too far and the isn't happened with a single click of the finger of fate.

Of course everyone rallied round. Friends, relatives neighbours. The trouble was, they knew me too well. Knew of my predisposition to clumsiness. Possibly guessed it would be my undoing. And sometimes I saw it in their eyes, reading it between their ostensibly generous and sympathetic lines. If you really were a half-decent dad you wouldn't have let it happen, they seemed to say. Parenthood's more than love and commitment and devotion. It's about making sure the right hand knows what the second left foot's doing.

Louise and I made it a rule never to say if only. Never to talk about how it could have been avoided. Never openly to relive that day. Never to widen the wounds or open fresh ones. But as far as Louise was concerned it came at a price. She wanted another. I told her I wanted to leave it a few more years and when the time did come, if it did, I would want a boy. I think even the adoption agency thought she was rushing. But it was as if having robed herself with motherhood and having had the robe ripped from her, Louise was too frightened to stay naked, and needed the silky caress of its warm fibres. She begged me to agree to go ahead with the adoption and I heard myself say yes.

Once, only once, I articulated my reservations to her but once proved once too often. It was just before we met Katie for the first time. They were bringing her round to our house shortly after lunch. We were having minestrone soup and Camembert and cream crackers and I remember slicing my finger with the cheese knife and saying I didn't know if I could do this. Louise turned to me and said "You will do this." Then she got up and reached for the first aid tin and bandaged my finger and we finished our lunch. And I found myself being carried along with it. Producing the right answers to the agency, not giving them a moment's concern as to my fitness to fulfil my responsibilities as an adoptive father. I kept thinking, I've got to own up, I've somehow got to arrest this process, but my thoughts never translated into deeds. I did begin to confide in a work colleague who'd had an adopted son but before I'd got as far as voicing my worries she squashed me flat by telling me it was the best thing that had ever happened to her. The child she knew she'd never be able to have for herself. And that sort of got me thinking I must be the one that's wrong, that my inability to accept an adopted child as my own was something I needed to conquer, needed to be cured of. So I let it happen.

I didn't necessarily mind that she wasn't my own flesh and blood, that she was the product of someone else's business, someone else's relationship, someone else's love. I still don't. It doesn't bother me that my eyes are brown and hers are bluey-grey. It's not a problem that I'm below average height and she's twice ended up as the Giant in *Jack & The Beanstalk* and is on course to make that part her own throughout her life. It makes no difference that my hair is straight and black while her ginger locks are so tufty you could lose a golf ball in them.

And it's not as if she's difficult, or lazy, or spoilt. She's none of these things. She's polite and intelligent, finds it easy to make friends, and her school reports have always been exemplary. Fenella, who was her class teacher when she was in year four, has already planned out a future for her as teen model, Cambridge graduate, film star and Prime Minister. More than once she's been described to me as a model child. "You must be so proud." "She's a credit to you both." "She's going to go such a long way." If I've heard these words once I've heard them two hundred times.

No. The problem was simple. Katie wasn't Isabel.

I've never hurt her. I've never been nasty towards her. I never would be. I hope she can see my strengths, shafts of light among the mists of failure. I work long hours to ensure there's enough money to provide for her. When we go out as a family I'm never slow to put my hand in my pocket for ice cream and chocolate and other treats for her. I've never intentionally put her in danger. But all the time Louise and I both know that my relationship with my daughter, a little girl so dependent on our both being more than half-decent parents, is built on incomplete foundations. The rooms are warm and carpeted and comfortable and furnished but I fear for what happens when something happens that calls on me to prove my love for her and I dread the crash of the house when the torrent strikes.

A kind of implicit pact developed between Louise and me. She, the one so desirous of the motherhood bit, the one forcing unwanted adoptive fatherhood onto me, found herself doing the lot. Literally, everything round the house. From catering, vacuuming and washing to cleaning, shopping and mending, from recreating Caernarfon Castle on Littlehampton beach to football in the back garden with gnomes for goalposts. Me sitting indoors trying to remember who kept goal in Arsenal's opening League match in 1955-56, Katie keeping goal outside the window between Bill and Ben. In the four years we've had Katie, 87 Park Drive has become a kind of School of Childhood Excellence and Louise is the sole lecturer, facilitator, director and administrator. She sees that Katie's homework is done, not just to a bog standard but to Masters degree level. She probes her on things she's learnt at school and makes her use Google to expand her levels of knowledge so by the time she goes back to class next day she can actually teach the teachers. And she's tapped skills I might never have thought possible in her: the ability to make blue jam tarts and paint sunsets in six different shades of pink and to know where to look for caterpillars and glow worms and grass snakes.

As for me, my tasks could be, still can be, summarised in seconds. To provide financially. To be at home when dinner was in danger of appearing on the table. Not to wait till there were no clean boxers in the cupboard before mentioning the fact that I was getting low on clean boxers. Not to leave my *Arsenal Complete History* cluttering up work surfaces, dining table, settee arms or in such places as shall at any time appear expedient to the Plaintiff on the First Schedule annexed hereto hereinafter referred to as Schedule A and hatched in red. To request sex as little as possible, ask me as far as possible to make my own amusement in that regard, preferably with nobody else involved, and to prepare myself for the menopausal years and possibly beyond when I shouldn't ask for it at all.

And not to come between mother and daughter. Not to impinge on their friendship. They've always been friends, Katie and Louise. Yes, Louise has taught her boundaries as well, and is strict with her when she needs to be, but they still have this friendship. Louise has taken such care to nurture it. I can see why. Louise has got no relationship with her own parents any more. They live abroad and she's not spoken to them for at least fifteen years. She's an only child, as I am; she's determined that Katie, as her only child, will always stay close to her and sometimes I think she forgets I'm part of the set-up as well, even if only a walk-on part. They talk in code. They steal secret glances and smiles and clearly hope I've not seen them, and I pretend I haven't. But the fact is I don't live in that particular world, and I'm never likely to. Louise says it's different for me as I've always got on well with my mum and dad. Or did till dad died last December. But his passing hasn't changed how Louise sees it. I doubt it ever would. And this unspoken pact has gnawed at the foundation of our marriage, leaving something that's still there, that's visible and can be touched, but needs rebuilding. To rebuild, though, would involve making an effort. And it was never part of the pact that I should make an effort to do anything.

It was even too much of an effort to be unfaithful. I had the option a few months ago. Rebecca her name was. I met her on a train and we agreed to go for a pizza a few nights later. And as we sat there that evening, I just knew from her body language and her words that the pepperoni and extra pineapple was the appetiser and there was a main course waiting. After our second coffee and third liqueur each, she hit me with it. "If you want me, I'm yours," she said. "But you'd better be in it for the long haul." She told me she wasn't interested in users and I didn't know her well enough to anticipate what she'd do if I leapt out of her bed and went back to Louise next morning. We may not have had a pet rabbit but I reckoned my reproductive organs would have been more than acceptable substitutes. So I thought about the long haul, which in her case, meant her two boys. I've always disliked boys. Even when I was at school in a class of thirty-two of them I disliked boys. And she said nothing about Reece and Tyler to make me think they were worth trying to like.

Perhaps it could have worked, I thought, as I watched her flounce out of the pizza restaurant, her four-inch heels slapping against the wooden floor. Perhaps there was enough there. Perhaps the boys wouldn't have got in the way. But it was just too much of an effort to find out.

And now through one act of idiocy on my part I'm seeing Louise, poised to rip our pact to shreds, challenging me to make some semblance of an effort to save what we have, and I know that although I'm not drunk I am incapable.

*

She comes back in and sits down where she was. She turns her body away from mine.

'I know I've let you down,' I mumble. 'I'm sorry. Really sorry. I do care. I mean it.'

She spins back towards me. 'Where was the care today?' There's fire in her voice. 'Standing on that platform. Never felt so humiliated, so ashamed. Ashamed of us. Ashamed of you. I've been trying. Telling myself that even though you contribute nothing to Katie's upbringing, to her daily needs, to her love, we need to stay together for her sake.' Her tone mellows just a touch. 'Listen, Mike. I know you'd never hurt her, and you look out for her, and buy her things, and make her laugh. But then I see you sometimes, and I can see the resentment just simmering, and I can see you don't want her, and given half a chance you'd take her back. And I can cope with that, just. But what's happened today, no. Can't have that. No way.' She throws the cushion down. 'Face facts, Michael. We're finished. This is it.'

There's a silence. My chance to disagree. And I'm wanting to, no, needing to disagree, wanting, needing to salvage some pride from the torn scraps of our relationship and our family life. But I can't even locate the sticky tape.

'So ... so you've really made up your mind?'

She rubs her fingers together. 'Katie and I will move out on Monday. Best if it's us that go. If we wait for you we'll all be sitting here on Doomsday.'

'Bit sudden, don't you think.'

She shakes her head. 'No point in reaching the decision then trying to live with each other after that. Be unbearable for all of us.'

'And how's Katie taken all this? Shouldn't we kind of talk to her?'

'No, I think we should keep it as a nice surprise for her. A sort of late Christmas present.' She sighs, then glowers. I've never seen such steel in her eyes before. 'Of course I've talked to her. Just now. Said all the right things, naturally. That we still loved her, that it was you and me that didn't love each other any more and it was best we lived apart for a bit, saw how it went.'

'And how was she?'

'Upset, of course. So am I. I don't want this any more than she does. But you've left me, left us with no choice.'

'Where will you go?'

She sinks deeper into the settee. 'It's in hand,' she says. 'You don't need to worry about us. I'm more concerned about you. How you'll manage.'

'I'll be okay.'

'Don't be ridiculous.' There's not a trace of a smile on her face. 'I'll write some instructions for you before we go. How to use the washing machine. Where I keep the vacuum cleaner and the ironing board. The dishcloths, the teacloths. And where the cooking utensils and saucepans are. I'd hate to think of you living off Chinese takeaways for the rest of your life. Especially at breakfast time.'

'Hardly a hanging offence.'

'Anything else you'd like me to teach you while you've still got me? Making a bed? Putting the dishes away? Separating recycling from the rubbish? Hanging clothes in the wardrobe? Changing light bulbs?'

'I've done that.'

'Oh yes, silly of me,' she retorts. 'Mustn't forget that anglepoise lamp in 2008.' She rises from the settee and stands, her arms folded. 'You don't care.'

'Of course I do.'

'You've never properly cared about Katie. You don't care about me any more. And you know what? I don't care now. Not about our marriage. Not about you.' She stoops down and begins to gather up the portions of Lego that Katie has left scattered around the floor. 'I've met someone else.'

'Who?'

'Bloke.'

'Kind of got that. What's his name?'

'Paul. Paul Faraday.'

'Would I know him?'

She permits herself a light laugh. 'I doubt it. I met him down the gym.'

In that case I know I wouldn't know him. Louise and I had had this argument only the other day about the gym. I told her I couldn't believe that anyone in their right mind actually paid to sit or stand for hours at a time inhaling the stench of synthetic fibre and other people's sweat, and spent good money on petrol to get there and back. I'd suggested that if she wanted to get fit, she simply jogged to the gym, turned round at the front entrance, and jogged home again. No cost at all. Now of course I realise why the take-up on my suggestion had been a big obese zero.

'So how long have you been studying the Epistles of St Paul?'

'Come again?'

'How long have you two been working out together?'

'A few weeks.' She finishes gathering up the Lego and throws the pieces into the plastic container then gets up and stands there, avoiding my eye. 'Look. I was going to tell you. We've slept together.'

'Guess that's cheaper than the gym as well.'

'Ha, ha.'

'And I suppose he's all the things I used to be. Go on, say it.'

'I'm not saying he is or isn't,' she says, 'but I can tell you he's a hundred times the man you are now.'

I spot a piece of abandoned Lego by my chair and throw it at the container. The umpire signals a wide. 'Has Katie met him?'

'Of course. They get on really well. In fact, she ...'

'I know. She loves him and she's already calling him Daddy.'

'He does a lot of charity work. He cares, really cares. He does something with his days. He believes in things.' She gets up and goes to the kitchen. 'Hot or cold drink?'

'I'll have a beer if you're having one.'

'I've already had a glass of wine today, that's enough.'

'Coffee then.' I wander in after her and watch her get a couple of mugs out of the cupboard. 'What sort of things?'

'Things. Causes. Ideals. Friends of the Earth. Animal welfare. Greenpeace. Things like that. Things you've never ever cared about.'

'You'll be telling me he believes in God next.'

'He does as it happens.' She spoons instant coffee into one mug and drops a tea bag into the other. 'He's actually a Quaker.'

'Won't that be a problem for you?'

She shakes her head. 'It's hardly a deal-breaker,' she says. 'Your trouble is you don't believe in anything. You don't even believe in non-belief. You're a sort of walking apathy, moving indifference. Always have been.'

'I was in the college Christian Union.'

'Good God, they must have been desperate. How much did they bribe you?'

'There was no bribe.' I smile. 'There was Alison Wicks, Joanna Burrows, Susie Clarke. You're never going to get a better pick of wise virgins than that.'

'If you're trying to annoy me, you're wasting your breath.' She fills the kettle with water. 'But that's you all over. In it for what you can get out of it. No self-motivation, no ambition, no vision, no nothing. I'm fed up with it. Fed up with the excuses. Fed up that you don't care.'

*

We set off next morning and are home and unpacked by early evening. Then the following day it's an ordinary Sunday. Louise gets the bagels with scrambled eggs which we eat in our dressing gowns, then she pulls on her burgundy tracksuit and I throw on my rugby top and jeans. I read the football reports in the papers while Louise cooks the lunch and helps Katie add cuttings from the colour supplement to her scrapbook. We eat at one o'clock and it's gammon, one of my favourites and Louise's desert island food. At one thirty the live footie coverage starts on Sky which will take care of the whole afternoon. After Louise has washed up, she and Katie bake a pineapple cake then sit down for an electronic Scrabble session; after they've thrashed the computer, albeit on Easy setting, they're getting out their paints and brushes and are continuing their joint project, a Sussex Dawn.

It's as if none of us believe it's actually going to happen. Perhaps it won't. Perhaps this would be the time to try and ensure it doesn't. If I were a half-decent husband and father I'd be interrupting their game or their artistry, and saying to Louise come on, let's not over-react, let's see if we can make this work, let's put Katie first, are you really so fed up with me that you want to throw in your lot with a geezer suffering from a severe case of do-goodery and a splash of religion mixed in for good measure, and are you really so turned on by the patches of sweat dripping down his Adam's apple.

But Man City are three behind at the Etihad and have now been awarded a penalty and it's game on and it's just too much trouble to know how or where the hell to start.

*

After the football we sit down and watch a Disney film together and Katie cuddles up to Louise when we get to the scary monster bit. Louise makes us all cheese on toast and cuts us slices from the pineapple cake, and we watch the first episode of the new Sunday evening TV drama set in the Lake District in the early 60's with shots of Derwentwater and Coniston Old Man and the melodies of Vaughan Williams and a genial back announcer telling us to press the red button for in-depth profiles on the farm sheepdogs. Then it's Katie's bedtime, and I give her a hug and tell her to sleep well, and by now I'm wondering if Louise is really going to go through with it.

I come down then Louise goes up to say goodnight to her and returns to the front room with a pen and notepad in her hand.

'I've made a start,' she says. She doesn't sit down, but just stands between the settee, where I'm sitting, and the door.

'Sorry?'

She taps the notebook with her pen. 'Page one, you'll find how to microwave and how to work the vacuum cleaner. Page two, changing the duvet cover and the bedding. Then I thought how about something really gripping for page three. Setting up the ironing board, perhaps.'

'Sweetheart, I've been thinking.' I motion to her to join me on the settee.

'Oh, silly me.' She doesn't move an inch. 'There was I assuming that to wash clothes you needed a machine to do it. Or to iron clothes, you know, get rid of all those naughty creases, you needed a nasty hot silvery thing called an iron. And all I needed to do was think. What a waste of so many years of my life.'

I get up and walk towards her. 'Look, sweetheart, it's late. Why don't we discuss this tomorrow evening. When I get back from work.'

'Katie and I are going in the morning.' Now she does move, but it's back towards the door.

'And do you know where you're going yet?'

'I spoke to Paul this afternoon. We're moving in with him. I'll take what I need for now, come back for other stuff as and when.'

'Is there any point in …?'

'No Michael. No point at all.'

*

Monday morning starts just like any other, with a family breakfast accompanied by Radio 2 after which I'll get the train to work and Louise

22

will drive Katie to school, her first day back after the holidays, then go on to her work. I have my usual bowl of Cheerios, Louise her Weetabix and Katie her Cocopops. Louise makes me four granary bread sandwiches and I throw them into a tupperware box, pick it up and put it in my bag, and Louise tells me she's ready and Katie's nearly ready, and I kiss Louise goodbye and wish her a good day.

And a good life.

I'm not sure what I should say or do to Katie when she appears. It's too difficult. It's too complicated. I take the easy option and go and sit on the loo. If she wants to see me she'll wait.

She doesn't wait. By the time I've come out she's gone. They've gone.

I'm about to leave the house when on the table by the door I see the notebook Louise had last night, with my name written on it. I sit down in the front room and start to read. She's filled virtually every page and covered every household eventuality, from washing dishes to mending holes in socks, from how to clean up tea stains in mugs to wiping down the hob. There are lists, tables, headings, sub-headings, diagrams, arrows, and flowcharts. It's like a cross between a GCSE mathematics paper and the Cluedo rules.

I wonder whether at the end I might find, if not a revelation of who did the murder and with what, perhaps a message of affection, of encouragement or of support. There's a message all right. It consists of four words.

"Welcome To My World."

I should be bawling my eyes out. I should be running after them, begging them to come back, to save me from her world, and to try with me to create a new world where we can make things work and restore the love we've lost.

But my buttocks remain superglued to the settee.

3

Garadhban(n) – tough call as to whether to gamble on a path advertised as temporarily closed being passable, in the certain knowledge that if the gamble fails it will add at least two hours walking to the day

I put down Louise's instruction manual, stagger from 87 Park Drive to the station, hop on the next train and make it into my Portsmouth office at just gone nine fifteen. At least Howard's not in, but that's the only piece of good news this morning. Kevin's rung with one of his twenty statutory days' per annum sick leave so instead of a morning in the office spending some time on the Crisp file I've got to go into court. It's not an intellectually demanding list but it is a lengthy one, and by the time we finish our morning list I've barely fifteen minutes lunch break. Those fifteen minutes are only just long enough to open the Crisp file on my laptop and read the case summary and preparation for trial form, nothing else.

It isn't a difficult matter on the face of it. The case summary reveals we've one independent witness, Jasmine Pennock, who will say that she was on her way to a nightclub just before midnight, when she saw a lad, she reckoned in his late teens, stepping out into the road, looking right and left before beginning to cross. She then saw a car pull out to overtake a parked van. The car wasn't travelling that fast, she says, but the overtake was clumsy, and although the manoeuvre could have been completed without causing danger to oncoming traffic, the car ended up on the wrong side of the road and hit the teenager. He was killed instantly. Jasmine says the driver and sole occupant, wearing a grey top, black trousers and white trainers, stopped the car on the correct side of the road, got out, saw what had happened and, presumably from shock, slumped back onto the bonnet of his car. She called the police and ambulance service, and stayed till the paramedics arrived. Later she made a full statement to the police. PC Lilywhite will then say he duly appeared, prised grey top and white trainer man from the bonnet and arrested him. The vehicle matched the description of one that had been reported stolen earlier that evening from a multi-storey car park on the other side of town. Crisp, who's got previous albeit for different types of offending, gave a no comment interview and was charged. He'd pleaded not guilty and asked for magistrates' court trial. The preparation for trial form doesn't state what his defence is: he merely states he's "putting the prosecution to strict proof." In other words, he's hoping Jasmine Pennock won't turn up.

I emerge from court at five thirty and am about to start reading the witness statements when Andy Frost pings me from the next office and suggests a drink. I guess of all my colleagues Andy's the one I like and respect most. We first met at school, and though we went our separate ways after "A" levels we've stayed in touch all these years and by a twist of fate we're in the same class again now. We often remark that there's just as much homework and probably even more detentions. I'd mailed him at lunch and told him about Louise and Katie, and I liked that he was wanting to do his bit to help. With Crisp hanging over my head like some mythological beast half-remembered from one of my dad's Latin lessons, my first thought is to say no, not tonight, but I'm brain-dead and knackered and need some company and suddenly a beer becomes the best option. And fifteen minutes later finds me sitting in the Plough and Furrow while Andy gets in the Budweisers. A good place, the Plough and Furrow. For a city centre pub it has a relaxed and homely ambience. You can tell the landlord's a country lover: there are rural scenes depicted in the paintings and photographs on the walls, and *Country Life* and *Walking Today* magazines scattered over the tables. I pick up the *Walking Today* magazine that's on the table in front of me and run my eye over the delights promised by the blurb on the front cover. Fifty Great New Walks, Just For You. Twenty Bobble Hats Must Be Won. Your Nettle Rash Problems Solved In One Easy Lesson. I know a foolproof solution to nettle rash problems. Stay away from nettles. In fact, stay away from the countryside. Don't do the fifty great new walks. Don't do any walks. Be normal.

Andy joins me with the beers and sits down. 'Not worried about the Crisp case are you?' he says, chewing open the wrapping from his packet of Maltesers and stuffing a goodly proportion of the contents into his mouth.

'It's fine,' I tell him. But by the look on his face I can see he's not buying it. 'Andy, truth be told, I'm scared. Never been so scared.'

He smiles. 'Made a few enquiries this afternoon,' he says. 'I looked out some of his previous files. He's never pleaded to anything, relies on the witnesses failing to show or failing to deliver. Once they've come up to proof he changes his plea. Done it three times now. Then I checked with witness care. Jasmine's on the phone to them every day. Checking and double-checking the hearing date. You'll be fine. Just be professional. Put what's happened to you on one side, just for a few hours. You'll get through.'

'Wish it was that easy.'

He holds out the Maltesers to me. 'Mike, you're not the first and you won't be the last to go through this. So please don't expect the sympathy vote.'

I take a couple of chocolates. 'It's different.'

His eyebrows jerk northwards. 'You mean, because you're too bone idle to pick your own nose you're entitled to plead special circumstances?' He takes a swig from the bottle and slams it down on the table. 'Mike, you won't thank me for saying this, but the whole world is full of men in their thirties and forties who've settled down with their partners and think, great, they'll have everything done for them, their meals, their washing, their ironing, the lot. But they still recall the time before that when they did have to cook and wash and iron, and remember and occasionally practise these useful skills, so when their beloved decides to call time, they're not going to be completely screwed. Those are the sensible ones. And then there's Michael Partridge.' He sighs and applies himself to the contents of the bottle once more.

There's silence. The silence of the witness without a decent reply to the flurry of questions in cross-examination. When my response does come, I surprise even myself with its limpness. 'It was sudden. That's what makes it different. Friday morning, a happy family. Monday morning, a bachelor.'

He shakes his head. 'Don't give me that, Mike. This isn't just an overnight thing and you know it. It's been coming. It's you, you, you and it's always has been you, you, you. How many times have we sat here on a Friday evening and there's me looking forward to a Saturday morning standing on a muddy field freezing his balls off watching his son hopping from foot to foot on the goal line and seeing eight goals sail past him in the first twenty minutes. Whereas you, horizontal till mid-morning, a couple of beers in front of the lunchtime Sky game, an afternoon in the company of your good friends Mr and Mrs You Tube … Sorry, Mike, but the curtain came down on Act 1 a long time ago for both of us. There's good stuff in Act 2 as well but the play's moved on.'

He's always liked the sound of his own voice. 'There's nothing wrong with wanting to see Act 1 again,' I say. 'Another night, another performance.'

'Fair point,' he says with a nod. 'But you forget there's more than one of you who's booked to see the whole three-act farce. Mike, I'd love to go back to being sixteen. Friday, period 4, hot days in May, out on Parkes Court. Amanda Ferriby. Charlotte Robins. Julie Halstead. Private study. I tell you, wasn't nearly private enough.'

'Julie Halstead? Didn't you date her during sixth form?'

'Wish I had. Made a mistake there. Missed my chance. Don't get me wrong, Pippa and I are good, she wasn't a mistake. That's my point. I'd love it to be just her and me again, all passion, no strings. I'd love to be back at the point where even if she was dressed up in yesterday's fish and chip wrappings I still thought she was a sex goddess. And yes, it'd be great if just by dressing her up in a short skirt and a pair of heels you could forget the rut you've fallen into and think of her as a sex goddess again and in turn that seals all the cracks in your marriage. Trouble is, there's two of you, and thereby hangs the irregular verb. I try to turn the clock back, you objectify, he needs a reality check. It's not how relationships work, Mike. You've never seen that and you've left it too late. They've gone. Face up to it.'

I take a deep breath. 'I can't do it, Andy. I can't. I need them back. I need to get them back.'

He moves his chair a little nearer mine and his voice softens. 'Why?'

'Because … because I …'

He removes another pair of chocolate spheres from the packet. 'You're not getting it, are you. You should only have them back because you love them and can show them you love them. Not with cheesy cards and flowers. Not with gift-wrapped lingerie and boob tubes. But with the boring stuff. That blasted muddy field on Saturday mornings. Homebase rather than Sky Sports. *The Elves And The Shoemaker* at bedtime, complete with funny voices.'

'Katie's a bit old for that.'

'You know what I mean.' He looks me straight in the eye. 'Don't try to get them back. Not yet. Let them go for now.'

'Excuse me?'

'You heard. Start sorting yourself out. Show the world you've something about you. That you are capable of getting up off your backside. Capable of working to your potential. Capable of giving back. Then, only then, start to think about who you're going to share the rest of your life with.' He points towards my stomach. 'You want to watch that as well, you know. Overweight, no exercise, bad combination. Want to look after others, need to start with yourself.'

He's beginning to get on my wick. 'And join us next week for another edition of *In The Psychiatrist's Chair*.'

He doesn't bat an eyelid but smiles again and looks at his watch. 'Got to go. You're a good guy, Mike. You're a cracking lawyer. You've so much there to give if you'll only let yourself do it. But one step at a time, hey. Get the result on Crisp, that'll do for starters.'

I can't be bothered to argue back. 'And Jasmine will definitely turn up?'

'If she broke her neck she'd still find a way to get to court on time,' he says. 'Just focus, be careful, and you're halfway home.' He gets up, swallows the last of his Budweiser and shoves the packet of Maltesers into his pocket. 'You're not still in touch with Julie Halstead, are you?'

*

It's my first evening meal as a separated man. My starter's one of a multibuy pack of Kettle Chips; my main is a cheese sandwich smothered in Worcester sauce, washed down with an individual-sized carton of orange juice bought from the Co-op on the way home, one of my five a day; and for the sweet course it's the rest of the pineapple cake, another of my five a day. Then I sit down at the dining table with my laptop and open the Crisp file again. I move from the preparation for trial form to the witness statements. They're brief and straightforward, there are no complexities or inconsistencies in any of them, and they add very little to the case summary I've already considered. I wonder if there's a catch but there isn't. After that there are pages and pages of correspondence from the family of the deceased, and dozens of letters from members of the public demanding to know why Crisp wasn't charged with something he could have been beheaded for. After letter number twenty-three I'm beginning to wilt and I'm wishing I'd not had that drink with Andy after all. I flick on the telly and it's Chelsea against Liverpool starting on Sky in ten minutes. I use the ten minutes to reread the key statements, reflect that the guy would be a hundred times better off just admitting it and giving closure and peace of mind to everyone involved, and rip open the Carlsberg multi-pack.

*

It's time for bed. I wander round the house. The empty cheese sandwich plate is lying unwashed on the carpet, and the duvet's sprawled half on the mattress and half off it, and my suit's lying on the floor where I left it, and there's a newspaper blocking the path to the loo and there are three empty coffee mugs, two beer cans and an empty beer glass decorating the lounge floor. I can't find a clean shirt for the morning and my deodorant's run out. And although I've 37 freshly washed socks, none of them pair up with any of the others and rumour has it they're on the verge of forming their very own singles bar.

Welcome to my world.

*

I arrive at court next morning in good time. Immediately I enter the court room a dark-suited man comes over and introduces himself to me as Crisp's counsel. His name's Shatner, Stephen Shatner. I ask him if his client still wants to run it as a trial. 'He wants his day in court,' Shatner tells me. He lowers his voice to a whisper. 'I think he knows he's knackered. But he wants me to go through the motions. You know what some clients are like. Expect you to work for legal aid rates.'

He asks if I can scroll down my statements for him on my laptop to check that they accord with the paper copies of the statements he has. As he says, in the brave new digital world errors do occur. I'm happy to oblige. Then he goes out to take some further instructions. A moment later the usher comes in and tells me both my witnesses, Jasmine Pennock and PC Lilywhite, are now present. Shatner comes back and I expect him to tell me that as a result of their attendance his client's going to plead guilty but he doesn't. However he says he's taken some further instructions and is now able to agree that all the prosecution statements can be read aloud with no need for any live evidence. I go out and release my witnesses. Jasmine's delighted as it means she and her boyfriend can start their Center Parcs break a good three hours earlier than they expected. As soon as I've returned to the court room, Shatner starts asking me about good eating places nearby and I'm extolling the virtues of Mrs Peggotty's, especially her jumbo-sized plates of ham, egg and chips, and as it's Tuesday today it must be the hot spotted dick and Cornish ice cream. Then we move on to what turns out to be a mutual love for the Gunners and remark on their recent run of good form which we attribute to some robust and overdue defensive reorganisation. He points to the Crisp file. 'Sorry about this,' he says. 'We know we've both got better things to do.'

By now the court room is full and there's talk of fans being locked out of the stadium. The usher tells me that the victim's family are here, comprising not only his mum, dad, brothers and sisters but an assortment of cousins, aunts, uncles, grandparents and great grandparents. There's not a spare seat in the house, and hardly a dry seat either; the incident may have taken place more than nine months ago but you'd think it had happened yesterday. The immediate family approach me and introduce themselves. Father is white-faced and sombre while red-eyed mother looks as though the slightest provocation could precipitate an onrush of tears which if unchecked would threaten the courtroom with flood damage. The sisters each wear black dresses and matching court shoes. It's as if this is another funeral for the victim. Perhaps it is, in a way: it's the day when the perpetrator, the murderer, receives his dues, the equilibrium in society is restored, and those most closely affected can bury the past and try and move on. I tell them there's no change of plea but nor is there a defence so the outcome isn't in doubt. 'I don't mind what he gets now,' father says to me. 'I, we, just want him to know what it's done to us. That's all we care about. We want him never to forget. To live with this forever. To take his punishment, whatever it is, and reflect on what he's done and really feel inside.' I think I'll be the one bawling in a minute.

The magistrates come in. The usher calls Crisp, a shaven-headed brown-suited man in his mid twenties, into the dock, and away we go. I start with Jasmine Pennock's statement: the sickening bang on impact, the innocent young man left lying in a pool of blood on the road, and the shocked grey-topped white-trainered driver reeling back onto the bonnet. All the time I'm reading, the distress levels in the court are soaring well beyond those recommended in the latest European Union directive. I don't need to look behind me: I can hear the snivelling, the sobbing, the wailing, the weeping and the gnashing of teeth. I can feel the speed of my oratory increase and my delivery becoming more robotic with each line that I'm reading, and I just want to sit down and let someone else talk and not be the one responsible for prolonging the purgatory in which these wretched souls are trapped.

After Jasmine's statement, there's one from a paramedic confirming he attended the scene within five minutes and pronounced the victim to be beyond any medical help. Then I go on to the statement of PC Lilywhite.'"Following a report of a serious traffic accident on 14th July last at 11.57pm, I attended the scene at 12am on the 15th July last. There I saw sitting on the bonnet of the vehicle a man I would describe as being in his twenties dressed in a grey top, black jogging trousers and white trainers. He appeared from his facial expression and his posture to be in a state of some distress."' I feel a good deal more comfortable with his dispassionate and clinical tone, the style and terminology of one accustomed to dealing with tragic aftermaths and seeing it as just part of the day's work. Then I move on to the ensuing interview at 7pm on the 15th July, summing it up in barely more than two words, "no comment." I read one more statement, from the owner of the vehicle, confirming that he had returned to the car park and found it missing and nobody had permission to take it. 'And that concludes the case for the prosecution.'

I wait for the usher to lead Crisp round to the witness box. But then I see Shatner putting out a restraining hand. 'I'm not calling my client,' he says.

I don't get it. The statements have disclosed a clear case which demands an answer from the defence. I can only assume that Crisp's realised the hopelessness of his position, albeit later in the day than one might have hoped, and that he's chucking in the towel. I look towards his counsel, expecting him to ask the clerk to put the charge to his client again.

But he isn't. He's sitting down and the chairman's asking if I wish to make a closing speech.

'I think the evidence speaks for itself,' I reply. 'The defendant drove into the wrong side of the road in a car that he'd taken without consent. As a result, there was a tragic fatality. The evidence hasn't been controverted. I invite you to convict. What more can I say.' I feel goose-pimples run down my spine. It's a comfortable home win.

Then Shatner gets up.

'Your worships, I submit to you that the Crown haven't proved beyond reasonable doubt that my client was the driver of the vehicle at the material time.'

4

Rushock(n) – smug reference in walking magazine article or memoir to joyous comparison of the writer's lot with that of the less fortunate, eg "It was a brilliantly sunny morning at Great Missenden and I could only feel for the hordes of commuters piling on to the 7.57 as I shouldered my backpack and headed for the hills ... "

M y heart leaps three somersaults. I look again at the case summary. There's no doubt. He's got out of the car, he's collapsed onto the bonnet, and the police have been called, scraped him off the bonnet and arrested him. He's gone no comment, and he's not given evidence.

I look round. The tears have dried up but I can sense a smouldering apprehension on the faces of the victim's family, and heartbeats that are drumming with the intensity of a Seventies glam rock percussionist.

'My friend,' Shatner says, 'refers to the incident being timed at three minutes to midnight on 14th July last. Yet the statement of PC Lilywhite you have just heard read, and my copy of that statement, refers to the police attending at 12am on the 15th. There is no such time as 12am. It could be midnight at the start of the 15th, it could be midday on the 15th, it could even be midnight at the end of the 15th. In the latter two cases, that is ample time for the person who has left the vehicle to quit the scene and for another to take his place. Nobody has positively identified my client as the driver of the vehicle. His clothing wasn't unusual and there were no distinguishing marks. Miss Pennock does not say in her statement when the police arrived. She doesn't even say she was there when they did. Nobody else has given any evidence to the effect that the police attended at midnight at the start of the 15th. And neither Miss Pennock nor anyone else states that the man who got out from the driver's seat remained in situ until the police attended ...'

He pauses for breath and I leap to my feet. 'Your worships, I'm sorry, this is ludicrous. If my learned friend was taking a point on this, he should have done so long before today.'

The response from across the court room is instant. 'With the very greatest respect to my friend, it isn't for the defence to do the prosecution's work for them,' says Shatner.

'In any event,' I argue, 'you need only look at the surrounding circumstances of the incident to conclude this is indeed a simple error and should not impact upon your verdict. '

'I would respectfully venture to suggest that those are the words of a prosecutor grasping at straws,' Shatner replies. 'The case stands or falls by the evidence actually presented. Supposition has no place in your deliberations. None at all. I repeat, this case has not been proved to the requisite criminal standard. Doubtless your learned legal adviser will direct you in relation to the law surrounding adverse inferences from silence but in view of the evidential failure I respectfully submit that it would be wholly wrong to draw any such inferences. Please acquit my client of both charges.'

'Your worships, may I have a moment to check my file for some further supporting evidence of timings.' The chairman nods. I go through the evidence once, then go through it again, and once more with feeling, but it's as if the shock of this new development has translated all the material into an obscure foreign language. It's just random words on a page, devoid of substance, devoid of meaning, devoid of sense. I feel the sweat on my forehead, on my hands and on my feet, my heart not just somersaulting but doing bungee-jumps from my mouth to the bottom of my stomach.

I fire off a distress flare. 'Your worships, as I've intimated, this is the first time my friend has put me on notice of this. There's clear case law to support the right of the prosecution to reopen its case in order to deal with ambushes by the defence. The Crown were wholly unaware that there was an issue around timings and who the driver was. I therefore ask to reopen the Crown's case and exhibit the custody record which will give the defendant's arrest and arrival time using the twenty-four hour clock.'

'I can't agree the custody record by itself,' Shatner says. 'It's a computer generated document and as a matter of law I shall require a statement to vouch for the accuracy of the computer on the day in question.'

'In which case I request an adjournment so I can call the witnesses to confirm the timings and or obtain the statement referred to by my friend. Hopefully the case can be re-called later this morning with witnesses present.'

The bench agree to give me twenty minutes to make some phone calls. But Jasmine Pennock isn't picking up, PC Lilywhite's been called to the scene of another accident and he's not answering either, and there's nobody available to provide a statement to vouch for the accuracy of the custody record. So I go back to court and ask the magistrates for a further hour in the hope that the witnesses will respond to the messages left for them. They give me the hour. In fact they give me nearly an hour and a half. But when after that time there's still no response from either, I'm compelled to return to court and ask for an adjournment to another day

'Naturally I oppose that,' Shatner says. 'My client has simply sought to put the Crown to strict proof, as he is entitled to do. My client came expecting a trial today and does not expect to come back another day because the Crown has not put its house in order.'

The bench go out of court to consider. And barely have they closed the door behind them than father is coming up to me. 'What's going on? What's happening? Is he getting off?'

I tell him to calm down, that it'll be fine, that Shatner's got to do this, and that the bench will understand the gravity of the situation and won't let technicalities interfere with the course of justice. Then I have to get out. The usher finds me a private room and for twenty minutes I just keep pacing from one side to the other until I know the paint colour on the walls better than Mr Dulux.

And then the usher calls me back into court.

'Mr Crisp, remain standing,' says the chairman of the bench. 'We've listened carefully to everything that's been said, but aren't minded to grant the adjournment. This should have been sorted months ago. We've given the Crown most of this morning to put the defect right, but without success. On the evidence presented to us, which is all we are allowed to consider, we can't be satisfied so we are sure that you were the driver. We think it inappropriate to draw any adverse inferences from your silence at interview and at court today. The Crown were put to strict proof and have failed to discharge the burden of proof. We therefore find you not guilty. The court will now adjourn.'

The magistrates leave and in an instant I'm the one in the dock. And in place of the three justices of the peace I'm faced with a brand new tribunal which doesn't have law books but umbrellas and folded newspapers and faces scarlet with loathing and anguish. Father rounds on me and out of instinct I put up an arm to defend myself. 'This is an outrage,' he thunders. 'A travesty. You've not heard the last of this. Is this justice? Is this flaming justice?' A white-haired man who could be the deceased's granddad, great granddad, neighbour or window cleaner demands I drag the magistrates back into court and start the hearing all over again. A grey-haired woman clutching an umbrella waves it in my direction and suggests a number of locations within my person where she might be minded to insert it. The usher calls for reinforcements and three security men come in and begin to eject the breast-beaters while two others put themselves between the lynch-mob and my quaking body. A moment later, I'm the only one in the court room.

But even though Shatner has gone outside, he's left his file. I glance down at it and see, at the top, the defence copy of a statement I know I've not seen before. It's a further statement of PC Lilywhite dated a month ago. "This is by way of an addendum to my earlier statement. I can confirm that our time of arrival was at midnight at the start of 15th July last, some 3 minutes after the call from Jasmine Pennock. We arrived and spoke to Miss Pennock at the scene ..."

I go back to my laptop and check my statements again. I scroll down to the end of the statements but it's as if my finger's glued to the scroll key. I keep on scrolling and reach the letters. Letters and more letters and still more letters. All the rest of the digital file is letters.

Except the last page.

"This is by way of an addendum to ..."

Then Shatner comes back in. 'Anyone for spotted dick?'

*

It is a good decision, the best decision. Howard says that I'll depart with dignity, taking away a favourable reference and an effective performance marking from my previous review, with no allusion to my inability to read either page twos or electronic page eighty-twos. My pension rights will be preserved and they'll even do a collection and throw a farewell party in my honour. I'm fine with all of it. It's not going to bankrupt me; only a week or so ago my bequest from dad came through at last and although it's not enormous – mum's needs are greater – it'll do for the moment. Howard's also told me I don't need to work out the period of notice.

And according to my TV guide they're starting reruns of *One Foot In The Grave* on UK Gold at 9.30 on Monday morning. My gran was right. Everything happens for a reason.

*

Louise has been round to collect some stuff but always when I've been out at work. Now I've stopped work and am at home all the time she's not been round at all. She's removed all the photos of herself, of Katie, of Isabel. The only standing photos left are in a collage sitting on the mantelpiece, comprising pictures of my own family, my mum, my dad and my cousins. I need Louise and Katie back and I need them now. But all I get when I try phoning Louise is her voicemail. When three weeks after she's left me I've got voicemail for the twentieth time I decide I'll go and meet her as she picks Katie up from school. In the meantime, granted, there's today's *One Foot In The Grave*, but straight after that they move on to a quadruple bill of *Last Of The Summer Wine* so I'm forced to flick over and feed on a diet of women's magazine programmes and low-budget reality. The clock plods round to mid-afternoon. I now know, or should know, how to lose half a stone in seven days but still be able to empty down my throat as many Mars Bars as I please; how to lie in till noon after clubbing Saturday night away, yet manage to make the perfect Sunday lunch and remain throughout as unfazed and sexy as Nigella; and how to effect an emergency repair on my four-inch heel should I be so unfortunate as to catch it in a metal grille at three in the morning. But it's all washed over me with the coolness and smoothness of the water from the power shower that's helped to sell The Porter's Lodge to Leah and her partner Abigail in *A Place By The River*.

Nevertheless, I must have been more captivated by the fare on offer than I thought possible, because despite walking to St Cuthbert's C of E at a brisk four mph, I see no sign of either my wife or my daughter.

Though seemingly unable to speak to me on the phone or return my calls, Louise has at least given me a note of Paul's address which is also in Chichester, and while I've no desire to risk confronting her new guy I want to see her and Katie and I want to see them today. I decide to walk there; she's taken the car and I don't know how many decades I'll have to wait for a bus. I try the same technique as I do when I can't sleep in the hope that it'll make the miles go more quickly. Arsenal Cup Final sides. 1971 for starters. Wilson, Rice, McNab, Storey, McLintock, Simpson, Armstrong, Ball ... it works and I'm there by half past five and God willing, Paul won't be home from work yet.

It's a new-build detached house in a cul-de-sac. I see a Merc parked on the hard standing but there's no sign of our car. I ring the bell. The door opens and a man of about forty-five is standing on the threshold. He must be at least six foot three, he's got short tidy black hair and a tanned face, and wears a lime green polo shirt and light trousers. A few beads of sweat line his forehead. He's holding an orange document wallet.

'You must be Mike,' he says, extending his hand and smiling. 'Paul. Paul Faraday. Pleased to meet you. How can I help?'

I find myself taking his hand. 'I'd ... I'd like to see my ... my wife and daughter. If I can. Please.'

'Sure,' he says with a smile. He goes back inside and I hear him call for Louise to come to the door. A moment later he's back. 'You'll have to forgive me. I've got a planning meeting.' He points to the wallet. 'Might you be interested? Charity fun run, this Sunday morning, ten o'clock, Bognor seafront? All the proceeds to the local cat and dog rescue centre?'

'I don't think so.'

'Well, if you change your mind, pop down.' He points to my stomach. 'Might help shed the odd pound. In every sense.' He smiles again. 'We meet at the pier. Good to put a face to the name. Cheers.' And he offers his hand again and I find myself shaking it again. Then he walks past me and out into the cul-de-sac.

I watch him stride away and a moment later Louise appears. She's wearing her plain grey zip-up onesie. A pair of dark blue bedroom slippers dangle from her feet. She doesn't look me in the face. She stares right past me.

'Hi,' I say.

I move forward to hug her. She seems to anticipate it. She shrinks back.

'What's wrong?' I say. 'You are still my wife. I still love you.'

'Michael, it's difficult.'

'I want you back. I want you and Katie back.'

'Back for me to wash your shirts.'

'Not just that. Being on my own. It stinks.'

'Like your shirts presumably.'

'Sweetheart, I'm lonely.'

'Mike, don't.'

'Come on. Get in the car and come home.'

'We've sold my car. Anyway, this is …'

'Don't say this is your home now. You know it isn't.'

There's another silence and as I stand there gazing into her eyes I'm aware of a softening in her face, a ray of sunshine through the layer of stratus above a rain-soaked field. A moment later she's standing aside to let me into the hallway and then ushering me through into the living room.

It's almost empty: there are just a few boxes, a futon, green and red armchairs, and some pieces of coloured paper on the floor, cut into square and triangular shapes. We stand there in the middle of the room, facing each other, she with her back to the window.

'Darling, I want you and Katie back. I need you back.'

She forces a wan smile. 'Do you?'

Then Katie comes in. She's still in her school clothes. She wanders over to me and puts her arms around me. Then she releases her clasp immediately and sits down on the floor by the coloured paper.

'Come and play my game, Daddy,' she says.

I hear a ringtone from somewhere inside Louise's costume. 'I'd better get that,' she says. 'Perhaps you might condescend to spare your daughter a few minutes of your precious time while I'm gone.' She extracts the phone and goes out.

I wait till she's closed the door behind her then turn to Katie.

'Are you … okay?' I ask her.

'I'm fine.'

'You mean that?'

'Mmmm.' She doesn't look up at me. She's gazing down at the pieces of paper.

'Paul? Is he nice to you?'

'He's okay.'

'Looks after you and Mum?'

'Yeah, he's okay. Eric's nice too.'

'Eric?'

'His dad.'

'Are you happy? Living here?'

'Kind of.'

I look her straight in the eye. 'Kates, what's the matter?'

'Nothing.' Still looking down.

'Something's bothering you though. Isn't it.'

'It's nothing.'

'You can tell me.'

She sighs. 'It's fine. It's okay. You couldn't do anything anyway.'

'I could try.'

She takes a deep breath. 'It's Pamela.'

'Pamela?'

'I know Paul still loves her.'

'Does Mum know about her?'

'Mum says she doesn't mind. She understands. She says he's bound to still love her. I don't like her. I hate her.' She still won't look at me. 'Dad, will you play my game?'

'Not now, Kates.'

'It's the best game I've ever made. Please.'

Without a doubt this is top of the list of things that marked me out as the zero-rated adoptive dad, and Louise the adoptive supermum. I've lost count of the number of times I've returned from a day at work or looked up from the sports channel and found the dining room table protesting under the weight of paper, felt, glue, scissors, glitter, old newspapers, old magazines, Lego, plasticine farm animals, plasticine velociraptors, petrol stations made out of matchboxes … and it's never been a case of Louise seeing it as a sacrifice, a necessary parental duty. She joins in and she revels in each second, providing expert design advice, manufacturing assistance, and an instant no-call-out-fee repair service. She loves it and has always loved it. And I've loved never having to love it. But this is my probationary task and comes above Paul and Pamela and everyone and everything else.

'Of course, darling.' I sit down on the floor beside her.

The game's called Colour Blind and makes De Luxe 3D Monopoly seem as straightforward as Snap. From her initial exposition of the rules, it appears that the object of the game is to dispose of all your pieces of paper by matching them with similarly shaped pieces. I think I get that bit. But there are various colour inscriptions on the pieces and they're all coded and it's important not to have more than two pieces of paper with any red on them or I have to hold onto them as long as I've got them. The only way of being able to dispose of a piece of paper with red on it is to collect one with a blue circle on it. And if I pick up a piece of paper with yellow on it I pick up a penalty point which I can only cancel by accumulating four similarly shaped pieces of paper simultaneously. At least, I think so. Yes, that's right. It must be. Or is it a piece with purple on it …

No. Number 8 was George Graham. I remember Alan Ball playing at number 8 but George Graham was credited with Arsenal's equaliser and from my DVD of the match I recall the number 8 on his shirt when he was being congratulated. Something's gone wrong. It wasn't Ball. Why am I thinking it's Ball when …

'Dad.'

'Mmmm?'

'It's your turn.'

'Ah – er – yes. I've … um … two triangles to give in.'

'Let's see them.'

I produce the triangles.

'Da-ad.' She says it in the way she always does when I've displayed my abject parenting qualities before her eyes.

'What?'

'There's red on both of them.'

'Does that mean I can't give them in?'

'I've told you. I've told you. You didn't listen. You don't listen.'

'I'm sorry, Kates. I'm sorry. So what do I do now?'

'You've got to …' Alan Ball. You total fathead. Alan Ball never played in that side. He'd not even signed for them from Everton. It was the 1972 final when he played number 8 and George Graham was number 11. From the top, then. Wilson, Rice, McNab, Storey …

'Your turn again, Dad.'

Oh, God. 'Right. I've two hexagons. I've no red at all. So I'm going to give the two hexagons in. Right?'

'Dad, you need three hexagons.'

'So I can't give them in.'

'Dad, I told you. I told you just now. Why don't you listen?' As she speaks, Louise comes in and sits down on the arm of the green chair.

'What's going on?' She fixes her eyes on me.

'Daddy won't play my game with me.'

I rise to my feet. 'That's not quite true,' I say. 'I did try and play, but ...'

'But you didn't listen when I told you the rules,' Katie says. 'You were just ... just rubbish.' There's no playful affection there, but a kind of exasperated disdain, and I'm shaking.

'No change there, then.' The words fall from Louise's lips like shards of broken glass.

'Mum, can I go and get a jammy dodger?'

'All right. Just one. Get a drink of water as well.'

She leaves the room. Louise remains perched on the chair arm. I move a few steps towards her, then speak almost in a whisper.

'Sweetheart, come back with me tonight. Both of you.'

'Michael, I can't believe you're serious.'

'Of course I'm serious.'

'You just had a great chance to show Katie, show me, that you can actually do something for our daughter, and you do like you always do.'

'So that's it, is it? I don't pick up the rules from her *Isaac Newton's Top 575 Classic Unsolved Conundrums* and I fail the test?'

'Don't be ridiculous. There's far more to it. You know that.'

I reach out and take her hand. She doesn't snatch it away, but nor does she move any part of her body. 'I know there's more,' I say. 'That's why I want you. To work through the far more. Not run away from it. Face it all. See what's gone wrong. Start again.'

She just stares out to space and frowns. And in the silence that follows I find myself hating Paul, the charity king, for being so much better than me, so nice, so reasonable and calm, for not being a bully, for not slamming the door in my face, for not threatening me with summary disposal into the nearest underground sewer unless I placed at least three hundred miles between myself and his front door knob. And aside from the fact that anyone who organises a fun run, encouraging large sections of the community to subject themselves to a Sunday morning of self torture, must be guilty of an offence of some description, I've got nothing to beat him with. I know I've not got Pamela to beat him with. The forsaken ex-partner who for all I know may herself have started the cheating chain. I'm the Opposition election candidate who's unable to orchestrate any negative campaigning because for once the Government are actually getting it right.

The only decent card left in my hand is the one with the wounded kitten on it. Still holding Louise's hand, I kneel down beside her.

'Sweetheart, I need you. I really do.'

There's another silence.

'Do you?'

'Of course I do. I'm lonely. I can't do it on my own.'

Her frown melts away, and now she's looking into my eyes. And maybe the injured little moggy has trumped the Ace of Pauls. For as I look into her eyes I can see a beam of light and once more she's the goddess who taught me how to love.

'I'd like to think you really did mean it,' she murmurs.

'I wouldn't be here if I didn't.' I look closer into her eyes. 'I want us to try again. The three of us. To get it right.'

I see concern and care etched into her face. She squeezes my hand and sighs. 'This is so difficult, Mike,' she says. 'I know what I said when Isabel died, and I've tried, I've really tried. Don't think it's not tearing me apart. I'm sorry. I just think … things are different now. I can't get it out of my mind. You might have lost Katie forever.'

'It was a stupid mistake. I've said I'm sorry.'

'I mean, hell, it's been hard enough getting Katie to readjust. I don't know how she'd react if I told her we were moving back again. I'm not sure how Paul will react.'

'I'm still your husband. He's got nothing to do with it. Anyway. He's got …'

'What?'

'No. Nothing.'

'Pamela, you mean.'

I nod. 'Katie told me.'

'Everyone's got baggage, Mike. Paul wasn't the one who caused the break-up. He was the innocent party. Badly, horrendously treated. The love's still there. It's not like a bathroom tap. You can't just switch it off to order. I can't make him and I've no right to make him.' She sighs once again and a watery smile crosses her face. 'It's easy for you. You're not caught between partners the way Paul and I are.'

'I realise.'

'It's an awful lot to forgive. Despite everything, I'm not sure, I really … I'm not sure.'

'I know it's not going to be easy.'

'I don't think you've any idea, Mike,' she says. 'This is the straightforward bit, isn't it. The talking bit. The syrupy slushy bit. But Kates and I need to know you properly mean it. And the only way you can show that is by

41

doing. Doing for me. For us. Not just when you want to, when Arsenal aren't on. It's full-time work. Starts now. Goes on. And on.'

'It will. I promise.'

'Too right you'll promise.' Still holding my hand, she leans forward. Our lips meet and and we kiss.

'That feels so good. Feels so good.' I'm blinking back the tears. 'Honestly, you've no idea. It's been a nightmare, total nightmare, since you left me. I can't believe I messed up the way I did. But I'm starting again. In fact ... pause for effect, roll of drums ... I've already started.'

'What do you mean?'

'I've left my job.'

Her eyebrows disappear into outer space. She lets go of my hand. 'You've done what?'

'I've gone. They don't need me to work out my notice. I've prosecuted for the last time. Reviewed my last file.' I go into cod-States-side. 'Partridge's Last Case. Kissed goodbye to Godzilla Of The Central Southern Region.'

'They sacked you, didn't they.'

'No. I decided I'd had enough. Couldn't do it any more. Resigned. And you know what, it's the best thing I ever did. To be honest, I ...'

'So what are you going to do instead? What about the mortgage, the council tax, the bills?' There's more incredulity than anger in her voice.

'I don't know yet.'

'Great. Great decision.'

'I mean, there's you ... your job ...'

'That's pocket money and you know it.' She speaks quietly but now there's no mistaking the disgust in each syllable. 'Let's get this right, shall we. You're asking us to come back to you. Incapable of recognising your own daughter in a train corridor. Incapable of engaging with your daughter without drifting back into your own selfish little world. And it seems, quite happy just to throw away your training, your vocation, your pride. And your own family's future vanishes down the tubes at the same time. Would that be fair?'

'I wouldn't say that, sweetheart.'

With a torrent of sobs and expletives she lurches forward, and her hands are flying towards me, one blow to the head after another. I'm crumpling, the shock of the sudden aggression leaving me powerless to fight back. The physical pain, none to speak of; the anger that's crashed onto me, off the scale.

And I look up and I see Katie's come back into the room. She stands there, her mouth ajar, and I see her lips beginning to vibrate and her cheeks are frozen lard. Louise turns and sees her too. A moment later

Katie's run back out and I hear the banging and clattering of feet on the stairs.

Louise wheels back round to me. Her cheeks are purple and tear-stained, and loose hairs wander down her forehead. Her voice is almost a whisper. 'You're unbelievable, Michael. Unbelievable. Just get out. Get out of our lives. Go. Now.'

As I rise to my feet Paul comes in. For what seems like an hour and a half nobody says anything and nobody moves.

I look into his face and he's smiling again. I detect no malevolence in the smile. It seems more diffident, almost apologetic. 'Listen, Lou,' he says. 'Can I just have a word with Mike in private. Maybe if you could start dinner?'

She turns to me and shakes her head then staggers from the room.

Paul motions to me to sit in the red armchair while he sits in the green one.

'Mike, mate,' he says. 'Lou's told me a lot about you. You're a good bloke. Nice bloke. Need a few fireworks up you, but who doesn't. I appreciate what you're going through. What all this is doing to you.'

'I doubt it,' I growl.

'I just feel that all round it's best you don't trouble us. Not if it's all going to end in tears like this. It's upsetting for all of us. You just as much. If not more.' And he's looking into my eyes and there's that smile again, and I'm wondering if I ought to be asking him down the Fountain for a drink and requesting him to recommend a decent marriage guidance counsellor. 'For your own good. Please leave now. Good man.'

*

I try texting and ringing Louise the next day but there's no response.

I decide on a new strategy. We'll all talk, us three adults, like the mature, sensible individuals we are.

So that evening I go round to the house again.

I go up to the front door and ring the bell. There's no answer. There's no sight or sound of anyone in. I look round and notice the Merc's gone.

And peering through the window into the lounge I can see all the furniture's gone too.

5

Chartham(n) – irritating tendency for lack of decent path signage over several miles to be over-compensated for, on arrival at beauty spot, by massive profusion of signage which then confuses rather than assists when other tracks and trails overlapping with your route all start to be signposted as well

I get to St Cuthbert's at just before half past eight next morning, and watch the procession of vehicles and bodies approaching the main entrance. I know some of the mums and dads of children in Katie's class, although probably not as many as I should. I've never been a member of the saintly band who get involved with PTA stuff, helping at the Christmas fayre, organising the Easter Egg Hunt, dishing out burgers at the summer barbecue, or forgoing a Saturday morning lie-in for the get-your-hands-dirty-spruce-up-the-reception-classroom session. I go along to the odd concert and the occasional fete, but to be honest they all seem to mingle into one after a while anyway. I recognise just a handful of the parents arriving now, some dressing to impress with their designer tops and tailored jeans thrust into polished boots, others happy to slum it, putting comfort and convenience over appearance, with misshapen jumpers, tracky bottoms and paint-splashed Crocs. They gather in little huddles and there's me left apart from them; suddenly it's like being back in the playground at my own school, with its mixture of cosy cliques and the lone saddoes not quite knowing what to do with themselves. A few members of the assembled clans do acknowledge me and make me feel a little less uncomfortable, but I'm still the bloke on his own hanging around the school gates at the start of the day. A couple of mums flinch away, and there's another woman gawping at me, a mixture of wariness and suspicion written all over her face, clearly hating that I'm there and wanting me off the premises at the earliest opportunity. I've never rated her as head teacher.

There's still no sign of Katie at nine by which time the drop-off has finished and school has started. I try ringing Louise but she doesn't pick up, so I go into the school office and speak to the secretary Mrs Snelsbury, a grandmotherly figure with curly grey hair, sensible tweeds and too much perfume.

'Can I help you?' she demands.

'I'm enquiring about Katie.'

'Which Katie?'

'Partridge. Year five.'

'Who are you? Her father?' A burnt crust of irritability coats her voice.

'I'm beginning to doubt it. But yes.'

'Well? What is it?' She looks down towards her desk and sniffs.

'She and her mother have separated from me. I was expecting to see them this morning and I need to talk to them. I'm worried about them.'

She glances down at a piece of paper on her desk and then looks up at me. 'Wait here.' Then she gets up and disappears down a corridor and she's gone ages. I feel as if I'm the one in the wrong, the pupil left in the study while the principal goes to find the cane.

Mrs S doesn't come back. But Katie's class teacher Gemma Maxwell does appear. 'Michael, good morning,' she says, offering her hand. There's a businesslike, professional air about her. I've never liked her as much as I liked Fenella.

'Gemma, is my daughter in school today?'

She sits down beside me. 'Michael, this isn't easy.'

'Oh?'

'Katie's not going to be with us anymore.'

'How come?'

'I can't tell you. All I can say is that she's no longer a pupil at this school.'

'I'm her dad. I've a right to know. Tell me.'

'I'm sorry, Michael.'

'Can I speak to the Head?'

'You can but she'll tell you the same. We have to respect confidentiality. In this instance we're under strict instructions to keep this information confidential. I assume you can ring or text Louise. I'm sure she'll tell you more if she can.'

'If she's left this school you must know what her new school is,' I argue. 'Do you know? Can you tell me?'

She looks away. 'I can't help, I'm sorry.'

'You mean you won't.'

'I'm sorry.'

'Like hell you are.'

'Michael, I think you should leave now.'

'I'm going nowhere.'

She picks up the phone and presses four numbers. 'Craig, can you come to reception urgently, please?'

*

45

And later that morning I get a text from Louise. *We've moved*, it says. *Paul's work. Very sudden. I'm fine and Katie's gr8. Luv Louise and Kates xxxx.*

*

I never thought it would be this difficult to trace my own wife. At the touch of a button I can compare the prices of thermal underwear across the major department stores in Brisbane and can learn the number of score draws from last Saturday afternoon's fixture list in the fourth tier of the Mauritania National Women's Hockey League. But ascertaining the whereabouts of my own flesh and blood who for all I know may be less than an hour's drive away seems to be beyond the sum of all human knowledge. It's like the maze we visited a couple of holidays ago where every step I took either had me entangled in a cocktail of briar, thistle and gorse, or brought me back to the entrance where I'd started two and a half months previously.

I go to Louise's work but they stonewall with even greater robustness than the school. As for her parents, I've no idea where they are, or how to contact them. I speak to mutual friends, but they say they're just as curious as I am. None of the local gyms are prepared to acknowledge the existence of a Paul Faraday or Louise Partridge on their books, and all the enquiry agents I try require a significant Lottery win to cover their fees on account.

In the end I call the police and request their help, and find myself being shunted from operator to operator, at the same time being treated to 397 repeats of the opening bars of the Hallelujah Chorus. Finally I do find myself speaking to a sergeant who asks me what part of wasting police time I don't understand. They're not a free tracing service, he tells me. If a crime's been committed, the child's in danger or a court order's in force, yes, that would be different. Come back as and when that is the case, and we'll look at it. Now go away.

And I move to a different strategy. The chucking the phone across the room so that it smashes against the wall strategy. But it's a strategy that only brings short-term therapy and short-term satisfaction, custom built for the one who's fallen as far as he thinks he can fall but looks down and sees he's still nowhere near the bottom.

*

It's the day after the early May bank holiday. The weather forecasters promise a fine day with good spells of fresh spring sunshine and light north-westerly winds. But all I can see from my kitchen window is an arid plain scorched by the dull persistence of savage heat and depressions where rivers once ran and now bearing the dust of ten thousand rainless days.

I've reached my last clean mug in the house. It's the Chelsea FC, FA Cup Winners 2007 mug which I seem to recall one of Louise's friends paying me to take home from a car boot sale. To my list of attributes I'm now able to add the ability to accumulate not only record-breaking tonnages of skid-encrusted boxers but a uniquely ingenious variety of excuses for not putting on the washing machine. Starting with the very first line of Louise's instructions which invites me to turn the dial to the letter G. I can't see a letter G anywhere on the dial. There's a C. That could be what she meant but equally I've this vision of any setting other than G resulting in an explosion of apocalyptic proportions with Park Drive submerged in a mixture of water, Sainsbury's Basics No Frills Washing Powder and men's undies, and my neighbours having to charter a canoe to buy their Sunday paper. So another visit to the Saturday morning market in Winters Field beckons. Twelve pairs of cotton slips for £2. Nominations for the highlight of the day have been made, and the results are in. In third place, the lunchtime regional news read by flame-headed Vicky Rennison. Runner-up, the final scene of today's episode of the new supermarket soap *Checkout*, in which Leigh-Anne on Till 19 has accepted an in-store café date with Colin on the almond macaroon counter. And today's winner is … long pause, desperate yells from the audience … this afternoon's edition of *Warm Memories*, the thrice-weekly review of the contents of suburban airing cupboards.

Now it's nine in the evening. I'm unable to choose between rival offerings on BBC2 and ITV1 focussing respectively on Sydney ratcatchers and millionairesses masquerading as CAB volunteers in Hucknall. In the end I've switched to tonight's 1980's quiz rerun on Challenge. Then after Shelagh from Andover's won the star prize of a Betamax video recorder and a week for two in Magaluf with £100 spending money, I switch off and ring mum.

Mum lives in Buxton, Derbyshire, some two hundred miles from me. She and dad moved there from Surrey five years ago. They were close enough then for me to see them every month or so. Since they moved we've not met up more than a dozen times. But we've spoken on the phone most weeks and since dad died I've made the point of ringing mum every week. For obvious reasons I've wanted to avoid worrying her too much about the separation. I've told her what's happened and why it happened but I've pretended I'm managing okay both practically and emotionally.

Of course I ask her how she's coping, and I wonder by her answers if she's pretending a bit too. She keeps going on about how she's embracing her independence, and how now dad's gone it's a weight off her shoulders, and how she's determined to fill every hour of every day, whether it's bridge afternoons or her local church choir or the Diabolical Su Doku in the *Daily Telegraph*.

We're too alike in this regard. We're both too proud to admit things might be anything other than fine. It's not helping either of us and whether it's the sheer banality of the night's TV offerings that's done it I don't know, but suddenly I want to stop the pretence. I want to see her and put my arms round her and tell it to her as it is and trust her to do the same to me. She says she's busy over the next few days, but suggests I come up on Saturday.

I get straight onto Google to find the cheapest way of getting to Buxton from Sussex on Saturday morning and the only way I can do it without emptying my savings account is by overnight coach to Manchester and then a morning train or bus to Buxton, returning home the following night. I don't think I've travelled by coach since my schooldays. I certainly never got any encouragement from Louise to use the things. She reckons she's still not fully recovered from her coach journey to Dubrovnik when she was a student. She was sitting in the bus for 36 hours. And at the end of that time they were still sitting in the middle lane of the M20 just outside Dover.

*

I didn't expect much of a night's kip. I'd have hoped for a couple of hours. However, since my London to Manchester vehicle sees fit to proceed to visit every town in the West Midlands, garnering passengers not only from their bus stations but it appears every street corner in between, I never get beyond a state of semi-consciousness, my senses unable to confirm to me whether the next stop is one I should be getting out at, or just another housing estate in Dudley. Sleep only really threatens to wash over me at half past five or so when we limp out of Stockport and head for Manchester city centre. But that's all it does, threatens, and I'm no more refreshed by slumber when we pull into our destination than at the very outset of the voyage.

We reach the coach station more or less on time. I'd have been happy for us to have been two hours late. As it is, it's still six fifteen and I'm not due to meet mum till ten. I go for a sausage and egg McMuffin and coffee from a nearby McDonald's and manage to make it last well over an hour, thanks to my discovery of an abandoned copy of *This Month In Bolton* with its Wordsearch competition, my completion of which has lined me up for the month's star prize of a £10 John Lewis voucher (travel and tobacco products excluded). And following the high that this triumph brings me, the day just gets better as I sit and listen while a slight middle-aged man with satay-smelling breath furnishes his rotund multi-chinned female companion with a literally blow by blow account of his visit to the Sale and District Footcare Co-operative to have his ingrowing toenail repointed.

I order a second coffee and treat myself to a porridge and golden syrup to go with it, and the clock wends its way round to eight forty. I'm thinking about getting out to Buxton when my phone rings and it's mum saying she's had to go shopping and then meet a friend who's just come out of hospital so can we make it half past two. There's a train at one fifteen that'll get me to Buxton in time. So that's … for one insane moment, I thought that meant I still had three hours and thirty-five minutes to wait. 8.40, 9.40, 10.40, 11.40, 12.40 … no, not three hours and thirty-five minutes at all. So that's all right then.

I mooch around for a while. I find a bargain DVD shop but having worked my way through the first three shelves and arrived at their sixteenth copy of *Titanic* I decide to move on. Nearby is the free-to-enter New Arts Of Manchester which is just opening for the day so I go in and gaze at paintings of nubile females vomiting into a field full of Flake wrappers, and nails being driven into the feet of Christ on the seafront at Blackpool, and the Incredible Hulk having his torso wrapped in lengths of razor wire. Having completed my inspection, I ask a member of staff what other attractions are nearby which might help some of the remaining significant slice of eternity to disappear. She gives me directions to an area of specialist shops which will be good to browse in, and a couple more galleries. But I must have misheard her, for minutes later I find I've been sucked into a part of the city where people come out of necessity rather than for enjoyment. There's office blocks, industrial units, back yards where lorries go to die, warehouses, workshops and places where you part with £300 cash to collect your clamped car. I'm aware I'm getting further and further from the station but am driven onwards by the conviction that it can't get any worse. And indeed as I walk on, I notice a subtle change in the surroundings. I've entered an area of more individual houses and businesses, what estate agents would describe as "character properties" in blue and green and pink and yellow, and I'm expecting to round a corner and meet the entire cast of *Balamory*. Within the mix there's a family butcher, a Continental style patisserie, and … Jodie Carteret.

I'd not heard of her till a couple of weeks ago but discovered her through my new-found acquaintance with daytime TV, specifically a recent edition of *Loose Women*. She's a successful model, accustomed to catwalks rather than Wainwright walks, but someone sees her out on a Sunday afternoon's rambling in the Yorkshire Dales, she admits to a passion for hiking, and the next moment she's acquired the ability to turn windcheaters and gaiters into sex objects. She's now got her own show on Sky, she boasts a weekend column in the travel section of a national newspaper, her Twitter followers can be counted in millions with a substantial fan base in Uruguay, and as she says, she must be the only person to appear regularly in both *Country Walking* and *Cosmo*. And when she jumps into bed with an *X Factor* winner, one assumes she'll make the Guilty Pleasures pages of the *Metro*. But then if she helps to get more people out into the countryside, the happier our green campaigners are sure to be. For the walking fraternity it brings a whole new meaning to the concept of exposure.

It's not actually her I'm looking at now. But it's as good as her, no, even better than her: a giant representation of her in the window of a retail premises adjacent to the butcher's, called WALK THE WALK. A glance into it from the street reveals that it specialises in equipment and literature for serious hikers. I pause and study the range of designer walking wear in which the store staff have decided to kit Jodie out. She's modelling a bright yellow cagoule and matching leggings and sou'wester. The cagoule has a shiny finish, the leggings look like they're made of rubber, and the boots into which her feet have been thrust don't look quite like traditional functional walking garb. I can't recall seeing any committed walkers heading for the hills in such tall lace-ups with quite so great a profusion of straps, buckles, zips and tassels.

'Do you like the ensemble, sir? Or can I tempt sir with something else from our selection today?'

A suited man, mid-thirties at a guess, shortish with fair straight hair, has appeared beside me, clutching a carton of drink and a sandwich and pointing at Jodie in the window.

'Er … no. No, I don't think so, thank you.'

'There's forty per cent off most of our stock this weekend, sir. Fifty on some items. Is sir really not tempted?'

I grin and shake my head. Nonetheless, there's something immediately engaging, and, yes, likeable, about the guy. It could be because I've always been a fan of *Are You Being Served* and in bearing and appearance he has more than a passing resemblance to Mr Humphries. At any rate, he's the first person to take a genuine interest in my personal needs since the woman in the burger bar on Victoria station last night asked me if I wanted extra tartare sauce with my fishburger.

'Can I ask, are you a walker?' he enquires.

'No. Not at all.'

'But you're not from round these parts, are you?'

'Is it that obvious.'

'Well, your accent is a bit of a giveaway,' he says with a smile. He offers his hand. 'Gavin. Good to meet you. Are you just up for the weekend or are you here for longer?'

'Just for today. Meeting my mum in Buxton.' I take his hand then look at my watch. 'I've got just over three hours to go before I meet her. And probably about another five hours to kill after that.'

'Kill!' He looks at me as though I've just been found guilty of molesting his tortoise. Then he points up the street. 'There's enough out there to last you forever. Why not stay, enjoy? Live a little?'

'I'm not up for clubbing the night away, if that's what you mean.'

'I didn't mean clubbing. I meant walking. Out in the hills.'

'I've never walked.'

'More fool you.' He applies his teeth to his sandwich, the content of which could be beef, marijuana or something dug out of the Manchester Ship Canal. 'There's no magic to it. Just putting one foot in front of the other. Anyone can do it. I mean, if you're going into the wilds you need to be properly equipped, and know what you're doing. But if you make the effort, you'll love it, and once the bug bites, you won't want to stop.' He points to a colour photograph making up another part of the window display. A clear blue lake with snow-clad mountain faces shooting up behind. 'Look at that. Can you beat that? Where do you think that is? Austria? Switzerland?'

'Er ...'

'That is less than two hours from this very front door,' he says. 'The Lake District. Cumbria. What's not to love about it?'

I think back to my wanderings of the last hour or so. The rubbish we've clogged our cities with. Not just the landfill stuff. The lorry parks, the car pounds, the warehouses. The picture may just be a picture but there's something captivating there, the promise of a world that's greater and brighter than the world around me now. I like his passion, his enthusiasm for something better. I like his concern for me. And now he's beckoning me towards the door and I find myself following him in.

'You need to get the feet right first.' He pirouettes towards a display of red socks. 'What's your shoe size?'

51

'Ten.' And there's nothing I feel I can do about it. He's got me. I've not just fallen for his disingenuous sales patter. I've plunged with the effortlessness and focus of a deep-sea diver. I take my trousers and shoes off and moments later am tumbling into a pair of tight black breeches. My feet, duly wrapped in snug lambswool walking socks, slide into grey fabric boots; the next moment I'm being closeted inside a deep red windproof top, and following close behind is a floppy green hat. Then Gavin reminds me that my backpack, a relic from my schooldays, isn't big enough for the clothes I'm changing out of, nor does it go well with the ensemble into which I've now been poured, so I need a new rucksack as well. In exchange for my agreeing to provide my contact details so I can be made aware of other exciting future products, Gavin's applying sixty, even seventy per cent discounts and extolling his wares and their alleged qualities with such eloquence that I wonder if he's patented them all himself. But however unprovable the claims as to their soundness and durability may be, I just know all escape routes are barred and all avenues of appeal have been blocked.

The last strap is tightened and lace fastened.

'You really do look the part now,' he says with an approving grin. 'Mirror over there. See what you think.'

I go to the mirror and all I'm seeing is somebody else. Somebody I've never met. Somebody I'm not sure I would ever want to meet.

'And it's four pairs of socks for the price of three this weekend, so it's your lucky day.'

'One pair's fine.'

'No, it isn't,' he says, reaching out and grabbing a handful of them from the adjoining shelf. 'Now two things. Make sure you remember to peel the label off the back of your new trousers before putting them on. You don't want to look a complete jerk. And before you can even think about setting off you need your GPS navigator.'

'Navigator?'

He burrows in his trouser pocket and produces a device of black and yellow, its shape and size not dissimilar to a mobile phone of the late nineties. 'The compass of the twenty-first century. A child could do it. Dead easy. Allow me to demonstrate.' He takes me out into the street – 'to get the satellites,' he explains – and tells me he can get me to his favourite place on Earth, the summit of Haystacks in Lakeland, in twenty seconds. I don't set the stopwatch, but it seems in barely more than the blinking of an eye that an arrow and a mileage indicator are showing on the screen, and the explanation going with it doesn't require a BSc in interpretation of technobabble.

'I'd give you this one,' he says, 'but it's mine and I'm a bit attached to it. I never leave home without it. Especially after I've had a few and I've forgotten where I live. It's got me home more than once. But,' he says, waltzing towards the display at the foot of the stairs, 'there's plenty more where this came from.' He whips a box from the display and glides to the till. 'Now, how's sir going to pay?'

*

We reach Buxton shortly before half past two and I then have about a half-mile walk from the station to Mum's semi. It's no palace but mum and dad couldn't stretch to a palace. For years and years they'd wanted to move to the Peak District, specifically Buxton with its gracious architecture, operatic traditions and green spaces. They'd both retired from work and with not a massive amount of savings had difficulty in finding something they could afford and which they could maintain in future. It had meant downsizing significantly from their house in Surrey but they were happy to do that. Having made the move they built a little extension which is now a sort of sitting room-cum-library. Despite his declining health dad had driven the whole thing, even done some of the work himself. Mum refers to it as dad's room. I'd been up to see her here after we lost him and came and just sat in the room for a while. My own personal last respects I suppose. As I'd looked up at his prized collection of *Wisden Cricketers' Almanac* on the bookshelves, his Best Batsman in Fourth Form and Most Runs In South Surrey Village League trophies on the mantelpiece and pictures of him on every wall, I could feel him, thoughts of him, memories of him, in every square foot.

Mum ushers me not into the extension but into the front room. She's looking well. She may be nearly seventy-three but she still doesn't need glasses and her hair remains a resolute curly dark brown. Perhaps dad's passing really has been more beneficial for her than I thought. He was always the dominant force in their household and I think she felt quite overawed by his personality, his achievements, his friends and indeed his height, his six foot one to her five foot four. Now she can be her own person. I sit and listen while she talks to me for a good hour about her new outlook, her new friends, her new activities and a hectic list of social engagements, the next of which, she only now informs me, is a U3A event in Chesterfield, departing at four thirty this afternoon. Coming back on Monday. Great, thanks for telling me, mum. They'll feed and water her well, apparently. So there was no need for me to bring the malt loaf and butter. Or the buy one get one free packet of six Mr Kipling apple and blackcurrant pies.

'Well, that's me,' she says, glancing at her watch and offering me a fourth slice of malt loaf. 'How are you?'

I've been rehearsing this moment most of the way here on the train. The Moment The Son Actually Told The Truth To His Mother. Mum, I don't know where Louise and Katie are and it's really getting to me and I can't think about anything else least of all finding another job and I've not a clue where to turn, and I've come to you in the hope that you'll listen and understand so we can work it out together.

'I'm good, thanks. Yes, great.'

She smiles. 'That bad, is it?'

'Come again?'

'Mike, I am your mum. You can talk to me. I may be a drain on society and no use nor ornament to anyone but I do still have some brain cells. I know.'

'Know what?'

She puts the plate of malt loaf down on the table. 'I know it's not like you're making out. I know you're not telling me what's really going on. I think you're missing them, really missing them. Right?'

I nod and gaze down at the apple pie crumb-festooned yellow rug beneath my feet. I don't know what's worse, mum reminding me of the gravity of the situation as it really is, or her seeing through the pretence. Right from when she caught me with traces of blueberry sponge cake mixture on my face at the age of five, and proceeded to demolish my alibi in her first question in cross-examination, I've always wished I could pretend to her better than I really can.

'But ask yourself why they've gone. You've never given to Katie at all, have you. Not like you should have. You leave her with a complete stranger on a crowded train. You let her walk out the door without even saying goodbye. You chuck in your job. You go round to get her back and lose interest as soon as she tries to engage with you. Then she sees you and your wife, her mother, start fighting. Fighting, Michael. Grown adults.'

I lick some stray butter off the corner of the malt loaf. 'Not fighting. She was hitting me.'

'This isn't a police interview or court of law, Mike. It's not about apportioning blame. Katie's frightened, scared. Her mum's scared for her. She needs her safe. Protected. Loved. Cared for. She's contacted you and said they're both okay. If I were in her shoes I don't think I'd have done anything differently.' She checks her watch again. 'I hate to say this, darling, but I see only one name on your agenda and it begins with

Michael and ends with Partridge. What would you do if Katie came in now and asked if you'd play a game with her?'

'I'd play, of course.'

'But what if you had the football on the telly and it was a match you'd been looking forward to all week? Would you play with her then?'

God. All that's missing is the wig and the gown. 'Yes. Yes. Definitely. Of course I would.'

'No. I thought you wouldn't.' She was wasted as an accounts manager. 'Mike, they're safe, you know that, they've told you. Louise has met a good man, a kind man. She and Katie are settled, secure. So wait for them to want you. Or if that doesn't happen, wait till you're up for playing the game.' Then she looks at her watch once more. 'Mike, I need to get ready.'

It's on the edge of my tongue to say, I'm so glad I've come all this way, to be made to feel the size of a premature newborn stick insect and then find the jury's returned its verdict before I've even opened the case for the defence. Then I remember that part of it is supposed to be about her. My newly-widowed mother. About making sure she really is adjusting to life without dad. About trying to claw through the membrane of her pretence. About honesty. About truth.

'Mum.'

'Yes, darling.' Now she's on her feet.

'I ...'

'What is it?' Her blue eyes look directly into mine.

No. There's no need. She's happy, relaxed, alert, rational, sensible. Just a few words and my work here will be done. 'Anyway, mum, I'm so glad you've adjusted so well to ... to ... being on your own. It's great. I'm really pleased for you.'

'I'm pleased you're pleased.' She picks up the tea-tray and walks towards the door. Not the door to the kitchen but the door to the extension. She closes it behind her. And through the silence, broken only by the ticking of the clock and the rustle of the wind in the pampas grass in the front garden, I hear a snivel and a muffled sob.

I'm about to go after her but as I begin to haul myself out of my chair the door opens and she comes back in. Her eyes are dry and if anything she looks brighter than when she was dispensing the tea and non-sympathy.

I open my mouth but the words just won't come.

*

I'm on my way back to the station and my phone rings. I pick up and it's Gavin. He says if I'm at a loose end this evening would I like to go walking with him. I tell him where I am and he suggests Shining Tor. He says the start of the walk is just a few minutes' drive from where I'm standing, he's shutting the shop now and could be with me in less than an hour. According to him it's a very short easy walk and starts and finishes at the Cat & Fiddle Inn. There, he says. A great walk and a great pub. A no-brainer.

My first thought is he shouldn't be ringing me for personal reasons when I gave him my number purely for business use, and anyway given the choice I'd rather be filling in pot holes on the outer ring road around Ouagadougou. But I've underestimated his powers of salesmanship. I suppose I should have divined from his performance at his store earlier that he could flog Big Macs to the International Veganists' Conference. And he squashes the sandcastle of my resistance with the gentlest of neap tides.

Eighty minutes later, we're drawing up at the Cat & Fiddle and I'm scrambling into my newly purchased walking clothes and sliding my feet into my new boots, and gazing at a reflection of myself in the car window again wondering, as I was this morning, who the hell is this person and do I really want to know him. I just thank the Lord that the fresh dry conditions obviate any need for that ghastly floppy hat.

I guess there are worse places than a pub to start and finish a walk. Gavin tells me the inn is the second highest in England. He explains its unusual name may be a corruption of "*le chat fidele*"(the faithful cat), "*Caton le Fidele*" (a former governor of Calais) or "*Catherine la Fidele*" (Catherine of Aragon, Henry VIII's first wife). It may also be a reference to the once popular game of tipcat, with the fiddle representing dancing, that might have attracted customers to the hostelry. I don't doubt any of it for a second. But having set off along the roadside path, leaving my day clothes in Gavin's car, I do begin to doubt my own fitness to remain at large in the community. I'm allowing myself to be carried off into this unknown world and don't know where I'm going or why. We leave the roadside, the cars and buses and lorries, things that intelligent people climb into in order to travel from one place to another, and having followed a clear path up a hillside, we bear right onto a clearly-defined track passing above farm buildings. Gavin points down at the farm and starts giving me another history lesson, or is it a geography lesson, but he might be speaking in one of the more obscure tribal dialects of Equatorial Guinea because nothing's going in, nothing at all. Then he starts on about the origin and former usages of the paths we're following and there's me wondering why with the silky smooth roads and motorways that have replaced them we should actually be choosing to use our leisure time retracing the old routes, and in the process find ourselves turning over our ankles, tripping on loose rock, skidding on patches of mud and wading through ten-foot deep puddles. It defies good sense. It defies any sense at all.

We reach a path junction and a signed path to Shining Tor heading off to the left, and keeping a dry stone wall to the left, we begin what Gavin assures me is now the final haul to the summit. Now I'm paying with interest for forty years of not-so blissful indolence. To a seasoned walker I've no doubt that this final haul, as he describes it, is a Sunday afternoon stroll. To one whose most demanding recreational exercise away from home is climbing the stairs to my hotel room because the lift has broken, it's punishment more exacting than as a prosecutor I ever felt able, in the interests of the maintenance of decency and decorum in the court, to recommend to a sentencing tribunal. My knees start to grumble, then my ankles are protesting, and before long my thighs are petitioning Buckingham Palace. My boots aren't just pinching now, they're stabbing, and I have to stop to check that the soles haven't been pierced with complimentary tin tacks. Having seen how far it is to the top, I've just decided to gaze downwards, take a step at a time, and look out for the next species of trip hazard that has somehow eluded the relevant Health and Safety department. Gavin does his best. It'll be worth it, he keeps saying, just another five minutes. I know from the time requested by defence lawyers to ready themselves that five legal minutes equates to about thirty real minutes. I'm hating to think what five hill-climbing minutes are but if we're still here this time tomorrow I'm not sure I'd have any right to be surprised. The futility of the pain and the pointlessness of the task set my mind racing around other bits-of-my-life-which-I'll-never-get-back moments, and I'm just coming to one of the stronger candidates for top place, queuing all night to pay by Barclaycard for an Arsenal 6th Round FA Cup ticket only to find seven hours later that they didn't accept Barclaycard … when Gavin announces that we're there. We find ourselves at a triangulation point, or trig point for short, which Gavin explains is a stone pillar used by the Ordnance Survey for mapping purposes. He says this marks the highest point in Cheshire. 'Just look,' he says. 'Enjoy.'

It's as if a curtain on a giant stage has swept open. The ground has fallen away in front of us. And as the curtain opens, the orchestra are striking up a symphony, a sparkling fugue with dancing strings and cavorting woodwinds, and there's so much to listen to, so many contrasts of sound and movement, so much light and shade. We're gazing down on what seems like half of England. Before our eyes there's green, light green, dark green, verdant green, dusty green, pale green, the greens of hills and of valleys, of fields, of trees and bushes and shrubs. And between the greens there are greys and reds of farmsteads, hamlets, villages. Gavin looks straight ahead and indicates the townscape of Macclesfield, the radio telescopes of Jodrell Bank and the sprawl of Manchester, then guides my eye to the left, and points out the highlight of the symphonic work, a distinctive green hilltop, the elegant and beguiling summit of Shutlingsloe, so shapely that it's known as Cheshire's Matterhorn. There's more than a hint of the volcano about it and I'm kind of expecting an explosion of molten lava to shoot from it, the grand percussive finale of the piece.

I stand and stand and stare and I feel the aches and the pains dribble out of my body. Then I look up at the sky, and the grey and white beasts that have scudded and teased the hilltops earlier in the day have disappeared and there's blue, whole blue, nothing but blue.

I almost can't bring myself to admit it but it's beautiful.

'There,' says Gavin. 'Can you see now why we do it?'

I think back to the climb, to the toil and the pain and the sense that nothing could render that amount of discomfort worthwhile. But as a lawyer I've been taught to watch out for what might just be a single tiny piece of evidence, maybe a chance comment, a single line in a police pocket notebook, a fleeting figure in a piece of CCTV footage, a four word text message, which changes my perspective altogether, which turns an innocent defendant into a guilty one or which at the touch of a button blasts the prosecution case into oblivion. For the first time since leaving the pub I feel that something's been given back to me. That there's been a return on my investment of time, of expense, of hard labour. That there may be a method in the walker's madness after all. That there's a spark of rationality in what I'd perceived as Gavin's unhealthy exuberance and enthusiasm. From not wanting to leave the car park I now don't want to leave this spot. I turn to him and nod and smile and his eyes light up in pleasure and for one hideous moment I think he's going to kiss me.

Now he's secured my membership he's determined to provide the full welcome pack. As we make our way back down the hill he's indicating the grass on either side of the path, pointing out clumps of yellow flowers of the birds' foot trefoil and the creamy petals of white clover. He stops suddenly and directs my attention to an orange tip butterfly. A little further down the hill he lets out a whoop of excitement and points up into the air at a plump-bodied bird with a woodpecker-like bill and feathers of blue-grey and orange, which he says is a nuthatch. 'First I've seen this year,' he says, with a broad grin of triumph. I admire his joy in these simple things, I suppose I kind of envy him for it too, but I can feel the spikes in my boots beginning to reappear and indeed multiply, and various parts of my anatomy are balloting their workers on industrial action, and working-to-rule, overtime bans and lightning strikes can't be ruled out.

*

We get back to the Cat & Fiddle at just gone seven thirty and enjoy a celebratory pint apiece. By the time we've reached the bottom of our respective glasses, Gavin's planned a whole year's worth of walks for me, from yomping across the Falklands to a quick lunch-hour scramble up Mount Fuji. As we rise to leave I look at my watch for the third time since we finished our walk, hoping we've made some significant progress towards quarter to midnight when my coach is due to depart. But the little hand is still lingering obstinately around the eight as if reluctant to don its crampons and take up its ice axe for the rest of the climb.

Gavin seems to read my thoughts. 'I know it's still early,' he says. 'I would suggest a curry or cook you something at my place but I'm going out tonight. I can obviously drive you back to Manchester, no problem. Or …' He frowns and strokes his chin.

'Or what?'

'Why not stay round here another day.' The frown gives way to a broad smile as he warms to his theme. 'You don't want to be stuck on a coach two nights running. Tell you what. Give Kinder Scout a go. Fantastic walk. Starts from a place called Edale. I know a great B & B in the village, Greenfinches. I can drive you there, no problem. It's not that far out of my way. It's on the railway, you can easily get back to Manchester from there tomorrow.'

I don't know if I ought to feel flattered or worried. 'What's Kinder Scout?'

'The highest point in Derbyshire. One of the last great wildernesses in England.' He chuckles as I flinch. 'Don't worry, it's not that difficult. If you can do Shining Tor, you can do Kinder Scout. Give me your navigator.' I reach into my pocket and pass it to him. His forefinger flies around the buttons. 'Stage 1, go to the café in Edale and ask for a map and directions to get you up to Kinder Low. Very straightforward all the way up. Just a bit steep in places. Once you hit Kinder Low, you'll be right on the edge of the Kinder plateau. Then if you want to get to the highest point on the plateau, switch this fella on and let him do the rest. Don't get me wrong. Rain, snow or mist, you'd be a fool. The plateau's a peat desert and in bad weather you don't want to be anywhere near it. Tomorrow, warm and sunny all day, you'll do it. It's quite dry up there in parts, hasn't been any rain to speak of for a week. It's not mountaineering but you need stamina, you need patience. I'd come with you but I'm busy most of the day. What do you think?'

I'm thinking, don't push your luck, you may boast a new convert to the faith but he isn't yet ready for full immersion. Then however I catch a whiff of my underarms, fish-baskets dragged from a North Sea oil slick, and can feel my boxers now welded to my buttocks, and I daren't unlace my boots for fear of causing a stampede of eager food shoppers believing there's a new cheese market in town. And my thoughts move to the prospect of a hot night date with the suburbs of Dudley, and Wolverhampton, and Walsall, and I can smell the stale sweat and cigarette-stained jackets and jumpers around the coach and hear the incessant bang of the toilet door and the crackle and hum of the tablets and iPads from the seats in front and behind and feel every dull jerk as we stop at traffic lights and roundabouts and contraflow systems. Five minutes later I'm rebooking my coach for tomorrow night and have a bed at Greenfinches, Edale. Gavin doesn't only drive me to the village, he takes me right up to the front door. It's a creeper-clad grey stone cottage, bathed in soft welcoming light. Birds chorus and the air is heavy with the scent of early flowering roses. My first floor bedroom has matching bedding and wallpaper of bright cherry blossom, and I walk across the butter soft carpet and drop onto a bed that sinks so deep I expect to find myself back in the guest lounge downstairs.

*

I enter the breakfast room at half past seven next morning. It's a lot earlier than I need to be – Darshan, the owner, serves breakfast between 7 and 10 – but it's a bright sunny morning, I don't feel like lying in, and having skipped dinner last night I'm hungry. And my hunger seems to increase at the sight of the array of food on the sideboard: individual cereal packets, jars brimming with eighty-three different types of muesli, labelled jugs of whole, skimmed and semi-skimmed milk, a jugful of yogurt, two glass dishes overflowing with prunes and grapefruit segments, and a basket stuffed with croissants and more types of roll than a PE instructor could ever find use for. There's jars of jam, strawberry, raspberry, blackberry, loganberry, elderberry, Newbury, Westbury, change here for Trowbridge and Bath Spa. A menu invites patrons to choose between various combinations of boiled, fried, scrambled or poached egg with bacon, and in bold type, smoked salmon and kedgeree, open brackets, order night before please, extra charge payable, close brackets. I need the food and I need the energy. I go for the muesli jar with the largest number of pieces of dried fruit per cubic centimetre and empty the top third of its contents into a bowl. Then I splash on a swimming-bathful of semi-skimmed milk and bring a blizzard of white sugar down onto the ensemble, leading to significant accumulations on higher ground and risk of widespread travel disruption.

It's as I pick up my bowl and a spoon that I see there's one other person in the room, at a table by the window, toying with what looks like a bowl of rice flakes. A woman, possibly in her early thirties. She wears a grey T-shirt, black leggings, and black low-heeled leather boots. But the hair that caresses her shoulders is blonde; not just bushy blonde, it's jungle blonde. Her green eyes have the lushness of a glenside meadow at daybreak and her cheeks have the glow of an Auvergne sunset …

6

Clenrie(adj) – description of dejection you feel on multi-day long-distance footpath walk when, owing to the route layout, you realise that as the crow flies you're further from your ultimate destination at the end of your day's walk than you were at the start

... **B**ut I see worry lines drawn all over her face and a tinge of sadness in those lush bright green eyes: a salmon that's leapt out of a Scottish mountain stream and hit dry land.

And as I'm looking at her I realise she's looking up at me.

I stand there torn between not wanting to appear impolite but not wishing either to disturb her melancholy reverie. She's the one who breaks the silence.

'Morning.'

I nod towards the window and smile. 'Looks like a lovely day.'

'Fine. Just fine. Fantastic.' And the next moment she pushes her cereal bowl away. It slides along the table and in a split second it's flying across the room. Then without warning, it nosedives and hits the deck, and an individual packet size consignment of soggy rice flakes cascades onto the carpet, turning the worst affected area in an instant from deep green to milky white, and sending streams of liquid across the surrounding plains.

Darshan comes in at that moment bearing a plate with a boiled egg and two slices of chunky buttered granary toast. He's a short man in early middle age, and with his white shirt, bow tie and black trousers I wonder if he's doubling up as the cabaret act. 'Little accident?' he says, looking at the debris. There's no reproach in his tone. He looks more amused than angry.

'It was my fault.' The words are out of my mouth before I've had the chance to think.

'Do you know, we brought this carpet over from Karachi. It's been in our family for the last three hundred years and never so much as a mark on it,' Darshan observes. I gaze at him in horror and start to reconsider my antipathy towards the EuroMillions. He retains a straight face and watches me splutter and squirm, then breaks out into a smile. 'I only jest. I'll mop it up later. It was the full English for you, wasn't it?'

'Please.' He puts the egg and toast down on the table next to my new dining companion and departs stage left.

She looks up at me again and her face has turned white. 'That was kind,' she murmurs. 'God. I'm sorry. I'm so sorry. I just ... just can't help it. Not at the minute.'

I retrieve her bowl, place it on a nearby empty table, and point to the vacant chair at her table. 'Can I?'

'If you like.'

I put my bowl down on her table, sit down opposite her, and with my spoon begin the demolition work on my cereal skyscraper, starting with the east wing. 'Do you want to talk about it?'

'I'm ... I'm not sure where to start.' She picks up her navy serviette and wipes a tear from her left eye. Then she shakes her head. 'No. I don't ... don't want to ... oh, God.'

I slice two storeys off the tower and empty them into my mouth.

'I miss him,' she mutters. 'I can't believe I'd miss him this badly.'

With my pre-molars grinding half a hundredweight of innocent hazelnuts into submission, I'm unable to do any more than look into her eyes, hoping she'll feel able to continue what she's started.

'Toby. I love him. Never knew I loved him so much.' She shoves her cooked breakfast aside but with more finesse and less brute force than she applied to her cereal bowl and there's no need to check the *Times* ski reports for further avalanche warnings on local slopes. 'He was writing this book. *High And Wild*. The best views and the wildest spots in Britain. Then he went off to Canada. Last December. For six months. He worked for a bit, then went travelling. He was travelling three weeks ago on an internal flight, that ... that's when it happened. The crash. Whole plane, it ... it burst into flames. Then exploded. No survivors. Bodies turned into ash.' She sits back and drags a gallon of air up her nostrils. 'I'm sorry. You don't need this.'

I begin work on a couple of extra-chewy sultanas. 'So what brings you up here?'

'I wanted to finish his book. I wanted something of him around me still. Pretending, I suppose. Pretending he was still there writing it himself.' She smiles and sighs. 'I thought if I could do the rest of the walks in the book, if I could complete it for him ... so I asked the publishers and I guess they just assumed I was a keen walker like he was so this guy Steve, one of the editors, okayed it. I found what he'd done, what was left. I was looking forward to it. Thought I'd start with the summit of Kinder Scout. Came up from home in Hampshire on Friday, tried to do it yesterday. Truth is I've hardly walked at all. I've done some, but always with Toby. I hoped someone else might be doing the same walk but no. So I went off on my own. Was okay to begin with. Then it got so hard, so steep, really steep, and my boots were pinching, I was sweating, and hot, and thirsty, and I kept on stopping for water, and food, and at last I reached the top and found myself on the plateau.'

'You made it that far then.'

'Mmm. But then I knew I had to go into the plateau to get to the highest point. Nothing but heather, and peat, and rocks, and mud, and water. And I just wandered into it, and I lost all sense of direction. Never been so scared.'

'Did you have your compass?'

'Yes.' She pours some tea from the teapot into her cup. 'But I couldn't get it to work. I panicked.' I see tears filling her eyes and her cheeks are reddening. 'Now I know why people talk about going round in ever-decreasing circles. That's what I felt I was doing. Then I lost my grip on reality. I found myself wandering around the plateau. Looking for some ground that was vaguely higher than the rest of it. I knew there was a cairn marking the spot. I saw no cairn. No nothing. Just lots more heather, and peat, and rocks, and mud, and water. Then a mist came down. Started to swirl around. Nobody to help. Nobody to guide. I read something once about how you're never lonelier than when you're in a crowd. It's rubbish. I've never been lonelier than I was then.'

At length my spoon makes contact with the bottom of my bowl. 'So what did you do?'

She seems to have second thoughts about her cooked breakfast. She manoeuvres it back towards her, slices the top from her egg, breaks off a small piece of her toast and lets it down into the egg. I've never known a process of this nature take so many decades as it does now, and the silence echoes round and round the room. But just as I begin to feel I can take no more, she resumes her narrative. 'I thought, I'll just keep walking in a straight line. Thinking at least if I do that, I'll hit something eventually. Only of course there was so much mud and so many streams that I just ended up taking whatever line was the easiest. And at last I came to a path and followed that but I had no idea where it was taking me. In the end I just came to a lump of rock and sat down and cried like I'd never cried before. I just sat and sat there, wondering what to do. I must have been there hours.'

'Why didn't you phone for help?'

She shakes her head. 'I didn't want to. Didn't want to admit I couldn't do it. Not to me, not to anyone else. Anyway, then a couple of walkers found me. Told me they were walking back to Edale. I asked about getting to the summit cairn but they said it was some way off. Told me I needed to go with them for my own safety. Knew then I'd failed.' She chokes back a sob. 'I knew it was a stupid idea, this walking malarkey. Guess I'll just have to forget it. Find some other therapy. Get a good shrink. I don't know.'

Out of the corner of my eye I see Darshan coming in with my cooked breakfast and it's hard to see his face behind the concentration of bacon, eggs and mushrooms. He sets it down on the table and then goes out.

I take a deep breath.

'I'm going up Kinder Scout today if that helps,' I say. 'Come with me, if you like.' Correction. Mike, you berk, you're not going up Kinder Scout, you're going to be trying to go up Kinder Scout. The sight of that cholesterol slag heap that's just arrived may have inspired you to greater heights of optimism that you've got it in you, but you can't be certain. And there's no way you can be sure you'll be able to guide anyone else up there. In any case, you ought to know better than to choose someone lying at the bottom of the pit of vulnerability. She may have the blondest of jungle blonde hair, the most verdant of green eyes and red and orange fire in her cheeks but Mike you're not that shallow. The woman's grieving and fearful and anything which might be seen as an attempt to exploit her situation in any way for your own benefit is unthinkable. But the words have motored out of my mouth before I can apply the handbrake.

'I'm going home today,' she answers. She looks at her watch. 'Got a train to catch.' Then she sighs. 'Messed up, that's an end to it.' She puts her elbows on the table and rests her head between her hands.

It's pointless to argue. 'Understood.'

'Anyway,' she says, and now she's looking straight into my eye, 'you wouldn't want me holding you back.'

And once more my brain is lagging behind my lips. 'It's no bother. I can guess how much this means to you.' I see her looking down and now I'm wishing that carpet would assume magic powers and smother me. 'There's no pressure. If you don't want to, I get it.'

'My socks are ruined. I've not got another pair.'

In the tunnel of embarrassment and helplessness I see a microscopic shaft of light of encouragement.

'I think I can help there.'

She breaks off another chunk of granary toast and puts it in her mouth. She's not saying anything but then just as I'm about to apologise for my insensitivity, ask her to forget I ever mentioned the idea, and make a tactical withdrawal to the next county, she looks up at me once more. 'Okay,' she says. 'So long as you're sure. Just ... just don't expect me to be the greatest company. By the way, I'm Natalie. Natalie Bradshaw.'

'I'm Michael Partridge. Mike, if you prefer.'

And we find ourselves shaking hands across the breakfast table. But I feel like I'm grasping half a wet turbot during a November downpour.

*

We're now a good mile beyond Edale, walking a little way above a valley towards the farm buildings at Upper Booth, the expanse of pasture dotted with clumps of silver birch and bracken, gatherings of dandelions and buttercups and pools of cow parsley, while gentle green hills bubble up beyond. It's a wide path that throws down a serious challenge to the genius in the art of losing his way. The route ahead, for the time being, is clear, and other walkers stroll and stride, and frolic and laugh like models for an advert for the latest brand of foot embrocation cream. For me this is a new world and I think to myself what I never expected to think to myself, that Gravel Voice had it right. The valley sparkles with sunlight. Every stream glistens. Each oak and ash has been clothed in a new leafy cloak of spring, and revels in its fresh green apparel. The sky isn't quite cloudless, but the white strands of cirrus complement each other's artistry and add to the pattern of the heavens and dynamism of the landscape rather than threaten to engulf us in deluge or suck us into an all-consuming mist. The grass is a deep emerald. It rains a lot up North, so my late uncle Gerard from the Wirral was wont to say. But, he would go on, the rain, the hail and the snow nourishes, cleanses and nurtures, and when the last fragment of precipitation has fallen from the sky, and the clouds have melted away, and the sun breaks over the Pennines, you can forgive every drop. You need a smelly dungheap for the best roses. Actually that bit was my aunt Margharita. Probably just before they sectioned her.

We arrive at the Upper Booth farm buildings and bear right onto a firm wide track and although we are continuing to climb, this does seem almost too straightforward still. We cross a proud, sturdy packhorse bridge; given the right circumstances, it would be an ideal spot for a picnic or just a rest and a drink, with the sizzling waters of the river Noe below and precipitous green fells rising up immediately behind. Then it gets harder, much harder, as we embark on Jacob's Ladder, a relentless ascent up an almost vertical hillside on a path with flagstones as hard as frozen diamonds. Its name is derived from the pony herder who took a short cut up this same hillside in preference to the longer gentler route so as to give him sufficient time for a smoke before his pony, who'd chosen the lengthier option, caught up with him. And just as the original Jacob's Ladder of the Bible was supposed to extend into heaven, I feel as though I'm climbing into outer space and expect to need oxygen supplies at any moment. The sun continues to shine and as we wage war against the forces of gravity, clawing our way up the boulder-clad hillside, I'm captivated and I'm elated and I'm so proud that I'm doing it and I'm managing it; more than managing it, I'm embracing it. This is a world of magic, of intrigue, of a thousand coffee-table books suddenly bursting into life. The guidebook, which I'm sure was written to take into account the very worst weather, seems almost superfluous.

But while I may be ascending the heights in mind as well as underfoot, Natalie is clearly still several thousand fathoms beneath the sea. Throughout the climb, she's hardly said a word to me. "If you say so" has been as good as it's got. She's certainly been talking, talking lots, but chiefly into her mobile, sorting out a revised late afternoon journey to London. All the conversational avenues, streets, boulevards, parades, and out-of-town retail complex approach roads I've tried have met with the same reinforced steel wall, with strands of barbed and electrified If You Say So coiled round and round it. She mutters, in answer to question 251 of my interrogation, that she vaguely remembers this landscape from her efforts yesterday, but it would seem that as far as she's concerned anything that separates her from her objective, however it might excite the aesthetic sensibilities of the average visitor, could just as well be the unclaimed baggage office at East Midlands Airport.

But since Toby was her world, and still is her world, and she and I are strangers, and I can claim only the most temporary membership of her world, it's crazy to even contemplate that it might be otherwise.

And then it's the plateau, and the white triangulation point of Kinder Low. It may be just a stump of rock amongst an explosion of rocks and stones, a stump which some thoughtful local has daubed with bright paint, but to me it's a beacon. I want flames to shoot from it to celebrate our arrival at base camp from which we're to make our decisive assault across the plateau interior. Kinder Low: who on earth gave it that name. There's nothing low about this landscape, with its peat-stricken heights lingering on one side and Manchester and its surrounding countryside laid out before us on the other. And yet this isn't the end. There's still work to do, work which involves our having to probe the interior of the plateau. The summit it has to be, and with it the satisfaction of being able to say that we've made the roof not only of the interior itself but, at 636 metres high, the entire Peak District National Park as well as the county of Derbyshire. Nothing less will count. No cribbing from other sources will do.

I keep looking at Natalie. Over the past few minutes she's been studying the ground beneath her feet as though something down there holds the key to the Holy Grail. Every so often she winces. I've no doubt that even with the stockings I've donated to her, her boots are giving her a taste of purgatory. But she chooses to remain silent. And with every breath she makes, every step she takes, the certainty intensifies that only if we make this summit will I have any chance of finding a way over her Toby-shaped castle battlements.

I withdraw the navigator from my pocket and remind myself of the instructions. Switching it on is easy enough, and I can do that bit. Wait for satellites, thirty seconds but seems like thirty Stone Ages. Ready to navigate. Press, press, press again, Find Waypoint. That precious reference. Index number 1. Now pray for the arrow, the arrow that'll point us to the summit cairn, and an indicator of distance.

There's the arrow. It seems to waver and spin, and for a moment I panic, but then it appears to settle on its desired direction and there's also a distance indicator showing me that no more than half a mile separates us from the big prize. But there's a catch. While a proper path continues round the sanctuary of the plateau rim, a factory manager who takes care to avoid any contact with the shop floor, there's no path to the highest point, a piddly but infuriating three metres higher than the Kinder Low triangulation point. How generations of pedants must curse the pedant who measured it in the first place. It would be pretty much a formality if it were just a walk across heather, but it was never going to be as simple as that. As we make our way into the plateau interior, we walk into the peat, harsh relentless peat, with the texture of cake icing but the smell and sensual appeal of the cesspit of the underworld. There's channels, and ditches, and mini-valleys, and they're all going the wrong way, and although there are dry patches, each step seems like a lottery, where a misjudgement could see either of us sinking through an invisible trapdoor into a sticky black-brown abyss. And every one of the boulders, placed where I least expect them, seem to be waiting to do a Chinese burn on my right ankle. If we wanted to take the mystique out of it, we might liken it to a puzzle in a kids' magazine, the mouse trying to get through a maze to a piece of cheese, though I can't imagine that or indeed any of my boyhood conundrums bringing the threat of mud interment with each false move. It's fearsome enough under the cloudless sky with which we are blessed. But just the thought of being benighted here in rain or mist or both sets me quaking in unison with the tremble and shudder of the ground beneath our feet.

Looking around me, though, I begin to realise that the dark brutality isn't just scaring me, it's kind of exciting me at the same time. The mix of peat and heather has a masculine, aggressive edge and my vulnerability and sense of insignificance in its face leaves me exhilarated, not shrinking from the fear but embracing it, afraid to ask for more yet wanting and needing more. It's the thrill of coming out of normality and into a different and unimaginable world, the terror generating in me a bizarre sense of pleasure. Around me now is a landscape that is noble in its desolation and in its nothingness. Life is stripped bare just here. There are no verdant fields or buttercup-clad hillsides, no riots of foxgloves and azaleas, no waterfalls bouncing down purple-headed mountains, and no fast-flowing rivers brimming with trout and bream. It's a landscape that doesn't ask to be liked but defies you to stay indifferent to it. It would prefer you to hate it.

And we're getting there. The arrow's not dancing and the mileage is reducing with each act of boghopping, with each mini-valley and channel and ditch. Natalie's pace is quickening now, and she's looking up, and there's a light in her eyes, and I make up my mind that even if I never have the chance to do anything more for this girl, and even if the moment we get to the summit she tells me to shove off and throw myself under the Brighton Belle, I can at least say that I've made something happen for her. Now the ground's getting less squashy and the fractions of miles on the navigator have turned into yards, and the yards now turn into feet. 340 feet, 200 feet, and suddenly we don't need the navigator because there it is: a modest pile of stones in the middle of nothing, just heather and standing boulders and water and muck and much more muck. I reach out and offer my hand to Natalie. Maybe not ten minutes ago she'd have recoiled from it as though it were a risk to public health but now she clenches and squeezes it and nothing will make me release it.

Hand in hand, we walk the remaining twenty yards to the cairn, we both lean down and place our hands on it, then we draw ourselves up to our full height.

Now I gaze at Natalie's face, and tears are pouring from her eyes and cascading down her cheeks.

'I've done it, Toby,' she whispers. 'I've only gone and done it.'

And as her face becomes an ocean, she's smiling, she's smiling like I've never seen her smile before, and I stretch out my arms and envelop her in them, and yes, I know I'm taking a chance and she may be revolted and strike my brazen cheeks with thunderbolts from her fingertips, but she drapes her arms round me and here are these two troubled strangers standing in embrace.

7

Merstham(n) – malevolent piece of pathside vegetation that waits till you think you've cleared it before inflicting maximum damage on your skin, hair or clothing

We come apart again and just stand there for a few minutes. Then she gets her mobile out and begins taking pictures of the cairn. Three, six, nine, twelve, then a couple of selfies. Were it not for the significance of the achievement for her I'd be suggesting, once the first half dozen are in the can, that she's got more photos than she really needs; other than to seekers after peat-clad summits it really could be anywhere. I content myself with a single pic using my own mobile, and I just don't feel it appropriate to include her in it. This isn't about us. For her it's a mission, for me it's a voyage of discovery, but there's no us in this at all.

All the while I've been careful to keep the white Kinder Low trig point in our sights. Gavin reiterated before leaving me last night that he'd never send anyone onto this plateau in mist unless they were experienced and confident in the use of the navigator. We're blessed with such clarity today that there's no need for a navigator to get us back to the trig point. Eyesight alone will do. As we begin our walk back to Edale, my eyes stay fixed on the white stone column as though looking away for a second runs the risk of turning me into an Old Testament-style pillar of salt. The peat and heather hold no fears for us now, and in fact Natalie's marching ahead, as if the triumph of achievement has given her legs an injection of Sherman tank fuel. The walk from Kinder Low to the top of Jacob's Ladder seems almost too short, and as we descend to the packhorse bridge on the flagstoned path I'm having to call out to Natalie to slow down as she skips from stone to stone, only too aware that one misjudgement might send her into free fall without a parachute between the pair of us. I follow at a more discreet pace but my feet are fireballs and I need to stop for a rest. The packhorse bridge over the cool gliding waters of the river Noe, nestling between steep green banks, seems like the ideal spot. I'm able to catch her up just as we reach the bridge and suggest we sit by the bridge and dip our feet in the water. Natalie glances at her watch and tells me she's worried about her train. But sweat is etched into her face, she's panting like a champion greyhound, then she's reaching for her water bottle and throwing the liquid at her mouth. A moment later she's sitting down with me on the bank of the river, just upstream of the bridge. I get my boots off and it feels as though the weight of the Emirates Stadium has fallen from beneath me. Natalie removes her boots but then also peels her socks to expose her bare feet, and begins to bathe them in the water. I can see her pleasure and her relief.

'Better?' I ask.

'It's good,' she says with a smile. She takes a deep breath. 'Listen, Mike, I'll never forget what you've done for me. Never forget it. Toby would be so proud.'

Toby, Toby, Toby. Always Toby. No, Mike. No right to judge. No right to try and staunch or redirect the flow of grieving. You've never been there. Don't presume to show her round it, still less try and escort her out of it. Help her. But on her terms, in her way.

'Tell me about him,' I say.

'What do you want to know?'

'Anything. Your first date. Maybe.'

A smile plays on her face. 'It was a geography camp in my GCSE year. Fifteen years ago. Lulworth Cove. A Wednesday morning. We'd just had another hateful night in a bunkhouse and we were fossil hunting. And we noticed Toby was missing. Nobody had the foggiest where he'd gone. There was a search party, the whole shebang. Turned out that he'd bluffed his way into a restricted area of clifftop and was shinning up and down these cliffs with soldiers firing ammunition round his ears. He was a born explorer, adventurer. I fell in love with him that day. I made the first move. I asked him to have coffee with me in the village next morning.'

'The Costa del Lulworth?'

She permits herself a simper. 'Hardly. Just a takeway from the burger van if I remember. When everyone else was mopping up sick in the bunkhouse dormitories. That night he and I went for a moonlit walk on the cliffs. Was crazy really, we only had this poxy torch. Could easily have gone over the edge. But it just made it more special. Made the first kiss more special.'

'And you've been together ever since?'

'Yes.' She gazes up towards the fluffs of cloud playing in the spring sky. 'We went to different universities. Suppose it crossed our mind that we might drift apart in that time. But no. Then we got jobs in the same town. Wasn't planned. Just happened. Moved in together, stayed together. Never married.' She looks at the ringless fingers of her left hand. 'Didn't bother me. We didn't need a priest or registrar to remind us that we loved each other. I mean, yes, it would have been fun. My mum kept on asking when it was happening, had the whole ceremony planned for us, had the hat on order, agreed the eight flavours of cake icing, couldn't decide between the limo and the pony and trap. Wasn't to be. Never worried me, we were still partners, we were never not going to be partners ...' And now she runs the fingers of her right hand across her wedding ring finger. 'He was quite unconventional in lots of ways. Didn't want to just conform, follow the crowd. He wasn't a career guy. I remember him telling me what his ambition was. It wasn't to earn loads of money or live in a nice house. It was Everest. To climb Everest.'

'And he achieved that?'

She yawns and stretches out her arms. 'Got so close. Couple of years ago. He got himself on an expedition. Made it to base camp but the organisers said it was touch and go because of the weather. Then suddenly there was this massive snowstorm. Much worse than forecast. They had to call it off. He was heartbroken. Couldn't afford to try again. He's done a lot of the other big peaks. Kilimanjaro. McKinley. Mont Blanc. All over Norway, Switzerland, South America. And of course most of the summits he'd been planning to include in his book. He mopped all but one of the Scottish ones up in a single expedition. Just left a few odd ones here and there, one in Wales, the rest in England. He was a big kid. Tearing open the big Christmas presents first, leaving the small ones for later. He lived for his walking. Dreaded getting hurt so he couldn't walk. Hated anything that came between him and his walking. Obsessive at times. Watched starving Africans on TV without batting an eyelid, then next day in fits of rage because the outdoor goods shop was out of dubbin. So single-minded, so determined. Had so many grand plans, visions. The entire west coast of the USA. Going right across Africa from west to east. Exhausted me just talking about them.'

'And you didn't mind all this?'

'Not at all. The rugged explorer. I was proud of him.' Now I can see tears assembling round the corners of both her eyes. 'When he came back from a long walking expedition we'd celebrate by going to our favourite restaurant and gorging conchiglie carbonara and gooseberry and elderflower ice-cream and drinking Chablis while he told me where he'd been. Then we'd just spend all our evenings, all our weekends together, just talking, just loving. He was an amazing guy, brilliant guy. I mean, don't get me wrong, he was a human being, for crying out loud. That was what was nice. Certainly no geek. He had needs, like everyone else.' She giggles. 'He had this obsession with power dressing. Smart business suits. Crisp white shirts.' She sighs and gazes heavenwards. 'I disappointed him there. Didn't have to power dress for my work. Roving reporter for the local rag. Jumper and jeans girl, me. Look a bit daft turning up at church bazaars in short black skirt and heels. It became a standing joke between us. We laughed about it. But underneath, I don't know … Anyway, I guess we all have our … our …' She tails off and sighs.

'And you didn't mind him going to Canada alone? Couldn't you have gone together?'

She gulps and I can see it won't take much to release a Niagara of sobs. 'We couldn't both afford to go. He was being made redundant from his work, decided to use most of his payoff and go out there alone. So wanted it. We spoke almost every day and he told me he was catching this flight then going off into the mountains after that. I was sitting at home with the radio on, had just tried ringing him actually, see how he was, but it cut out and I couldn't even leave a message. I thought, that's not right. I'd just hung up when it came through on the radio about the crash. When they said where the flight had started and where it was going I knew, just knew, it was his flight. I rang him again straight away, nothing. Then again a few minutes later, still nothing. I rang the airline, they confirmed it was his flight. No survivors at all. Bodies burnt to a crisp. Nothing left of him at all. Bereavement. Widowhood. It sucks. Whatever bad things he's done, I'd forgive him every single one if he could just walk through our front door again. That's what it's like. He encouraged me so much. Now he's gone, I'm scared … so scared …'

I place my arm round her. 'It's okay,' I whisper. 'You'll be okay.' Just words. Words of the helpless helper, words demanded by convention, by politeness, but I can feel the emptiness in every syllable.

'I keep telling myself he's at peace,' she says between sobs. 'I wish it helped more. Maybe it will in time. At the moment it's still hurting so much. And so many reminders. Even just before you first saw me. Was fiddling with my phone. Found a whole load of texts, pictures from him I'd never got round to deleting. One on the top of Snowdon and guess what, it was snowing. Another that he'd booked a weekend in early July in Edinburgh. For my birthday. Just one thing after another. Hurts so much. So,so much.'

I look around me. The surroundings are perfect: the effervescent glide of the mountain stream, the contrasting greens of hillside and the leaves on the clumps of trees, the sun coating each rock, each hillside, each movement of the water with a smooth sheen of light. Other walkers have passed and continue to pass us, their faces filled with anticipation and elation and enjoyment. But as far as Natalie and I are concerned it's the absent figure and her love for him that draws a dark cloud over the scene and the longer we stay the darker and more invasive I think the cloud could become. And I'm the one who suggests we need to move on.

*

Natalie has a train to catch so tempting though it is to call in at the pub or the café in Edale village centre for a celebratory drink we agree we'll walk straight through the village and out towards the station. I've spent the first part of the walk back from the bridge making further changes to my travel arrangements. I don't want to spend another night on the coach and it's actually cheaper to stay up here a further night and transfer my coach booking to tomorrow than it is to travel by train this afternoon. Darshan's full tonight but he's fixed me up at a place in Manchester and assures me their breakfast is even better. But once that's sorted, we've continued in almost total silence, in my case the silence of fear that any topic I raise will seem banal and insensitive. There's so much I'd like to ask her. There's so much, as newly single people, we might find we had in common. But I'm no nearer than I was on our ascent of Kinder Scout to discovering the woman behind the grief and cutting through the stuff she's put round herself. And the tiredness which has diluted the thrill of achievement has robbed me of the ability to apply the boltcutters. It's only as we follow the road leading to the station that we start talking again.

'What do you do, Mike?' she asks.

'Me?'

'Yes, you.'

'I don't do anything. Really.'

She screws up her face. 'Nobody does nothing.'

I smirk. 'I'm a specialist in it,' I tell her. 'No work, no leisure interests, no beliefs. My w … my ex-wife was right. Not even a believer in non-belief. I'm a nothing, I do nothing in particular, I believe in nothing in particular. My granddad, he was a great fan of Gilbert and Sullivan. When I was about six or seven, he used to play bits of it to me. Well, more than bits sometimes. He used to laugh like mad at the songs. He kept playing this one called *When Britain really ruled the waves* or something like that, and there was a line which went something like "the House of Lords throughout the war did nothing in particular, and did it very well." That's me. Except I don't really do it that well. I don't do anything that well. Certainly don't do marriage well. Do fatherhood even worse.'

'It's not easy being a father.'

'I was a great dad once. To my daughter. My real daughter. We had the one child we wanted. Then she died. We adopted another. I couldn't love her, Natalie. I gave up on trying to be a good dad. Trying to be any kind of dad. And I tell you this much, if I'd not had the snip, they'd have enacted a special law to make sure I had to have it. That bad. Louise, my wife, she did everything. For all of us. I did nothing. Nothing. Anyway, now they've left me. Result, my house is now a health hazard. Attracting interest from environmental pressure groups. And I certainly don't do work well. Not working now, never likely to be again.'

'You've done something pretty well today.'

'I certainly didn't do it for me.'

'You must be good at something. Everyone's good at something.'

'I'm honestly not. Unless you ... no.'

'Eh?'

'No, it's ...'

'Go on. I'm interested.'

'Arsenal Football Club. Anything you want to know about them. Top scorer in 1937. Result of their first match with Tottenham after the war. Anything.'

'Oh. Right.'

'Exactly. It's a nothing. It's an embarrassment. That's all I'm good for. A load of useless tripe nobody cares about. Does it take civilisation forward? Does it make life better for anyone? Feed the hungry? Heal the sick? Raise the dead to life?'

'You never know. It might. It's ... well, it's different.'

'It's not Toby though, is it.' Thank God I just stop myself saying it out loud.

*

A few minutes later we arrive at the station. It may be one of the more rural on the network – there's hardly a house in sight – but being a natural base for Peak District walkers and on a line linking two major northern cities, it's bound to get busy. Both platforms are crowded with walkers reliving their weekend explorations, bronzed by the sun and wind on their faces, weary, triumphant, doubtless counting the hours to the next time.

While I'm heading to Manchester, Natalie's bound for Sheffield, and her train's due to leave just ten minutes before mine. I walk with her to the far end of her platform, trying to think what to say, how to bring a dignified curtain down on the scene we've been playing out. But again the right words, if there are any right words, just seem to elude me. And again she's the one who speaks first.

'I'll never forget what you've done for me, Mike,' she whispers. 'Thank you.'

She places a hand on my shoulder and kisses me on the cheek.

And whether it's the kiss, or the realisation that we're likely to have only five more minutes in each other's company I don't know, but my words are racing ahead of my senses once more. 'Can we do this again sometime?'

'Do what?' There's genuine puzzlement on her face.

'Go walking. Perhaps tick some more off your list.'

She kisses me again. 'You're a very kind guy, Mike,' she says. 'A very kind guy.'

Though mists of disappointment and anti-climax are closing in on the golden sunset of our farewell, I manage a smile. 'It's a no, then.'

'Mike, we're both in crap places right now,' she says. 'You've been great today, and put up with me and done something for me I'll never forget, but I think … oh, God, it's hard to say this … I think we'd just be a disappointment to each other. I think you need more than I can give, and I …'She tails off.

'I know. I get it.'

'Best leave it, hey.' She puts her arms around me and I feel the gentle caress of her hands on my neck and upper back.

At that moment the train comes into view. She draws her arms back and looks into my eyes. 'Nobody does nothing very well, Mike,' she says. 'Stop doing nothing so badly. Start doing everything and doing that really well.'

The train's arriving at the platform. Now I kiss her on the cheek then watch her pile in with the other ramblers, and watch her as she scrambles into a window seat and places her backpack on her lap. She looks at me and smiles and the next moment she's disappeared from my sight.

8

Morvah(n) – where a village with pub you and your walking companions are desperate for is signposted as 1 mile away, mysterious second mile which will always interpose between you and it

The Manchester train comes in more or less on time and we proceed on our way but after a couple of miles come to a halt and sit outside a tunnel for twenty minutes. I've heard of the owl that was afraid of the dark but never a Great North Western Transpennine Turbo.

Having thought that Darshan's breakfast this morning would last me till some time next January I'm hungry again. On the way to my B & B, which thankfully is within walking distance of the station, I find a Co-op. Here I secure myself a plastic carton of succulent chicken pasta in luscious tomato sauce with separate helping of crisp Caesar salad in creamy dressing. I decide I'll smuggle that, together with a family-size apple pie for pud, into my room and eat it there. Then I trudge on towards my night's lodgings. I'm still trudging when my phone rings. It's Gavin.

'How did you get on?' he says.

'I got there, if that's what you mean.'

'Kinder Scout?'

'Yes.'

'Good man. Where are you now? Still oop North?'

'Somewhere.'

'Where you don't want me to be?'

'Something like that.'

'Fancy a walk?'

I'm about to hang up. I don't want to talk to him again, still less walk with him again. Then I think ahead to the evening that's yawning out ahead of me. I doubt I'll want to eat again tonight and I'm in no mood to kill more hours traipsing around the city looking for other things to do. I'd done enough of that yesterday morning. I may have the prospect of a hot bath, a bed, and, if Darshan is to be believed, a breakfast fit for Billy Bunter, but there's still an awful lot of lonely idleness in the way first, and I've already had a substantial ration of same on the train coming here just now. So I give in. We agree that Gavin will pick me up from my B & B at three thirty, which gives sufficient time for me to get there and unpack, meet Mrs Freeman and eat my late lunch. There's a freshly-made bed, a choice of 738 television channels, four kinds of speciality tea among the sachets provided as well as at least sixteen portions of UHT milk, a basketful of funsize Bourbon biscuits, and the entire Luxury Book Club Library collection of Catherine Cookson. Mrs F's also promising me frothy coffee and extra-rich home-made fruit cake in the lounge at 9.30 tonight sharp. She says she's always in bed by ten so can't make it any later.

Gavin's on time. 'Got a little surprise for you,' he says with a grin.

'How do you mean?'

'We're off to the Lake District.'

*

I don't know why, but I just assume the Lake District is far too far away for us to get there and back and do a decent walk in the space of a single evening. But Gavin assures me that it really is only two hours by car, and starting our walk at five thirty we'll finish comfortably in daylight and be back in Manchester before half the decent clubs have even opened. I can still hardly believe I'm to be undertaking a second piece of hill-climbing in one day but the ride in the car, on the back of my refreshment in Manchester, is helping me to refocus and re-energise. Gavin's right about the two-hour outward journey, although it needs a creative interpretation of motorway speed legislation to achieve it. We're fortunate with light traffic on the M6, which we follow as far as Kendal, and it's also a clear run up the A591, the main road through the Lake District; most of the vehicles seem to be going the other way. By five fifteen we're embarking on the road which heads south-westwards out of Keswick through Borrowdale and signs are proclaiming our arrival at the Honister Pass.

As Gavin yanks the gearstick into first to get us up the almost vertical incline, I become conscious for the first time that the landscape's been closing in on us. On the M6, it was safe, bland fields stretching out on both sides. Up the A591, mountains and lakes have been in sight throughout, but the road has been wide and confident. Now, the fells and hills seem to be right on top of us. It's a kind of towering disdain on their part, an assertion of their grandeur and timelessness and man's futility in believing he could ever compete with them. I've not been to the Lake District before. Mum and dad were never card-carrying hill walkers and although we might go on short walks when we went away together, the idea of a walking holiday struck them, just as it has gone on to strike me, as a contradiction in terms. They weren't lured by the rugged and the inhospitable, neither in Britain nor abroad. So my arrival in Lakeland is an introduction to a new world. But it's as if everyone's being introduced and offering the hand of welcome at once. There are the hills, fells and mountains stretching to the skies, no tops the same, some flat and some proudly volcanic, some clothed with smooth sloping turf, tangly rich grass or fresh green bracken, some scarred, bare and battle-weary from countless confrontations with Nature at its most vengeful, some sporting random rushes of loose stones and boulders, some etched with outcrops of battleship grey rock, some boasting plantations of spikey deep green conifers, some ripped in twain by paths and tracks and wandering becks, whose waters hurl themselves towards the valley floors. Then there are the lakes that give the region its name, lakes whose waters host a thousand sparkles gifted by the sun, whose waters shimmer in the early evening light, whose waters bear apparel of purest blue, pale blue, deep blue, turquoise blue. And there's the road we're following now, a miracle of engineering, yes, but still a mere token attempt by man to match the untamed and untameable ingenuity and artistry of what lies around him. Gavin says there aren't many roads in the Lake District apart from the ones we've been following, and even those that exist are forced to give way to the whims of the contours of the fellsides and the playful inlets of the waters. Gavin's a model tour guide and indeed has been enhancing his credentials as such at each jerk of his steering wheel, naming and extolling each landmark, man-made and natural, as though every one was part of his own close-knit family. Ambleside, Grasmere, Helm Crag, Castle Crags, Seathwaite, Seatoller – it's a new language for me and I've been striving to master some of the more common nouns and irregular verbs. And I'm feeling the adrenalin pumping harder and harder with every corner we turn, every hill we negotiate, and every yard of metal ribbon that brings us closer to the moment when we'll need to rely on ourselves to make further progress without mechanical aid.

Having got us over Honister Pass, Gavin drives us on to Gatesgarth close to the eastern end of Buttermere, and our base for the ascent of his favourite fell, Haystacks. He's suggesting we do a circular walk, which will take a little longer but gives more variety. We'll be ascending via the Warnscale Beck crossing, Green Crag and two tarns, Blackbeck Tarn and Innominate Tarn, then coming down via Scarth Gap and High Wax Knott. It's about five miles and should take roughly three hours, allowing time to linger at the summit. With the sun not setting till around nine, Gavin says we'll make it easily providing we don't dawdle. I don't like playing beat-the-clock, particularly as I'm not sure I can trust my body to do what's going to be asked of it, but there's no point in arguing. He's the boss.

The start of the walk seems almost too straightforward. It's good fast walking on an excellent green path. We pass numerous other walkers, most coming the other way, their gait noticeably more laboured than ours, but there's a sweaty contentment on their faces. As soon as we've left this path, forking right and soon crossing a wooden footbridge over Warnscale Beck, the number of other foot travellers diminishes significantly, and the really hard work begins. We proceed more or less parallel with the beck for a while, then bend sharp right, left, and right again, and left again. We look down to the frolicsome waterslides of Warnscale Beck on our left, and across the beck to Fleetwith Pike; at 2126 feet high it's a real mountain, Gavin says, and with its thin dignified peak, separated from the valley by cascades of stone, it has the appearance and stage presence of a proper mountain. We're now over a thousand feet above sea level and we pause and look back to admire Buttermere, its serenity and placidity seemingly undisturbed and not intimidated by the presence of so many monsters pressing on its banks. Keeping a ravine to our left we continue to climb then veer once more to the right, passing an old quarry and beneath a stone shelter, once a quarryman's hut. We make the top of the ridge but Gavin announces it's too early for a celebratory rest and the work's far from over; we must now follow the ridge top, proceeding round the back of Green Crag and going on to the first of the ridge-top mini-lakes or tarns, this one being Blackbeck Tarn. Here Gavin allows us to pause, wipe the perspiration off our brows and truly appreciate the uniqueness of these surroundings. He quotes from Alfred Wainwright's description of the variety of features around us: "'Sharp peaks in profusion, tarns, crags, screes, rocks, heather tracts, marshes, serpentine trails … surprises around corners, and there are many corners.'" Having enjoyed the view down the Blackbeck Ravine, we walk on beside the shore of the next tarn, Innominate Tarn, from which Gavin points out one of the most shapely and photogenic of all the Lake District mountains, Great Gable, a giant loaf of bread, a satisfying rectangle of deep green on deep blue. Then we begin the final push to the summit, and as we continue on our way, Gavin warns me that it's always the last part of the task that's the hardest, one final challenge from nature, questioning our determination and our will to succeed. The map, depicting the path with a small succession of innocuous green dashes, makes it look no more than a stroll, but the path becomes stonier and more tortuous; it really does seem that each yard gained requires ten or twenty actual yards' work, but finally a wooden post among the boulders signifies that, as far as Haystacks is concerned, we can go no higher. There are other summits overlooking Buttermere that are taller, but Gavin's quoting Wainwright once more, telling me that our summit "'stands unabashed and unashamed … like a shaggy terrier in the company of foxhounds.'" I see what the man means. It's different. It's distinctive. Special.

We stop by the summit tarn. There's nobody else about and for a while we just stand there in silence. I see Gavin blinking and I wonder if he's got something in his eye. Then I remember that on the way here he told me that he was born and brought up in Carlisle and not only has he grown up in these surroundings but they truly are a part of him and even now coming here on a cloudless evening brings tears to his cheeks. As I gaze out towards Buttermere I can understand it, and looking round me I wonder if it's going to be my turn next. The summit is a giant work of art, where on a grand canvas the artist has determined not to be restricted by one particular school but rather to depict as many styles and moods as the size of the canvas allows. There are paths that snake and curl. There are patches of heather which clothe a black marshy flesh. There's the summit tarn, its gently swaying pure blue waters jealously protected by its own bodyguard of rocks and boulders. There's the prospect of loftier peaks around us, and from where we stand we can look up at the gloriously proud green bulk of High Crag. There are the small rocky outcrops, some smooth and elegant and inviting, others rough and shapeless and hostile, and there are great crags, some gentle and welcoming but others steep-sided and sheer and stark. Just looking at some of them turns my knees to aspens. I've been on clifftops nearer home, but these have tended to come complete with fences and warning notices and ice cream vans and, on occasion, posts in the grass bearing Bible verses and the phone number of the Samaritans. There are no fences or signs to be seen in this place. It's an environment where nobody or nothing seems to care whether you choose to remain on your feet, where no warning notices seek to dissuade you from certain crags and certain slopes, and one false move sends you off balance and to annihilation. Meanwhile, the evening sunshine, the clear skies, the soft air and the meek coos of the curlews above are playing with us, trying to have us believe that no danger exists. Gavin points out the clumsy mass of rock just a little lower than the summit, called Big Stack, and at his suggestion we clamber from rock to rock, from boulder to boulder, and stand on the edge. And as I stand and look down, and see the expanse of fresh air immediately beneath my boots, I feel spasms of fear in every finger tip, on the edge of each of my toes, and my shoulders, while my mouth is dry, and beads of perspiration queue up across my forehead to drip down over my eyes and my cheeks.

God, I love this place.

'Glad you came?' he asks.

'Just a bit,' I murmur.

He pulls a bottle of water from his pocket and takes a swig then passes it to me.

'No, ta. Not thirsty.'

'If you wait till you are it's too late. You're dehydrated by then. Worst thing to be on a walk. Leaves you thinking about nothing else.' He presses the bottle into my hand and watches while I drink. 'These hills just give so much. So much joy, so much wonderment.' He points to his boots. 'Friend of mine, he goes out walking in bare feet. He reckons that there's a load of energy, knowledge, primal wisdom coming from the ground. Says it's another way Nature gives back to us. And Nature asks for so little in return.'

'Just a few bloody toes, presumably.' I say.

He doesn't smile. He takes the bottle from me and puts it back in his pocket.

'I've met too many walkers who give nothing back in return,' he says. 'They never properly engage with what's around them. Too wrapped up in themselves. There's miracles every minute of every day. Sunrise and sunset. Clouds. Birdsong. Wild plants and insects. Rock formations. And, yes, what's beneath our feet. Unremarkable sometimes, okay. But still there. Still reaching out to us. But so often taken for granted. If walkers learned to stop, to watch, to listen, to respect, maybe get their feet dirty, take a joy in even the simple things, and then sought to protect, safeguard what was all around them … it's like any relationship. If you love, you show your love by giving. Giving lots.'

Watching every movement of the foot, but keeping our boots and socks on, we scramble and inch, clamber and slide round each pocket of rock and through each chunk of heather to return to the summit for the second and last time. Now we turn our attention away from the immediate surroundings and are looking further afield. Gavin's pointing out many of the features of the wider Lake District that, despite our being dwarfed by High Crag, we can enjoy from here: not only Buttermere lake itself but two other lakes, Crummock Water and Loweswater, Great Gable once more, and other fells including Grasmoor, Eel Crag and Pillar. There's a lifetime's worth of exploration and discovery in a single unforgettable panorama. Then Gavin suggests we concentrate on the horizon, and through his binoculars we're able to look far beyond Buttermere and far beyond the Lake District; so far in fact that we're able to look across the Solway Firth to the mountains of Dumfries and Galloway in south-west Scotland. There's a part of me that would love to move on along the ridge, to High Crag and High Stile, and beyond, not just a little beyond, but far beyond, right round, to observe the waters of Buttermere from every angle and watch the evening sun throw its final exuberant rays of the evening onto the fellsides. But Gavin points to the sky and reminds me that Nature's most lethal and unstoppable weapon, darkness, is heading towards us. The setting sun may be casting a pink beam on the tips of the hillsides, a layer of icing on the sponge of heather, and provide another image of Nature's serene and inscrutable power. But as he says, whatever I might wish to believe, there's a world down there, a world which we've no choice but to go back to, like it or loathe it. I find my hand clasping his. It's not so much a clasp of affection but profound gratitude that he's opened out to me this new world and taught me about a new kind of love.

For the first time on a walk this weekend, we're not just turning back. This is a round trip, so the thrill of discovery will be sustained till the very end. Accordingly, instead of retracing our steps towards Innominate Tarn we're going straight on, or as straight as straight on can be in this environment where every path has to contend with Nature's own walls and barriers and barricades. Initially we follow the ridge onwards, beginning with a drop down to the col, or dip in the ridge, known as Scarth Gap, effectively our exit gate from the ridge. Drop is the right word; it's a steep and perilous descent, the loose stones presenting another variety of obstacle and trip hazard, and every step has to be considered before execution. But as Gavin points out, time taken here is time better spent than on a stretcher or in a plaster cast. With a sigh of relief we reach Scarth Gap, but the relief is tempered with regret, because, like a child who reaches the ice-cream shop to find the shutters being pulled down, I have to accept that the joys immediately before me are out of reach for now. High Crag will have to wait for another day, another adventure. We must leave the ridge with its canvas of excitements and fears and surprises and alarms, and embark on a zigzag heading downhill to the boulders of High Wax Knott and neighbouring Low Wax Knott. The descent seems starker than the climb. We may have gravity on our side but Gavin says that's part of the problem. Controlling the pull of that gravity. Our feet might want to hustle us down the hillside at top speed but we're not going to thank them if they smash us to the ground. And it's the knees that take the biggest strain as we change down into first gear and ease our way away from the ridge and towards the bracken-clad lower slopes. We permit ourselves a pause at High Wax Knott, where Nature generously provides seating in the form of large boulders immediately beside the path. But I see a look of uneasiness in Gavin's eyes. He warns me that though the sun, unsullied and unthreatened by even the wispiest of cloud, is still casting its spell over the waters before us, its reign is almost at an end, and will give up its supremacy as readily as a candle submitting to a puff of cold air. There's still work to do. The gradient does reduce as we follow a path through the bracken and alongside a wall, but then there's a key right turn by a conifer spinney, which Gavin says we must not miss. In the end there's just enough daylight for us to identify the turning, complete the descent and bring us onto the runway for the taxi along the valley floor to Gatesgarth.

As we hit the valley floor, our desultory chat has dissolved into silence; it's the silence of tiredness and having no more to give, but for me it's also the silence of a contentment so profound that words no longer matter: contentment not only for what I've seen and for what more there may be to see, but for what I've achieved and the confidence that is now bursting out inside me. Then, nearing the houses of the village, we see headlamps of cars driving along the lakeside road, and lights in the windows of the farmsteads, reminders of the messy normal, reminders of the spell slowly unravelling and normal service now needing to be resumed whether we're ready or not. And moments later we're back in the car and Gavin's negotiating us down the far side of Honister Pass into Borrowdale, the peaks of the mountains and crags now lost in the march of dusk and darkness.

The rigours of the day's walks are catching up with me now I've stopped. I've not got the energy to initiate any conversation and as we leave the A591 at Kendal and join the M6 I find myself yawning and shutting my eyes.

'Sorry for keeping you up,' Gavin says.

I force my eyes open again. 'Not used to so much exercise.'

'Just be glad you're fit enough to do it at all. I try to tell myself that every day. Specially when I have a Bleaklow moment.'

'Eh?'

'A Bleaklow moment,' he says. 'A Bleaklow is that frisson of dread you get when you're passed by a Saga coach full of eighty-year-olds and it hits you that'll be you one day.'

He accelerates to pass a truck. 'Don't worry, It's this game that me and a couple of rambling friends made up one very wet Sunday lunchtime in a pub. Well, we didn't exactly make it up. It's a kind of spin on the idea Douglas Adams had in *The Meaning Of Liff*. But for walkers. So Walkopedia was born. You have to think up a situation, usually a bad or unlucky one, you as a walker might find yourself in but which there's no word for.'

Being stuck in a Ford Fusion listening to this being just one of them. And there's no obvious exit strategy. 'Oh yes?'

'It started out of nothing. I think it was me. We were onto our fifth pint. I asked what you call the selective memory which enables you to remember nothing about how wet a walk was or how many blisters are cluttering up your big toe, but every detail of the best pubs and the best beer. Or the inability to do any serious walking after drinking that beer. Kind of mushroomed from there. Reading a route guide that says "You can't miss this turning" and you do just that. Or that obstinate piece of mud on the sole of your boot which refuses to go away no matter how hard you bang the boot on the ground, then invariably ends up on your otherwise spotless living room carpet. So that's the first stage. Then, because there's no words for these things, you use place names instead. We use place names from long distance footpaths. Towns, villages, hamlets, hills, mountains, they're all in. Think up the situation, place name to match. That's Walkopedia.'

I can see this becoming a very long drive home indeed. My heart sinks when we run into a queue of traffic on approaching some road works. I yawn once more.

'I'm sorry,' he says. 'You must think I'm a right Mongewell.'

Best to humour him or he might turn dangerous. 'God, no. Perish the thought.'

He doesn't elaborate or explain. It's more serious than I thought. *I'm supposed to know what the hell he means*. Mongewell. Hmm. I'm guessing, only guessing, he's trying to own up to being someone who's taken his passion for walking to antisocial levels. I could just see him casting a reproachful glare at a would-be rambler kitted out with an inferior make of backpack or the wrong sort of water bottle. Or forming a pressure group to campaign for the reversal of a decision to close 5 metres of public footpath to create extra trolley space for the new Aldi superstore. Or sporting a T-shirt emblazoned with witty walking-related slogans. KEEP CALM AND CARRY ON WALKING. OLD WALKERS NEVER DIE, THEY JUST GET LOST. But hey, what's wrong with speaking in English.

We negotiate our way through the road works and are soon hitting ninety miles an hour. I'm expecting to be rechristened with some other obscure place-name, which in Walkopedia means walking philistine who doesn't know his Munros from his Marilyns and for whom a corrie is half past seven on Mondays on ITV1. But his flow of inspiration appears to have run dry. We proceed in blissful silence.

*

It's not till ten forty that we find ourselves back in the centre of Manchester. Gavin says he's got two or three good pubs in mind and then a club after that if I'm up for it. Up to about an hour ago I'd have been leading the way to the bar, but I think it must be the prospect of playing Walkopedia for the next umpteen hours because I find myself saying no, I'd rather be getting back to my frothy coffee and richer-than-Branson fruit cake. It'll be sitting there now, the coffee getting colder and, if made with hot milk, skinnier, but I'm hoping the fruit cake will be one of those which improve and mature with age and so be even sweeter and fruitier for its extended stay on the lounge sideboard. Gavin's fine about it. He says Sam's lasagne is never as good if it has to be reheated, and he's got to be up early for work next morning. He suggests next time I'm up in Manchester we do it all over again. I still don't quite know what to make of him and I wonder if now he's going to break into another sales pitch and tell me he'll be mortally offended if after all the trouble he's been to tonight, I'm not at his emporium tomorrow morning shopping for multi-pack energy bars and state-of-the-art pocket handwarmers. But he seems happy to confine his farewell to a handshake. Moments later I'm out of the car and he's pulling away.

Despite the absence of clouds in the sky, all traces of day have been blown away by the Manchester darkness. With no nearby street light it's as well that my B & B is marked out from its residential neighbours by an illuminated white sign advertising availability of ensuite rooms and full English breakfast. The sign throws a thin shaft of light onto the pavement and as I make my way to the front gate I see, for the first time, a figure caught by the light. The surprise of the apparition sends my heart whirling faster than it did at the sight of the drop off the edge of Haystacks and I flinch away from it.

Then I hear my name.

'Mike. Michael.'

And I glance back.

I have to look at her twice. I wonder if my senses have been numbed by the exertions of the last few hours and it's actually Mrs Freeman coming to chastise me for failure to make any inroads into her post-watershed banquet. But as I gaze into her eyes in the dim light of the signboard it's still Natalie and while her face may be tired and travel-weary it has for me the freshness and sparkle of champagne and the dazzling colours of a sun-drenched rose garden.

She holds out a pair of red walking socks.

'I forgot to give these back to you,' she says.

I find myself taking them. 'You didn't have to,' I murmur. 'I've plenty more.'

She just stands there. I stand there. The merest hint of a breeze brushes my cheeks.

'I … er … I suppose I'd better be …' Her speech splutters to a halt. But she makes no attempt to move.

'Do you want to come in?'

She smiles.

I motion to her to follow me up the path and she does so. I've my own key and let her in and we make our way upstairs and into my room. She sits down on the bed. I turn the bedside chair to face her and sit on it.

'I thought you'd be in London by now,' I say.

'I got down to Sheffield,' she says almost in a whisper. 'Train was badly late even before it got to us. We got in and they announced there was a fatality up ahead and they'd had to shut the line so there'd be a delay. We just sat there for hours. Literally hours. Then they started talking about getting us all into buses. But nothing happened. Everyone getting more agitated, restless. Some people were going stir crazy. Carriage was packed. It was hot, really hot. Babies crying, people swearing. It was hell. Sheer hell.' She gives a limp smile and gazes down at the duvet and begins tracing patterns on it with her finger. 'I had to get out.'

'What then?'

She's still looking down. 'I was just standing on the platform. Just standing there. Other people getting out now, shouting, screaming at the staff, in tears. Me just frozen to the spot. My mind a blank. Then I started thinking. Thinking back on today. Thinking this guy's climbed a mountain for me and I've not thanked him. Properly. I got here about an hour ago. Rang the bell. Nothing. Tried again a few minutes later. Still nothing. Kept trying … I was about to give it up. Force myself to get a grip and go home. But I just … oh, for God's sake, this is ridiculous. Look, tell me to shove off now. Tell me to leave you alone.'

And now I'm trembling. I hold my right hand out towards her, and now she is looking at me, and leaning towards me, and I see a look in her eyes, a look I've not seen before, a look of acceptance, a look of submissiveness. She takes my hand, and she doesn't just take it, she runs her thumb round and round my palm, and she's leaning closer and closer to me and I can smell the lavender fragrance on her glowing cheeks. Then my lips come forward to meet hers; to meet their softness, their gentleness, and their smoothness. After her lips, I move around her cheeks and neck, then feel her lips on my face, my neck, my cheeks, and my lips once more, and feel the thrill of exploration, but more than exploration, of arrival and discovery.

And then I strip naked and after I've stripped I begin to peel off her clothes, her black top, her T-shirt, her bra. She lies down and lets me remove her black boots and socks. She undoes her belt and lets me strip her of her leggings and knickers. We never make it under the warmth of the covers. The heat is inside us. She moves back and I glide into her arms and our naked bodies move and writhe round and round the top of the bed, and I feel the glorious pain of her nails digging their way into my back and watch her glorious pain as first my lips and then my teeth close in on her shoulders. Then I'm plunging inside her, going down deeper and deeper and our loneliness and our frustrations and our tensions explode into messy, stupid, reckless, unbearable joy.

We lie there in silence for what seems like hours, allowing our pulses and our senses to return to sane levels. Now I feel cold, and her skin feels cold. I manoeuvre her body under the covers and allow their comforting heat to glide over us. Then I enfold her in my arms and run my hands again and again through her jungle blonde hair.

*

The sound of footsteps on the staircase calls me from my slumber. I glance at the digital alarm clock by my bed and it says 5.50. I lie there in semi-consciousness for two or three minutes and only then remember I'm not in my bed alone.

Until I place my hand out and turn my gaze to my left and realise I am.

I draw back the curtains. The May morning sun streams through and there's no need of artificial light. I look round and all traces of Natalie have gone. There isn't even a note.

There must be a note. There must be something. I sweep the miniature kettle and cups and glass coffee and tea containers and unused packs of biscuits and UHT milk from the table, then turn to the leaflet display and the next moment the air is thick with two-year old flyers advertising local theatres and theme parks and pottery displays and model railway exhibitions. Then I comb every inch of the floor, the windowsill, the bedside table, the bed itself, the flooring under the bed …

There's no note. No nothing.

9

Meludjack(n) – sense of ethereal joy and relief when boots which have become a full-time blister factory are discarded halfway through walk in favour of trainers

It was the meat lorry driver's fault. He was the one who made the error which caused the Uncle Ben's transporter to tangle with it and the van carrying the spices to hit them both, turning the M1 into a giant Indian takeaway. There's plenty of words to describe the frustration of sitting in a stationary coach for three and a half hours and I don't need to be a genius in Walkopedia to bring some of them to mind. Instead of getting home by five thirty in the evening as planned, it's half past nine when I reach my front door. I've barely been away a weekend and it seems like a decade's worth of weekends. I'm anticipating there will be this vast accumulation of mail; instead there's just the one letter congratulating me on winning a once-in-a-lifetime, not-to-be-missed, fantastic opportunity to have my double-glazing needs satisfied by my electricity supplier. I feel sure the milk in the fridge will be coming out to meet me, bringing with it the block of mature cheddar and carton of natural yogurt plus separate helping of raspberry compote, but all three items are sitting minding their own business in the top compartment. I even expect the unwashed dinner plates in the sink to have taken advantage of their close physical proximity and started to breed, producing a small army of sideplates and saucers, but it seems that any attraction has been platonic at best. Surely I must have been gone longer than my mobile phone calendar and my digital alarm clock are both insisting I have. I thought it was only in the Bible that journeys like mine took as little as three days and three nights.

*

But my journey evidently hasn't been so long as to qualify me for an uninterrupted night's sleep. I must have got off at some stage but when I wake it's still only half past three and I'm lying there, lying there, wondering if anything I said to Natalie may have given her some clue as to how she might trace me again, wondering if I have the right to expect her to attempt to trace me again, wondering if her not staying around to say goodbye has effectively stripped me of any moral right to seek clues as to how to trace her. And five hours later the jury are still deliberating and even though the judge has indicated a majority verdict will suffice they're still no nearer to deciding the fate of the prisoner.

I get up and put the kettle on and there's a bleep from my mobile and it's a text from Louise. She tells me she's had one or two health issues, but she's very happy, so are Paul and Katie. She's given me the name and number of her solicitor to contact if I need. I don't want a text. I don't want to speak to her solicitor. I want her voice. I ring her to tell her so. I tell her about my new-found love for walking, hoping that that might push me up in her estimation to such a degree that she starts once more to acknowledge me as a human being with human needs. But all I'm doing is speaking into her voicemail box. I try again next day, and the day after, and the day after, if symptoms persist consult your doctor, but it's as if I've acquired the serving skills of Pete Sampras. Every one's an ace. There's never a return. I tell myself it can't go on but the stop switch has come away in my hand. I try Facebook, Twitter, tweet, chirrup, chirp, croak, quack. Nothing. I still have Vicky Rennison, I'm now hooked on *Warm Memories*, and the breaking news from the *Checkout* world is that Kelly on the pharmacy counter is expecting a baby with Carlton in Fresh Meats. I make a mental note to send in a card of congratulation. The trouble is I may not be able to afford the postage. The bills are raining in: the usual, and then some more. There's the Visa card, store cards, TV licence, garden fence repair, garden gnome repair, boiler breakdown cover, home insurance cover, extra cover, cover point, square leg, silly mid-on, the line of creditors now stretching as far as Penzance, and rumour has it that a private security firm has had to be parachuted in to deal with queue-jumpers.

I think about pulling on my walking boots and shouldering my backpack and heading back up north, walking away from the mess and the hurt and the disappointment. But Gavin was right. All the time there's the world to be faced, and it's no good pretending it isn't there because the world will get you somehow.

*

It's the morning of the last Wednesday in May and as usual I have the radio on while I'm getting breakfast ready. I always have Radio 2 playing but this morning when I switch on it doesn't sound like Radio 2. Then I remember that yesterday I needed someone in to unblock my waste pipes and he'd switched the radio over to Rustic FM and I've not got round to switching it back. While the toast is burning I'm being warned about three-car jams at the end of Acacia Lane, junction with the B2186, and the cancellation of the 10.37 shopper bus from the corner of Princes Drive, Oxshott, and the presenter's been trumpeting the treats in store on his programme over the next three hours. He's just moving onto the whistling burger maker from Fittleworth and I'm about to move off him. Then he announces what's coming after the burger prince. A manpower crisis in the local CPS branch, coinciding with an exponential increase in workload. So I keep the radio on and get the latest on the crisis. I hear the word desperate. Then I hear devastating. Then apocalyptic. By the time I've spooned the last fragment of sugar from the bottom of my coffee mug into my mouth they're quoting verses from the Book of Revelation.

I try phoning Howard as soon as the feature's over, but I get voicemail, and there's no response to my text or email. I want an excuse for a day out so I hop on the train and walk from the station to the CPS office. Lesley on reception gives me a smile, which fades as she explains that Howard is burning incompetent Crown advocates in Basingstoke today and won't be back till they've disposed of the remains. I tell her I'll email him again instead and I'm about to depart when Andy Frost appears through the door. A few minutes later we're sitting in the deeper armchairs of the town's Costa and I'm opening the bowling with a gentle delivery just outside the off stump, seeking his take on the current state of play.

'Usual.' He sips at his latte. 'Situation normal, all … well, you know the rest. Not enough funding, not enough time, not enough of us.'

'That's what I came in for. See if you could do with some help.'

'We could do with the help all right,' he says. 'Problem is, this is Mother Hubbard City. No money to take anyone else on, temporary or permanent. Agency budget, kaput. Howard told us the other day. One of our feel-good morale-boosting daily team energisers. Everyone sits there like good children then buzzes off afterwards and either bursts into tears or spews out their cornflakes. Nightmare. Disclosure, weeks behind. File allocation, pretty much doubled in the last quarter. Kevin and Alice both getting stress counselling, Kev just one bad day away from long term sick. Support and sympathy from the top brass, non-existent. Leadership, strategy, managing outcomes … well, I've seen car smashes that have been planned and co-ordinated better.'

'I'm well out of it, then,' I say with a smile.

He wipes a pocket of latte residue from his upper lip and shakes his head. 'Why, Mike.'

'Why what?'

'Why did you get out of it.'

'Well … wh … what you said,' I stammer. 'The … the stress, the sick, the … leadership, the …'

'The mortgage, the bills, the kids, the vocation, the status.' For the first time he looks me straight in the eye. 'Admit it, Michael. You screwed up. You got it all wrong.'

'I wouldn't say that.'

He rolls his eyes skywards. 'When you worked with us, you had the world at your feet. Experienced. Smart. Bright. And on your day, red hot. But look at you. You've imploded. First your marriage, now your career. Your profession. I mean, why, Mike? Why?'

I gaze down at my black Americano.

'There is a job going,' he says.

I look down towards him. 'In CPS, you mean?'

'I don't mean in CPS.' He unwraps his brie and bacon baguette. 'I mean the dark side.'

'In town?'

'Not this town. Bristol.'

'How did you find out about it? What's so good about it?'

'I'm always looking. Grass greener, you know. There's this guy I went to law school with, Marcus Kenton. We've kept in touch over the years. We're still mates. He's set up on his own as a criminal practitioner. Raking it in. Huge client base. They worship him. The police loathe him. He's reduced prosecuting QC's to tears. Anyway, he's just had to let his assistant go. He rang and asked me if I was interested in taking her place. Reasonable pay, big and varied workload, great location.'

'So what's stopping you?'

'Silly things. Leaving our home and our friends, getting the kids out of school, Pippa out of the job and house she loves. Whereas you …'

I wrinkle my nose. 'I don't know, Andy. I … I don't know.'

'I think you do know.' He pushes his now empty cup away. 'Mike, you've got to start walking back. You've too much upstairs. I take it you're still Law Society accredited for duty work?'

I nod.

'I know you. I know how good you are. Or at least, could be. I can help you.' He pauses and bites a piece of bacon off the side of his baguette. 'If you'll help me.'

'How?'

'Pippa's sister's helping to run a charity event next month. Drill Hall in Turnip Vale Road. Only a few minutes from here. It's a mind sports thing. Nerdalympics they call it. Scrabble, chess, bridge, quizzing. Profits go to the kidney unit at St Saviour's hospital. They're one short for the Mastermind quiz at the end. I thought you and Arsenal. You'd smash it. They need some new kids on the block. Tends to be the same over-competitive saddoes and the same saddo winning each time.'

'I'm not sure I want to be another saddo, thank you.'

'Trophy and champagne for the winner,' he says. 'Believe me, it's a fun evening. Better than sitting on your backside at home.'

I drain the rest of my Americano and push the cup away. 'Listen, Andy, I'm really not in the mood. Besides, my general knowledge isn't up to it.'

'You can be blasé about it,' he says, attacking a portion of brie that's worked free from the layers of white bread. 'But I've known two people who've lost children to kidney disease.' He puts his baguette down and looks straight into my eyes. 'They'd have lived if that equipment had been in place. But it's up to you. Of course.'

*

I've never been to Bristol before and have always had this ridiculous notion of it being a leafy country town populated by yokels who confine their offending to scrumping apples and unlawful fishing of the moon from ponds. But any such thoughts are dispelled by the jumble of multi-storey concrete that assails my eyes as my train makes its way along the home straight into Temple Meads station. And the vibrancy and urgency of city life hit me the moment I step away from the station forecourt and embark on the fifteen-minute walk to Marcus Kenton's office. I find it easily enough, a unit housed in a contemporary mock Georgian brick complex overlooking a section of canal, separated from it by a concrete walkway decorated with pavement art and modernist sculpture. Next door to the complex is a Starbucks and on the other side of the canal, reached by an elegant wooden footbridge, is a deli from which emanates an aroma of warm ciabatta bread mingled with steaming hot chutney.

I go into the office where the receptionist sits me down on a low purple armchair with a choice of the *Times, Time*, and *Time Out*. Barely have I turned the first page of *Time* and settled into a critique of the top US multinationals' record on reduction in carbon dioxide emissions than I'm approached by a man well over six feet tall in a light-coloured suit with creases you'd cut your fingers on. He looks about eighteen. I'm wondering if I should be ringing the manager of the local PC World to tell them that one of their staff has exceeded his tea break. But he announces himself as Marcus, shakes hands then ushers me next door to his office. He offers me a seat on a green leather chair and gets me a coffee, decanting a mugful of liquid from a cafetiere by the filing cabinet and plonking himself in a matching green chair behind his desk. It's plain he isn't a disciple of the clear desk doctrine which Howard embraced with such enthusiasm. The desktop is awash with files of many colours, red and orange and purple and green and pink and yellow and blue. There's a whole Lloyd Webber musical there. He explains he's not stopped since his assistant left, not had time to wipe his bum, let alone keep abreast of paperwork. Between slurps from his own hot beverage, he tells me how he started his working life as a trainee car mechanic. He developed an interest in the law from watching American legal dramas, carried on saving endangered Audis by day and studied by night, and having finished his training, built his business up from nothing, determined he was going to break into the toffee-nosed legal fraternity and kick the stuffing out of them. He explains how he gets an almost orgasmic pleasure from giving the police and CPS a really good beating, especially if it's some clever legal loophole they could never see coming. He says he never gets a conscience about seeing someone he knows has done it getting off, or someone walking free who should have got three years. It's not his problem, the problem is with the twits who haven't got the evidence together, or are so out of touch they've never heard of the Spice Girls. He says as a student he was always contemptuous of the establishment and if anything he's even more so now. As a result of his missionary zeal, he's become a victim of his success. He can't cope with the load. And that's where I come in. Or may do.

Now to business. It's just him, he explains, plus whoever fills the vacancy. I'm told I'd better not be doing much with my evenings and weekends, because I'll be spending most of them down the nick with our clients. And then going into court at ten o'clock next morning to get them all out on bail. Wages, I'll apparently get something if the legal aid fund ever get round to paying the bills. Holiday, I'll need to make myself useful about the place and I might get a week or two in 2023. Sickness, I won't be.

Any questions?

*

The Drill Hall is an Edwardian building so severe that I expect to receive a hundred lines for walking into it. It smells of wee. 'It always smells of wee,' Andy tells me after I've located him, Pippa and her sister by the refreshment area. 'When the foundation stone was laid, it smelt of wee.'

But the smell hasn't deterred people from turning out. The hall is full, and I'm told the attractions of the Nerdalympics, from Scrabble and bridge to chess and Cluedo, are such that it's been full all day. However I've decided to wait till the evening to make my way there on the train and present myself with my three fellow competitors for the ultimate nerdery assessment. I've thus spared myself the pleasure of spending the day learning words where there's no U after the Q or deciding whether there's more merit in the Strong No Trump Convention, Geneva Convention or Fairport Convention, or whether the Sicilian Defence is past its sell-by date. Sufficient unto the evening.

There are three rounds each, two tranches of specialist "nerdish knowhow" being the bread of the sandwich, the second tranche longer than the first, with a round of general knowledge being the unsavoury filling. I'm no more confident about my general knowledge than I was when I toyed with going on the real *Mastermind* but I tell myself that at least if I score *nul points* on that part I can rebuild some of my battered pride in the final specialist segment. I wish I'd been more discreet than to chuck out my furry-hooded parka and bobble hat, since my newly service-washed white shirt and dark trousers just make me feel more like the prat that doesn't belong and wants to be at home with the Sky cricket highlights and a family pack of Haribos. I'm introduced first to Dorian Cleverley, a bricklayer, in his late forties I guess; his subject is the films of Laurel & Hardy which he claims to know off by heart, every line, every shot, every piece of comic business. He comes complete with bow tie, inane head-scratch and reproductions of choice pieces of Stan and Ollie's comic business. And it doesn't take more than a couple of bursts of '"Well, here's another nice mess you've gotten me into"' to make me long to re-enact one of the scenes I am familiar with and place him under a fireplace while a shower of bricks cascades onto him from the chimney pot. Sid McGonagall is offering *Coronation Street*, boasting what he considers to be an unrivalled ability to impersonate the late Deirdre Barlow, although I'm sure I'm not the only one who hopes that it will not extend beyond his shouting "Shoot oop Kenneth" in cod-Lancastrian. Finally there's Letitia Colville, sporting a yellow moustache and spectacles tilting left to right, convinced that Western civilisation has been languishing in semi-barbarity as a result of failure to emulate her knowledge of Southern Railways since 1948.

And we're under way. The *Corrie* fanatic is first up. It's perhaps the most accessible of all the specialist subjects, but you'd need to be an obsessive indeed to know the colour of the wallpaper in the Rovers Return on the night of the Queen's Silver Jubilee or the destination of the tram that smashed Alan Bradley into the Great Soap Opera In The Sky. It's the more recent episodes that are his undoing, and he ends the round on twelve points. No better is the escapee from platform 16B at Clapham Junction, who may have impressed the milling hordes by her knowledge of the cause of the 2 hour delay to services at Surbiton on

February 23rd 1979, but whose credibility is compromised through her inexplicable failure to recall the precise month in which the old blue and white slam door trains were phased out on the Coastway West line. Just eleven points and a look of real dejection on her bowed head as she returns to his plastic yellow seat. But if I think her splashes of ignorance are giving me a real chance, I've reckoned without Dorian Cleverley who I can imagine putting his own father's funeral on hold in order to mug up on *Hog Wild* or *Night Owls*. The first person to get a faceful of rice in *The Hoosegow*. The thrower of the fourth custard pie in *Battle Of The Century*. The exact number of burning hot plates dropped and smashed in *Thicker Than Water*. It's machine-like and it's terrifying and it's given him a three point lead. But at least it should ensure there's no danger of me winning. I've done my bit by the taking part and the saving lives. I never did want to win. Seeing the fake gold trophy on the table in front of Adrian, the Magnus Magnusson of Turnip Vale Road, I want it even less.

And now it is me. An innocuous start. Arsenal's substitute keeper during the 1971-72 FA Cup semi-final. Then it gets harder. Scorer of their equaliser in the sixth round of their FA Cup tie in 1979. Pat Rice, blast it, no, David Price. Close but not close enough. The full backs in their 1969 League Cup final debacle elude me, and by the end I'm trailing in fourth place. Ten miserable points. I'm wondering if I'm going to be told I've missed the cut and am being sent home. But no, Dorian is buying me a consolatory coffee and telling me there's a long way to go, and we're off again, and let joy be unconfined, it's general knowledge. I'm first on this time, and from the outset I'm in the soup. To be precise, thick transatlantic soup. The first musical to open on Broadway, the capital of South Carolina, the location of the *Cheers* bar – I never knew I knew so little about affairs across the pond. Then it gets better. A couple of footie questions. A law-related teaser. A bit of elementary Sussex geography. Perhaps Magnus is feeling sorry for me. But before long the milk of human kindness has gone beyond its use by date. We're back in the USA, my brain dries up and my tally of points shrivels with it. And at the end of the round, Mike Partridge, you … are less smart than a six-year-old.

The other three take their turn and then there's a further break for refreshments. As Dorian Cleverley buys me a diet Coke I can see he's not only sniffing blood, he's lapping it up and is asking for another couple of saucerfuls. Even with his hesitant recollection of Elgar's Nimrod and lack of familiarity with Cromwell's Rump, he's amassed a further thirteen points to make him the clear leader with twenty-eight out of a possible forty. Letitia and Sid are joint second on twenty-two. Then me in last place on eighteen, and to be frank I think four and a half of those were erring on the side of generosity.

The last round. The sunshine outside is fading. The final dregs of plastic-cartoned coffee have been drained, the last broken pieces of Sainsbury's-50p-for-3-packs ginger nuts have been gorged, and all traces of Strawberries-And-Cream-With-No-Added-Sugar cordial have been wiped from the trestle tables; as Karen Carpenter nearly sang, there's a kind of hush all over the Drill Hall, the lights are dimmed, and it's my Arsenal and me again. The final opponents in their Invincible season in 2003-2004. Easy. The score of their first competitive victory under Arsene Wenger. Piece of cake. The goalkeeper in their 1987 League Cup Final triumph. Whereas Sid McGonagall seems to lose all his mojo when anything comes up in *Corrie* post 1990, I'm thriving on the Arsenal of my generation, visualising the TV coverage, the newspaper cuttings, the *Four Four Two* magazines, the videos, the DVD's. In a reverse of that classic Two Ronnies *Mastermind* sketch, I seem to know the answer to each question before it's asked. I'm aware of the taut atmosphere, the punters willing this newcomer, this makeweight upstart, to usher in a new generation and a new style of anorak. It's a clear round. Not even a fence grazed, let alone dislodged. Twenty-two points out of twenty-two. Forty to beat. As it's announced, the crowd are jubilant and rising to applaud, and you could hear their clapping and foot stamping on the Isle of Wight. I'm going to lose, I've more passes than anyone else anyway, and in the event of a tie the fewest passes wins, but anything to wipe the smile off Cleverley's face. I give him a glance as I return to my seat and I can tell he hates me.

And Letitia and Sid are rattled. I can see it in their faces and now for the first time the competitive edge comes to the fore. Adrian calls Letitia first. Letitia is outraged, claiming that as the higher scorer in the general knowledge she should go after Sid, not before him. There's an earnest discussion between Adrian and a bald-headed gent sitting in the front row of the audience. The ref's consulting the linesman, and oh my goodness, the linesman appears to have changed the referee's mind, and we have high drama here at the Drill Hall, and Sid will be incensed and he's every right to be incensed because the ref had quite clearly ruled that Letitia should go first. A major talking point on Twitter. Now, the question is, who's going to be the more affected by that. And it's clear they've both been shaken and stirred in their own way. Sid stumbles to an abject six points and Letitia just eight.

It's down to Dorian now. He marches to the chair and fires off seven correct answers straight away, bringing his score to thirty-five. He's within sight of the winning post. But while his encyclopaedic knowledge of the subject is beyond doubt, there's an arrogance about his demeanour and I'm sure a lot of people are willing him to blow it. If I weren't so anxious not to win, so would I be. On to his next question, in which film does Ollie prise Stan from his First World War trench and tell him the war ended years ago. *'Unaccustomed As We Are,'* Dorian responds without a moment's hesitation. 'No, the remake, *Blockheads,'* Adrian replies. Ooh, I say. An unforced error. It's thrown him. He looks rattled. A sucker punch has sent him reeling and crashing back onto the ropes. He splutters a succession of passes. I've counted and recounted. He's now got two passes more than I have. The clock is running down. Then he seems to get back into his stride. A correct answer. Thirty-six points. Correct. Thirty-seven. Correct. Thirty-eight. Correct. Thirty-nine. We must be deep into Fergie time now. Correct. Forty. Level but I'm still ahead on passes. 'What is the ...'

And then the pips. 'I've started so I'll finish,' Adrian says. 'The name of the actor who played the part of Jitters, the mad butler, in *Oliver The Eighth?'*

Dorian's not answering. Panic breaks out all over his face.

'Going to have to hurry you,' says Adrian. 'For the last time. The actor who played the part of Jitters, the mad butler, in *Oliver The Eighth.'*

'Jack Harty,' Dorian exclaims. 'That's it.' The angst falls from his square eyes and he smiles. 'Thank the Lord.'

'I'm sorry,' says Adrian. 'I can't accept that answer. The correct answer is Jack Barty. So at the end of the round, you too have scored forty points but with two more passes than Mike ...'

'That's what I said.' Dorian's facial expression doesn't change at all. He's still grinning. 'Jack Barty.'

The ref looks to the bald head. But bald head looks just as perplexed. Dorian is knocking his knuckles together. The appearance of a man who's got the Magnus Magnusson wannabe by the privates and is cueing in the Nutcracker Suite.

The rostrum is set up in such a way that my seat happens to be nearer than anybody else's to the Black Chair – well not so much a Black Chair as a Grey Padded 70's Plastic Orange Chair – and I know for a fact that he said Harty. Though I'm no expert on speech patterns, still less on phonetics, I know a B when I hear one. But here's my get-out-of-jail card.

'He did say Barty,' I say. 'Jack Barty.'

There's a sudden buzz round the hall.

'Are you sure?' The relief in Adrian's voice can be felt in Bahrain. 'I mean, it's hardly in your interests to ...'

'Jack Barty,' I repeat.

'Thank you,' Dorian says. He folds his arms and beams and I can reach out and touch the sense of perplexity and disbelief among the punters.

'Very good,' says Adrian. 'I will award you the point. So at the end of that round, Dorian Cleverley, your score has gone up to a winning 41 points.'

*

I lose count of the number of people who are coming up to me afterwards and telling me 'He never said Barty.' There are a few who tell me I must be an even sadder individual than they thought, to lie my way out of victory that I deserved. Dorian condescends to take his eyes for a few seconds from his Gold Nerdal to tell me that if I'm ever passing the Cow and Cushion at half seven on a Friday evening I should pop in and he'll buy me a pint. Next he's announcing his triumph on his Twitter page and talking about throwing a celebratory champagne party. The Scrabble players are planning a post-match all-night lock in tournament at the Frog and Truncheon, while Andy and Pippa are hurrying off for a Chinese with a couple of friends. Pippa's sister calls for quiet and announces how much has been made for the charity through entry fees, bar profits and audience tickets, then she's asking for help with stacking chairs and washing up. She gives me a hug and says I'm wonderful then walks off.

And the hall still smells of wee.

There's nothing more to hang around for. I amble towards the exit door, the hero of the hour but in second place, the gallant loser, fated to leave empty-handed and, this brief interval now over, to raise the curtain on the next act in a hundred years of solitude.

And as I walk, I'm aware of a figure sidling up to me. She's smiling a diffident, nervous smile, and her face is tinged with sadness, but there's still the same orange glow in her cheeks and playful randomness of each lock of her jungle blonde hair.

10

Betchworth(n) – Dog-owner unable to control his or her pet and whose words "He won't hurt you" begin to sound less than convincing as the animal starts growling and snapping at your ankles

For several seconds we just stand there, me gazing at her, she gazing down. The tension and the mystery of the moment sullied by the clatter of cups and the hiss of the tea urn. In the end I'm the one that speaks.

'How did you know?'

'I work on a paper, remember. Told someone at work about you. She works for one of our sister papers round here. She found out about this evening, press release I think. Knew it had to be you.'

'And you've been here all this time?'

She shakes her head. 'Wasn't sure if I wanted to come. I've been sitting at home. Staring into space. Usual thing. Then I thought … oh, God, doesn't matter what I thought. Thing is, what you asked me on the station. After our walk.'

The noise is abating and we're on our own at the back of the hall. 'You mean …'

'Yes, I mean your invite. Help me tick some more walks off my list.'

I shake my head. 'Forget it. I'm sorry I mentioned it. My stupid big mouth.'

'I don't want to forget it. It was … it was lovely.' She's still looking down. 'I want to finish the book. Want to do the walks. I just … just wish …'

Wish I, Mike Partridge, were half a per cent of the guy Toby used to be. Wish I could do something very well, something better than being the fathead who snatches second place from the jaws of geeky immortality. Wish I knew the right thing to say now.

'I guess …' I've no idea what's about to come out of my mouth but I've started and like Adrian I suppose I need to finish. But I can't. Not straight away.

'Go on.' And now she's looking up at me for the first time.

'I … I guess we could do just … just one more walk together,' I find myself mumbling. 'See how it … see whether it …' My cheeks feel as though they're on fire and in the colour stakes would put even the additive-laden Strawberries-And-Cream-With-No-Added-Sugar cordial to shame.

Then I look at her and realise she's smiling. It's the faintest of beams of a watery sun on a damp November morning but it removes a lead weight from my head. 'Okay,' she says, with a gentle nod. 'See how it goes. If you're sure you want to. I just wish ...' and thank God, this time she has the confidence to plough on, 'just wish I could promise to be half decent company. Just wish I could be sure it's not all going to end in tears.'

'We won't know till we try.'

She sniffs and looks down again. 'Suppose not.'

Another silence. There's nobody left in the hall now but us. I hear the occasional bang and crash from the kitchen as nerdery is finally put to bed, for tonight at any rate, but around us is the same sense of peace and space I felt with her on Kinder Scout.

And without the aftershave and the perfume of the audience and the sweat of the competitors, the smell of wee is now overpowering.

'Do you know where you want to go?' I ask her.

She nods. 'Brecon Beacons.'

'Where's that?'

'South Wales. About a hundred and fifty miles away.'

Not quite the ramble across the Hampshire or Sussex downland I'd expected her to suggest. 'So when were you thinking of going?'

'Wondered about tomorrow morning,' she says.

I stifle an expletive. 'Do you mean that?'

She nods. 'I want to get on with it now. Need to get the longer ones done while the daylight's still there.' She gets out her phone. 'You live in Chichester, right. I could come from me to your house and collect you.'

'Where would you be coming from?'

'My flat in Winchester.'

I shake my head. 'That's madness. Miles out of your way.'

'Doesn't matter. I'm always awake really early anyway. Give me something to do.'

She takes my address and phone number.

'Do you want a drink now?' I ask her. I've lost track of the time, God knows whether I'll make it back for the last train, but it's as if Normal has suddenly become a registered missing person.

'Better go,' she says. 'It's going to be a long day. See you later.' She kisses me on the cheek and walks out.

*

I'd better just go through all that one more time. She's suggested she comes to my house.

So there's a chance she may be walking about inside it.

The house has now been designated as an 18-rated movie, and unsuitable for those of a nervous disposition. I've become inured to the smell; to me it's the normal outside air that feels freaky and unnatural. But I know that behind my front door there's enough to secure me a bumper Christmas-length episode of *Life Of Grime*. On the morning Louise and Katie left, I think there were two coffee-stained mugs on the draining board. There's not just mugs covering the whole of the draining board, there's mugs everywhere: mugs on the kitchen window sill, mugs on the dining room table, mugs by the PC, mugs on the bookshelf, mugs on the mantelpiece, mugs in the shower, mugs under the bed, mugs in the belfry. There's cutlery and crockery decorating every surface. The two kitchen chairs don't need the specialist upholstery Louise used to keep on about. Every time I sit down for a meal I've got two weeks worth of used boxers parked up my bottom. As for newspapers, Louise has always told me not to throw them away, pointing out their recyclability potential, and here at least I've adhered to her principles. I've enough back issues of the *Metro* about the place to start my very own archive. I keep finding stuff I thought I'd lost not only between copies of the paper but welded to the pages of them too.

And in a few hours from now a simple request from Natalie to use my facilities will mean she'll be forced to wade into the undergrowth. Whatever equipment she'll have brought with her in readiness for the rigours of the day, I don't suppose it'll include a sickle or an elephant gun.

She won't mind. She'll understand I wasn't expecting her to invite herself to my house and she should take me as she finds me and she'll have seen far worse.

She will mind. She'll sniff the air. She'll look around her. She'll witness the confusion, the trail of devastation, the army of experts waiting to pass opinion on the long-term effects on the local economy, the members of the local community worst affected, the government ministers blaming the Environment Agency, the Environment Agency blaming the government, and the forecasters who say that there's even worse to come.

I remember *Challenge Anneka* where, for some good cause, the eponymous presenter would enlist an army of excavators, diggers, plumbers, painters, butchers, bakers and cabinet makers who in exchange for an enthusiastic hug at the start and finish, and the promise of lots of free publicity in between, would transform a previously derelict site, the victim of years of bomb damage and graffiti, into a cross between Sydney Opera House and the Bernabeu Stadium in twenty-seven hours. My site is worse than derelict and I've not got Anneka to call on. And as for knocking on the door of number 89 and attempting to hug Les Abercrombie in exchange for his drilling away into my overtightened widgets, it would be easier to just tear my toenails out myself and have done with it.

I make it home, grab a quick coffee, then get going. It's the hardest two hours' work I've ever done. I find buttons on the washing machine I didn't know existed. I'm able to remind myself of the colour of the kitchen work surface. Opening the sixth bin liner from the roll purchased on the way home, I can consign the Chelsea FC mug to the afterlife and make a note to engage the local priest to give it a decent requiem mass. I discover a scourer capable of penetrating the grease that has become such an established resident of the big saucepan that more than once I've thought about whether it should be applying for housing benefit, and I'm able to evict it without seeking a court order. And I find a cupboard I never knew we had, full of perfumes and scents with pretty flowers drawn on it, things you imagine having been bought from the Downton Abbey gift shop after a cup of Earl Grey and slice of carrot cake. As midnight comes and goes, the house is transformed into a fragrant garden with an intoxicating aromatic mixture of sandalwood and tarragon and I'm beginning to feel light-headed already.

*

At twenty-five to nine the doorbell rings. Her colours, red T-shirt and blue shorts, are as bright as the sunlight streaming from the cloudless sky. She gives me a kiss on both my cheeks but then retreats almost at once. There's a determined, businesslike look on her face.

She asks for a glass of water before we set off and while I'm getting it she goes into my front room. I bring the water to her and I see her wandering around, gazing at the shelving, the window sill, the mantelpiece. I hold my breath.

'Do you like it?' I ask.

She turns to me. 'Mmmm, good work,' she says. 'Must have been one hell of a long night.'

*

Thanks to my revision sessions yesterday afternoon and early evening I'd missed the weather forecast for today. So it's something of a shock when Natalie switches on the car radio and I hear that temperatures, which for the last few days have been ensconced in the comfortable low twenties, are today set to leap out of their indolent slumbers and spiral upwards, especially in the south and west of England and Wales, rocketing to thirty or thirty-one degrees. But rather than rejoice at the advent of summer, the news media have reacted with grim warnings, and you can almost hear the tremor in the voices of announcers as they counsel sun hats, sun blocks, sun screens, sun shades, sun spots, sun roofs, *Sun* newspapers … it seems the days have long gone when Health and Safety officials ever allowed us to enjoy any of our weather at all. With this increase in heat levels comes an explosion of M4 traffic, and even the lightest conversation must take second place to preventing ourselves becoming another travel news item. I guess it doesn't help that I've never been the best car traveller. When I was six I remember my projectile vomit being splashed all over the back seat of the car belonging to my best friend. Well he was my best friend at that time. Our relationship became rather more strained once his dad had obtained an emergency injunction banning me from coming within a hundred metres of his cherry-red Talbot Solara. Even as an adult, on journeys involving more than three double bends within half an hour of the blandest of light meals, I can tell that someone's switched on a Moulinex Magimix in my stomach. And my insides have been turning cartwheels again now, although that may have something to do with Natalie's Enya CD which I've now heard three times in as many hours and although I don't mind paddling with the Orinoco Flow on the odd occasion, I'm now wishing the boatman was calling out that number 7's time was up. We've allowed ourselves a service station stop but even then ice-breaking chit-chat has been frustrated by the need for us to hire specialist drilling equipment to break into our granary rolls. The result is we've hardly spoken since setting off from my home nearly five hours ago.

I suggest we break for lunch. I'm hoping that a decent meal in relaxed and congenial surroundings will rip away the invisible gagging tape. There's an A board beside the A470 advertising a café five minutes off route and we agree we'll give it a try. It's tucked away up a narrow lane, and its rustic setting is complemented by bucolic features: roughly plastered walls, wooden tables and benches, and menus not in Times Roman point 14 but copperplate handwriting. The A board has done its stuff, and many of the seats are occupied. A short bearded man emerges from a side door and announces the day's specials with a glint in his eye and a Welsh lilt in his voice and I'm tempted to suggest he might do even better in promoting his bill of fare if he were to sing it rather than speak it. We eschew the Welsh roast lamb and un-Welsh Wiener schnitzel and order soups and paninis.

For the third time this morning I gaze into Natalie's green eyes and for the third time I'm mesmerised. For the third time this morning I gaze at her jungle blonde hair and I'm almost sorry for the other guys in the café because none of their partners have hair like hers. I know it's not just the skin-deep stuff that's attracting me to her. I've had these tantalising samples of the person on the inside: this person who's shown she's bold enough to seek out the high places, independent enough to travel alone to Derbyshire, determined enough to have a second crack at Kinder Scout, daft enough to venture out late on a Saturday night to a nerds' convention in a suburban drill hall which reeks of urine, and crazily romantic enough to travel halfway across northern England to return a pair of red stockings. The outward beauty is there, yes, but I want more, so much more, of the person that I know lies within. I don't just want to sip the wine, I want a glassful. First back on Kinder Scout, then in Manchester, and now last night, I've felt her quivering hands stretching out towards me, drawing me to herself, but though I've been drawn, and drawn further with each look into her eyes, I can't seem to complete the journey.

The soup arrives, deep brown vegetable soup crammed with carrots and peas and parsnips and onions and mushrooms. Natalie tries a couple of mouthfuls then throws her spoon down. Toby's favourite, she says. Shouldn't have ordered it. Should have known it would bring all the Toby stuff back. And a moment later I find myself doing what I did on Kinder, getting her to talk but not about herself or about me but about him. In today's exciting episode, The Night He Came Face To Face With A Cheetah. This time next week, The One Where He Couldn't Find The Bridge Over The Amazon. She enthuses, she chuckles, she laughs, she runs her hands through her jungle blonde hair, once or twice she puts her hand on mine. But of course it's all cheating, it's the easy way to get her animated, to get her to talk. It isn't the medicine she needs or wants, it's the brandy to the alcoholic, the cocaine to the druggie.

That's the easy part, for me to realise it, for me to think it …

'It's not helping, Natalie.'

She doesn't react. She just sits there, gazing down at the bowl of congealing brown liquid in front of her.

'Natalie?'

'What?'

'I said it's not helping.'

She looks at me and for the first time I see the light of battle in her eye. 'It's helping me. It's helping me, okay.'

I pile a concentration of onions and mushrooms into my mouth. 'Natalie, I understand.'

'You obviously don't. If you did you wouldn't have said it.' She wipes her mouth with her serviette and starts to get up from her seat. 'I'll just … just go and sit in the car, all right.'

'Stay,' I bark. God. Where the hell did that come from. I see the fear on her face. I can feel the fear on mine. She sits back down. But if I feel I've done the hard part it's only a few seconds before I'm disabused.

'You don't know me,' she says. 'You don't know what I'm going through, you've got no right to tell me what helps, what doesn't.'

'I've a right to give you a different perspective, surely. I lost my little girl, remember.'

She picks up her spoon and brings it crashing down into her bowl, sending splashes of liquid and vegetables across the table and onto the floor. 'Yes, you did. And what's the betting you couldn't stop talking about it for weeks, months, years after? I've hardly begun, for God's sake!' Now she throws her spoon aside. 'Listen, Mike, I know you like me, I know you're attracted to me, and yes, I like you too. But that doesn't mean I'm going to be told how I can, how I can't grieve. Do you get that?'

I flick a stray piece of diced carrot from the zip of my trousers. Not daring to see just how many other diners are watching us. 'I just want what's going to help the most. That's all.'

'Fair enough,' she says. 'Help me get up the Brecon Beacons. Help me get down safely.' She looks at her bowl, grimaces and pushes it away. 'Just don't expect me to be the life and soul. What you see, what you get, okay.'

A celery ring drops from somewhere near my left earlobe and flops to the ground. 'It's fine.'

It's not fine, it's grey, it's grim, it's rubbish, it's going to be the worst and longest afternoon of my life.

'I can't do it yet, Mike. Can't do it. And if that's a problem for you, well … tough luck.'

*

Base camp is a car park beside the A470 between the towns of Merthyr Tydfil and Brecon, just beyond the Beacons Reservoir. The plan is to head first to Corn Du, then continue to Pen-y-fan, the summit of the Beacons, and go on from there to Cribyn beyond Pen-y-fan, making three summits in all. We change our footwear and set off straight away along the signed Beacons Way, initially skirting the south-eastern edge of a patch of woodland, then striking out north-eastwards, pulling away from the valley and heading for the top of the ridge. I can see worry lines criss-crossing Natalie's face and I try to soothe her anxiety with some reassurance; although Corn Du is 873 metres above sea level, considerably higher than Kinder Scout, we began at 425 metres, so in a sense half the climbing's been done for us. The path is dry and clear and firm and there's lots of other walkers about. But the fact is, my knees are knocking and my heart is sprinting. Three massive, unwelcoming, skyscraping peaks and it's thirty-one degrees in the shade and there seems to be like a whole stony rocky kingdom between us and that ridge top. There may be the odd puff of fair weather cloud but it's never going to challenge the ferocity of the June afternoon sun. We've hardly got going and already it's licking its lips and scratching me with its paw, setting off a waterslide of sweat down the front of my T-shirt. I remember Gavin's edict, drink lots, you won't get thirsty, but for God's sake we've not properly got going and even now my throat is as dry as a *Private Eye* editorial and of course my water bottle is stuck at the very bottom of the backpack. I plunge my hand into its recesses, yank the bottle free and unscrew the cap, and within seconds the bottle's almost half empty. The conventional wisdom is that it ought to take an hour to reach the first major landmark, the ridge and col at Bwlch Duwynt just below Corn Du, but it's half that again. We justify our frequent pauses by saying we should be admiring the increasingly panoramic views including the Beacons reservoir and the open expanse of Graig Cerrig Gleisiad National Nature Reserve to the north west, but in reality we're both gasping and our breaths are becoming more laboured with every lift of our feet. Part of my left boot has developed a fancy to an area of my skin just above the ankle, and now I'm raiding the first aid stores for an emergency application of Elastoplast. Natalie has no such problems but she's finding the going no easier than me and I can hardly bear to see the expression on her face, suffused as it is with weariness and distress. I glance at her as she takes ever more frequent gulps from her own water bottle and my worst fears are confirmed when, as we arrive at the col, I see her supplies are exhausted. I remember reading somewhere that when you're dehydrated, water becomes like a drug. It provides glorious relief for a few seconds but the moment it's worn off it's redoubled your need for more, much more. I've been doing my utmost to conserve supplies, taking an ant-sized portion every few minutes, and drawing comfort from the splash of the remaining liquid as it settles back in the base of the bottle. But now my determination to keep back some reserves from my own supplies is being used to feed her new-found addiction, and as we leave the col there's not a drop left between us.

From the col we have to dig into our mental as well as physical energy stocks for the final scramble to the flat-topped summit of Corn Du, well over 200 metres higher than the summit of Kinder Scout. Natalie wants to stop here but I persuade her not to, telling her the worst is over, it's only a short walk from here to the climax of our endeavours and we can have a good rest then. The reality is, I'm petrified that if we stop here we might not get going again. So we plod on. We veer sharp right to proceed just north of east for a few hundred metres to the summit of Pen-y-fan, 886 metres or just over 2900 feet high. I'm gushing my congratulations to Natalie, placing my arm round her, telling her she's a star and should be dead proud. But inside I'm freaking. There's terror stapled to each joint, each muscle. We have no water. It must be at least a hundred degrees out of the shade and we have no water. There may be little more climbing to do – although I wouldn't put it past Cribyn to spring a whole fresh set of challenges upon us – but I remember the descent of Haystacks being just as demanding as the ascent, if not more so, and the fear of what now lies ahead not only taints the excitement of reaching our highest objective, it's spitting its corrosive fluid all over it. I gaze out at the symphony of mountains and fields and farmsteads and woodlands and settlements that unfold before us. To the east lies Cribyn, our third and final summit objective, while we look down to the north-west at the lake known as Llyn Cwm Llwch, its refreshing waters calling and tantalising us even though it is well off our route. The town of Brecon lies to the north, while to the south-east there's another lake, Upper Neuadd Reservoir, and behind it, the massive wooded expanse known as Taf Fechan Forest. But it's a symphony that's being played on a scratched vinyl disc, where your enjoyment of the notes is marred by the crackling and buzzing and the constant threat of the needle getting stuck in a worn groove. It's not just the water shortage but the effect of the heat on the landscape. The views are there, yes, but in the far distance the panorama is enfolded in a soupy blur, and I feel Nature saying to us, you may have made the top, yes, we'll give you that, but we've no special in-store offers today, everything's full price. As we stand there, three men appear and claim that with the aid of binoculars it's possible to see Exmoor, on a good day of course, what a shame you've chosen a day like this, and for just a moment I want to wring their necks. We exchange pleasantries and compare notes on our journeys to this point. One of the men then lets out a whoop of excitement and says he's sure he has just seen a ring ouzel. I look in the direction he's pointing but from where I'm standing it just looks like an ordinary blackbird. He tells us the ring ouzel confines itself to mountain and upland areas and we'd never be likely to see one in Sussex, so we should feel very privileged, our whole expedition's worthwhile, and so on. But if that's the only real reward for our dehydration-inducing labours, I'm thinking of asking for my money back. We continue to chat. We bemoan the heat but acknowledge that rain or mist would be worse, so we should count our blessings. We agree we'll have to return on one of those crisp sunny days when there's no trace of cloud or haze, perhaps next March or April, when the purple saxifrage is at its best. I mention the discomfort above my left ankle and one of them counsels a tried and trusted remedy involving discarded sheep's wool which by the sound of it will make the discomfort a whole lot worse. Then they're gone and it's just us.

All this time Natalie's hovered on the edge of the group, contributing nothing to the impromptu summit cocktail party. I turn to her now and there's a vacant stare on her face. It's the stare of the condemned, the stare of one whose fate has slithered and then nosedived out of control. Her face is decorated with sweat and dust and flecks of saliva hang from her lower lip. Mindful that we've still got a summit to go, taking us even further from our start and finish point, I ask her if she'd rather turn back, but the vigour of her head shake in response makes me wish I'd never asked. I'll do this if it kills me, she seems to say, and there's an ever-burgeoning part of me that is afraid that that's exactly what it will do.

Cribyn, 795 metres high, looks straightforward enough from Pen-y-fan but looks are deceptive. We need to veer south-eastwards off Pen-y-fan, sticking to the Beacons Way, and as we do so the ground collapses away from us. Just like the walk from Haystacks to Scarth Gap, it's one step at a time. I'm leading the way but I'm watching her every move. And I'm shouting encouragement back to her, shouting, roaring, yelling, keep hanging in there, I'm so proud of you, you're amazing, you're a superstar. It's certainly enhancing my credentials required to fill the vacant post for cheerleading co-ordinator of the Brooklyn Dodgers but by the expression on her face it's clear that my words, far from getting inside her, are bouncing back off her, leaving not even a mark, still less any permanent effect, and disappearing into the sultry late afternoon sunshine. The path bottoms out, but after we fork left off the Beacons Way we're climbing again. It's now well after four, we're two thirds of the way through daylight, but the sun continues to throw down bombs of heat from the pale heavens. I abandon the cheerleading, grab my water bottle, open it and put it to my mouth, hoping, yearning, praying for one miserable drop that will give a square millimetre of relief to my frayed, burning lips. There's nothing, nothing, nothing, and looking at Natalie, I'm ashamed that I should have thought of putting my needs before hers, offering the bone-dry bottle to my mouth and not hers. She's keeping her head down, as though desperate to stop herself seeing how much more rock face is separating her from the top. She's sniffing and snivelling and brushing the sweat and grime from her forehead and her eyes. Then in an instant she's striding past me, her feet crashing into the hillside and sending showers of stones slithering away from her. There's an intensity of her focus which is at once stupefying and terrifying. I watch as she marches onwards and heavenwards, until with a final storm of earth and dust she gains the summit and flings herself to the ground. I follow at a more subdued pace, conscious of the work yet to be done, and again what should have been joy at arriving at one of our key objectives is polluted by foreboding. On our way in the car I'd been trying to take my mind off the traffic and Enya by reading the guide notes Natalie had downloaded, and the notes had exhorted us to look out not only for ring ouzels but wheatears and sparrowhawks. Above me now I can see a grey-brown bird with long yellow legs and claws and a black-tipped yellow bill and hear a harsh and piercing kek-kek-kek. It may be a wheatear, may be a sparrowhawk, may be none of the above, but every kek crunches into me, accusing, mocking, vilifying. This isn't your habitat, it's saying, you don't belong here, we didn't ask you to come, don't blame us. There's no other life in sight. And on this naked rock, this bare hillside, the solitude isn't something to embrace but something to fear. I look back towards the monster of Corn Du, no longer proud and shapely but a barrier standing between us and liberation from our thirst prison.

Now Natalie gets up and without a word starts to head back. It's as though an alarm has been triggered in her head. That was my rest time, she seems to say, now I've got to set off, to hell with everything else, if I don't follow what my mind's telling me to do, or should it be what the ghost of a certain late partner's been telling me to do, I won't be able to do it and will never be able to do it. Her single-mindedness may have attracted me to her previously but now it's scaring me. I've never believed in ghosts, have laughed away any suggestion of restless souls and spirit worlds, but watching her as she slams one foot in front of another, sending layer upon layer of surface debris shooting skywards, I can sense the presence of another being inside her head, driving her forward, propelling her knees and her legs and her feet. And I'm terrified all the time it's happening because I know the longer it goes on, the greater will be the explosion, the mess, the mayhem when this being is exorcised or exorcises itself. It's when, not if. It's got to stop. She's got to stop. I go after her, forcing myself to increase my speed from a gentle *andante* to *molto allegro*. I call out to her. And as I call out, she jerks her head round. Her focus seems to slip for a demi-second. Her left foot slides in one direction, her right foot in another. The ground beneath her seems to shake and then turn to ice. Her right foot swings outwards then inwards and smashes against the side of a protruding rock. The next moment she's off the ground and rocketing skywards. Her battered body becomes a maelstrom of waving arms and legs, and a split second later she's crashing to the ground with a thump and a blast of loose rock and dust and grass.

I yell at her to get straight up, now. But she doesn't. I panic. I shout and swear. I catch up with her and I see there's blood spurting from her lips and there's some substance now oozing from her chin and she's feeling her right rib. I pull her rucksack off her shoulders and rip it open and find her first-aid supplies. Where to start. Where the hell to start. God, this is my fault. This is all my fault. This was always going to happen, always, always, always. I yell again, not so much yells for assistance but yells of desperation, of a man who's lost his family's savings on the playful bounce of a roulette ball. And as I continue to yell, I see two figures approaching, thank God, two youngish women, they've heard my shouting and swearing and they're looking straight at us with expressions of alarm and terror. They get to us and my words all come out at once, she's hurt, she's badly hurt, you've got to help us, please do something, anything, anything.

Between us we're able to get Natalie to her feet and mop the blood and muck from her face and neck, and bandage her up. As she gets off the floor she's beginning to talk, saying she's great, she'll be fine, but she's wheezing and panting and her forehead is glittering. Our saviours converse in what I guess is German and produce two full bottles of iced water which they thrust into my hands. I squeeze open the top of one of them and pass it to Natalie, she snatches it from me and she downs every last droplet. Then I open the other and I hurl half the contents down my throat. It's cold, cold, cold, and I never knew I'd forget what cold felt like and how great cold is just now. One of the women takes me by the hand, applying a wet wipe to my forehead, and asks if I'm okay, and amid a sea of entreaties in broken English to calm down and not to panic I find my knees are shuddering and my eyes are shedding rivulets of tears.

We just stand there for a few moments, collecting ourselves, allowing the panic to subside. I've the presence of mind not to finish the water I've started but put it in my rucksack. I'm figuring it might just be the bottle that gets us home, that saves our lives. The women offer to get help, an air ambulance if need be, offer to find a stretcher to get Natalie off the mountain, offer to walk with us, everything, and I hate myself more than I've ever hated myself because I see more unselfishness in their left thumbnails than in my miserable body. But I see a renewed focus and determination in Natalie's eyes that is almost fierce. She'll do it, she says again and again and again, the studs of pain embedded right across her face. I can see that our new friends don't believe her. I perceive their anxiety as they watch her starting to walk off down the mountainside. She's said I'm to tell her to keep going, whether she's nursing a bruised rib, cracked rib or spare rib, even if I find myself being hauled before the Jockey Club for excessive use of the whip. I compromise. I ascertain that the women are going the same way back. I wait till Natalie is out of earshot, and ask if they'll keep a discreet distance behind so if we get into trouble they'll be there for us.

The procession begins, Natalie leading the way, me just behind her, the women bringing up the rear. And as we proceed, I'm conscious that the heat is starting to decline, chunks of white cloud are bubbling up to the south, and there's a healing breeze which strokes against our faces, an invisible balm for our reddened skins. But I just know that each step remains a supreme effort for her, each groan and sigh of pain giving me as much torture again as that which I know is weighing upon her. Especially as there's a stone lodged in my boot and my plaster has worked loose and is flapping about inside my sock and there's no sheep's wool to be found. But I tell myself that each step is a step nearer our salvation. We're able to use a more direct path heading south-westwards from Pen-y-fan, avoiding having to go back over the summit of Corn Du, and from the col at Bwlch Duwynt it's a straight repetition of the climb up from the car. The going gets easier beyond the col. The water supplies are holding out and talk of hosepipe bans is premature. There's a couple of evening dog-walkers who catch us up and see our laboured steps and offer to give us some company as we descend. We talk about the surroundings, about the countryside, about the weather, about Arsenal. It's helping to make us feel like human beings once more and even Natalie joins in. We arrive at the car park, wish each other well, give a farewell pat to the golden retrievers and sink down inside the car. We've made it.

*

She'd planned to drive us home this evening, ready for her to return to work on the Monday morning. But there's no way she's up for that. As a result of the volume of traffic on the way down and then her injury we're way behind schedule and neither of us fancy driving home tonight. I'm covered third party to drive her car and I get us to the next town where we find a B & B with no difficulty. Separate rooms is a given, but I'd not expected separate mealtimes: barely have we signed the forms at the reception desk than she declares she's not hungry and tells me to go and grab some food from the pub or takeaway if I want it and she'll sleep off her pain and with luck she'll be okay in the morning.

It's very late but the chippie's still open. There's a park nearby where I take my chicken quarter, large chips and a can of liquid calling itself

Fizzeroonie. It's the only drink they had left, albeit in considerable quantity, and judging by the its flavour, a kind of surreal taste sensation mingling essence of rotting apples, Windolene and paraffin, I'm not hugely surprised it's been left on the shelf. And seated on the bench that overlooks a waterfall, watching the graceful glide of a family of swans, and the soft play of the breeze on the silver birches, and two hoodies giving a beating to an innocent seesaw, I chomp, and slurp, and think. I'm thinking, the physical and sexual attraction is almost unbearable, and I see so much I could do for her, so much she could do for me, but there's still this massive border fence between us and though I may have been led to think that by her seeking me out last night there were any gaps in that fence, I've watched while the contractors have been flown back in and not only mended it but reinforced it and added a couple of tiers both on the top and the bottom. And if it's clear the only way is backwards, I'd rather turn round now and head for home alone – although even that option is not without its logistical issues. I've not seen a railway station, don't recall a taxi rank, and there seems to be no regular bus service, unless you count the shoppers' service to Merthyr Tydfil leaving at 9.21 on Fridays, public holidays excepted. Minutes later I'm wandering back to the B & B and trudging upstairs to my room.

She's in there, sitting on the bed. She's removed her pumps and just wears T-shirt and shorts.

She motions to me to come and sit beside her.

So I sit, and wait for her to either make the next move or tell me what my next move should be. But nothing happens. We just sit there, five minutes, ten minutes maybe, ten minutes of ignorance on my part as to whether she's any plans to get out the pliers and start hacking away at that fence or whether she's supplementing it with an electrical charge and a forest of landmines.

Finally she speaks.

'You don't deserve this.'

'Deserve what?'

'Everything.' She leans across and places a kiss on my lips. 'I remember us lying there in Manchester. You kept on saying it. Perfect, this is perfect.'

'I did?'

'And you're right. It was perfect. It was just the perfect ending. And that's exactly how I saw it. An ending. I couldn't see what came next. I'm sorry, Mike. Must all have seemed so final to you. I thought, I've been so unfair. Thing is ... .'

She seems to hesitate.

'What?'

113

'I ... I didn't see there was enough there. Enough for us. I wanted more. More from you. More than I ever thought you could give me.'

'And you still feel that way?'

'I don't know. I'm sorry, Mike, I really don't. It's got more complicated ... I mean, take the thing last night. I thought, if you can enter that, not because I've asked you to but because you thought it was right. And then letting the other guy win, I thought, what the hell possessed you ...'

'I never wanted to win.'

'Like I believe that. And then today, all you've done today, making your house look so nice, putting up with me over lunch, helping me do the walk, driving me back here...' She sighs. 'There's still Toby and he's all around me still and I'm frightened. I loved him, more than I thought I could love anyone. And I'm scared ... frightened ... I just don't know. I'm sorry. I know you'll say I've got to move on. Turn the clock back. So easy to say. Too easy. I can't do it.'

We stay silent for a few minutes. In my case it's the silence of fear that my time's running out and in a moment Natalie will be going back to her room still not knowing and perplexed that I've not started to help her to try to know.

But it's still not too late.

'Wasn't easy for me,' I say. Already I can feel the heat on my forehead.

'What wasn't?'

'When I lost Isabel.'

'Who?'

'My daughter. I told you.'

'The one who died.'

'You don't know how.'

I can't bear to look at her. I try and focus on something else. I gaze around the room. It's white. White white. White duvet, white towels, white walls, white curtains, white coffee cups, white teapot. All is calm, all is white. But my heart has the blackness of treacle.

'Do you want to talk about it?'

'Of course I don't.' And the simmering anger of years is now a steaming, bubbling cauldron. 'It chews me up even to think of it. But I've got to, Nat. Got to. She was beautiful. She was everything to me. To us.'

'How ... how did she die?'

'It was an accident. A stupid, avoidable accident. Louise said I was an accident waiting to happen. And sure enough it was an accident that did for Isabel. She was sitting on a wall. Picnic lunch. She's just sitting there, eating a sandwich. And she starts rocking back and forth. Not sure why, just the kind of thing children do. She was only three, for heaven's sake.

She leans too far back. And she goes over backwards – and it's not just a short drop onto the grass or something. It's a thirty-foot drop into a river. A rushing river. She gets swept away. She's screaming, yelling. You could hear the screams in flaming Beijing. Then they stop. She's smashed her head against some boulders. By the time the ambulance gets there, it's too late. So yes, Nat. It's not been easy. It's never going to be easy. I live with it every day. Every hour.'

She reaches out and squeezes my hand. 'And Louise has blamed you for it all these years?'

'No. Not at all.'

'You must … must be grateful to her for that. Would have been awful if she'd held it against you.'

'You're not getting it.' I prise my hand from hers. 'I wasn't there. I was at work. Isabel was with her mum. With Louise.'

'Oh, my God.' Her whole body starts to quiver. 'Oh, my God.'

'Louise took her for a walk and a picnic. She saw this wall, just thought, a nice place for their sandwiches. Isabel's doing this rocking thing but Louise has seen her doing it before, no problem. She gave Isabel a sandwich then turned to her bag, just for a second, to get one out for herself, and then turned back and Isabel wasn't there. Then there's this splash, and the screams, and … I had to live with this for days and days afterwards, her just going on and on, about how she'd always been the careful one and I was the accident-prone one as if some referee's going to step in and award me the blame on points. Sometimes I wondered if it really had been my fault. But no. She knows that. We know that. And she knows, we know, that because of what happened, we were incomplete and would always be incomplete and whatever else Louise gave me, did for me, in life would never be enough.'

'Couldn't she have given you another child?'

Now I'm studying the white carpeting beneath my feet. 'I didn't want her to give me one. Anyway, I'd had the … the procedure, remember. I knew nothing could replace Isabel. And I just had this awful premonition, that the same thing might happen, but that it would be my fault this time. Of course she kept on at me. Trying to get me to reverse my procedure. In the end I lied to her I'd had the reversal done. Just to shut her up. They say anyway that there's no guarantee it'll succeed. So I hid behind that. And then she hit me with it. She said she knew she'd never mother a child again, so we should adopt. She said if we could just do that, that was all she would ever ask for. Give another child a chance. I said it was too soon. She wouldn't listen. Turned on the waterworks. It was blackmail. Sheer blackmail. So Katie came along. I mean, she's a lovely girl, that's what makes me feel such a scumbag. She's kind, and polite, and really intelligent, and tall, and pretty, and makes us laugh, and would never hurt me. I just don't love her and never can.'

'But you stood by them.'

'Only because by then I was too bone idle to not stand by them. Needs less energy to stand than to walk.' I turn and look into her eyes. 'People keep telling me to move on, not to turn the clock back. And I want to tear their tongues out. So don't worry. You're quite safe.'

She's looking out into space. 'I've been so selfish.' Her lips hardly moving. 'All me, me, me. What must you think of me. I hate myself … just hate myself.'

'It's called grieving,' I say. 'Once it starts, it's a full-time job. And there's no retirement age.' Now I take her hand. 'God, Nat, I've not talked like this to anyone. I never thought I would. Ever.'

She smiles.

Then with the soft orange glow of the evening sun cascading onto the crisp fresh white covers we ease ourselves inside their tender embrace.

*

The reliving of Isabel's accident may have sent a rusty needle through my soul but it's as if a light has been turned on in Natalie's heart. I wake at seven next morning and she's there beside me, and as we scramble on our T-shirts and shorts, and have breakfast, and set off for home in the car, we've discovered how to talk to each other. We're delving back into our pasts and beginning seventy years' worth of catch-up. We go back to our childhoods, hers first, her stranglehold on the school sports under 15 long jump, her collection of Boyzone CD's and her pre-teenage crush on Gary Barlow. And then we talk about me, and my witnessing Arsenal's clinching of the Double in 1998, and my teenage appearance on *Blockbusters*, and my granddad's own rather more worrying crush on Gary Barlow. It's still not even ten thirty in the morning and I'm already hating the thought of her decanting me back onto my doorstep and our being apart. I want to put it off, put it off forever. So I suggest we leave the motorway and detour to Marlborough. We stroll up the shady side of the street, her hand in mine. It's not long since breakfast and neither of us are that hungry but it's another scorcher today and when we pass a café which doubles up as a second-hand bookshop we agree we could each use an iced coffee. We squeeze through the narrow door into an even narrower passage combining the smell of freshly poured cappuccino and mildewed

Dickens. We have to negotiate our way round a cardboard box and I see inside there's a whole load of maps. We have a random look inside the box to see if there are any of places left on Toby's to-do list but they're all for the far north of Scotland and the Western Isles. Natalie says there's only one on his list in Scotland and the walk in question is in central Scotland. We order our drinks at the counter then go and sit down. She puts her hand in mine once more.

'I know what you're thinking,' she says in a whisper. 'You wish this was new love. Clean, fresh love without the crap. Am I right?'

'I don't know,' I say. 'Does it matter how new it is? Should it matter?'

'Depends on how you define love, I suppose,' she says. There's the slightest mark on her lip from her fall but no other sign that less than twenty-four hours ago we'd been in such danger. 'If you just think of love as the physical, the sexual, I guess it probably wouldn't matter … but I think you know it's a lot more than that. If you define it as commitment, no strings attached, giving your whole self to the other person emotionally as well as sexually … well of course it matters. Because I can't promise that.'

The iced coffees are set down in front of us and my taste buds tingle as the freezing jet of caffeine smothers the roof of my mouth.

'I know you can't, Natalie. Not yet.'

'Don't say yet, Mike. I can't do yet.' She sips at her iced coffee then studies its surface. 'I don't want you thinking one day I'm going to click my fingers and say that's it, end of mourning, off with the grey clothes, I'm free and ready to start all over again.'

For a moment I'm hurt that she believes I could feel that way. 'Natalie, I know it's not like that. You need time, need as long as it takes.'

She shakes her head. 'I still don't think you're quite getting it,' she says. 'You said it yourself. Last night. There's no retirement age. You've never stopped mourning for Isabel, I hope you never will. You've got to see it's the same for me. I guess it'll get easier, but I can't promise anything … can't promise what I might be able to give back to you, Mike. I can give you friendship, and companionship, and yes, I can give you the physical, but as for my own self, my heart …' She tails off and shakes her head again.

'I'm not expecting it, Natalie.'

'I wish you meant that.' She looks up at me. 'I know you want me, Mike, all of me.'

My defences are shattered and I can feel the caress of the tears on my cheeks. 'You're right. I do want you. I'm falling in love with you, Natalie. I know you can't say it back, but I am.'

She picks up her serviette and wipes the tears away. And her other hand is still in mine.

*

We carry on through Wiltshire and into Hampshire and then move into West Sussex. The weather seems to be breaking and there are two flashes of forked lightning from a bank of deep grey cloud to the south. The temperature eases, and the air freshens, and we go on talking, yes, the superficial, the unremarkable, the prosaic, but still talking, and we're laughing, and teasing, and playing games that we used to play in the car as children, and it's all the companionship and friendship she promised, and more. Already we're planning further walks, and not just stuff from Toby's wish list, but beach walks, harbour walks and park walks, interspersed with Sunday lunches and cream teas and Natalie's favourite Italian fare. And now I don't mind today ending because I know it's really only the ending of the beginning.

*

She gets me home at six thirty. She says she'd love to stay but needs to get herself sorted for work in the morning. We agree we'll meet up again in Chichester next weekend. We kiss and she drives off home to Winchester.

I go back indoors and check my emails. There's one from Marcus Kenton in Bristol.

Dear Mike,

Thank you for coming to see me. I'm delighted to formally offer you the vacant post of assistant solicitor. I attach a draft contract. Can you start next Monday? We'll sort out the boring stuff then. Call me as soon as you get this.

11

Crig-a-tana(n) – Rather cloying congratulatory comment at end of last section of long-distance footpath guidebook, e.g. "On reaching the Sainsbury's car park you can officially be said to have finished the Breaker Way. Very well done indeed!"

I draft an emailed refusal to Marcus next morning but delete it almost at once and don't actually send him anything. I think it was sixty-nine letters I wrote seeking employment when I was leaving school, getting zilch back, not even an acknowledgement. So why should I respond now I'm not interested in the one offering me the job.

The only regret is that I've no hidden camera in Marcus' office so I can see the guy stewing and for a while at least having that arrogant smirk erased from his face.

Then I ring Natalie.

'Mike, get real.'

'Say that again?'

'I'd rather not. Mike, I was beginning to think you had a bit more about you than that. I really was.'

'I want to be with you. Near you. Around you. Isn't that enough.'

'Mike, grow up.'

*

There's no time to do anything about letting my house in Chichester, having mail redirected, and all the other responsible things one's supposed to do when vacating a property. I do remember, prompted by Natalie, to do the essentials. I tell Louise's voicemail where I'm going. Then with Natalie's help I manage to assemble together enough washed and ironed shirts for the first week, and sufficient clean underwear to hopefully avoid becoming a danger to public health for about a fortnight. She drives me down to Bristol on Saturday morning, we buy the local paper and we place red rings round the bedsits that appear tolerable to live in until I'm able to afford a decent set of rooms. But we've clearly not been quick enough and pretty much everything's been taken. So when Major Crosby-Williams says his room is still available, and I find it's within easy walking distance of Marcus' office, Natalie more or less tells me to take it. It's that or the St Mungo's night shelter in Rodney Street.

One look at the place tells me it's a step back; no, it's about six steps back. A family man who once had a wife and child and nice home with garage and washing machine and garden now reduced to renting a room in a house surrounded by lots of other men who were family men who once had a wife and child and nice home with garage and washing machine and garden. As a law undergrad I couldn't wait to get out of my hall of residence into a place like this. Granted, the halls were comfortable and convenient and great for making friends. Nothing bonds like a half-mile queue down the corridor for a lukewarm shower. Or the collective realisation that there's only five slices of processed cheese and half a small split tin loaf between ten of you and all the shops within a three-mile radius have shut. The trouble was that none of the others on my floor ever seemed to be the ones with the processed cheese and the half loaf. It was always me. So to get my very own bedsit where I knew the food I bought would be going into my own mouth and nobody else's, and only three others were competing with me for bathroom facilities rather than what seemed like thirty-three, felt like a real achievement. I had thrown off the shackles of institutionalism and for the first time in my life believed I had properly come of age. But now my new residence stinks of regression and failure. I'm thinking of putting a nameplate as well as a number on the door. Dunfamily. Done all that, the wife bit, the child bit, now as you were but with a heap of debris of hate and resentment and regret dumped on top.

The Major's rules and regulations make the legislative impositions on the people of Stalinist Russia seem like trifling inconveniences. I had anticipated, and indeed welcome, an embargo on smoking. As for no drugs, I can't afford them, certainly not now, although if I manage to keep the city's principal suppliers out of jail, I may be in line for mates' rates. So far so good. But those are only rules one and two out of eighteen thousand and twenty-nine. No more than one guest at a time, no overnight visitors, no animals, no alcohol, no parties, no shouting, no loud music, no custard creams after 9.45pm on alternate Wednesdays except that following the first Sunday after the feast of St Augustine of Hippo. I guess I can live with it, or rather without it, for a bit. It'll get trickier when I want to pick at that scab on my left buttock, in flagrant contravention of rule sixteen thousand and forty seven. At least I won't be suffering alone: during our briefing at HQ the Major gives me a pen-picture of all six other tenants with whom I'll have the pleasure of sharing my roof. I meet a couple of them as I depart after signing the paperwork: firstly Lucas, a Bulgarian with a boil above his left nostril, and secondly an OCD sufferer named Ernest, clad only in purple Y-fronts with a matching purple bath towel and carrying two family-sized bars of soap and bottle of shampoo. We exchange pleasantries in the mess hall, then I take my leave, promising to look out for them on the parade ground when I report for duty the following afternoon.

There's still a lot left of the day so Natalie and I go out and about. We lose our stomachs by looking down from the top of Clifton Suspension Bridge. We find a boutique whose ground floor offers leopard skin dungarees and red leather flying suits and blue knee-high lace up boots – then go upstairs and spend even longer in the womens' wear section. And we explore flea markets and antique collections that go on along corridors and further corridors and still more corridors again until I start wondering when we're going to see signs welcoming us to Cardiff. We book in at the Garden Hotel and close our room door behind us and it's the best ever, better even than with Louise beneath the olive trees. But I know all the time the clock's winding down and as the last spoonful of Sunday lunchtime treacle pudding and custard disappears from my bowl in the Royal Oak there's this vile certainty that this same afternoon she's going to be getting into the car and driving away from me. I ask her when we can see each other again. She says it's Sod's law that the moment we've fixed up to meet I'll find I've got a queue of clients being booked in at the cop shop. So we'll play it by ear, she says. Take a rain check, she says. She may be content with that but it's not what I want to hear. It's a million miles away from what I'd ever want to hear.

I watch her driving away and as her car disappears down Carterbar Road I know I'm more in love with her than I thought I could ever be.

*

It's five o'clock on the same afternoon and here I am, staring at the cracks in the mile-high ceiling and down the left-hand wall and above the mantelpiece painted in rabbit-dropping brown. There's a shelf with sachets of tomato soup at one end and tins of pineapple chunks at the other, and an unmade bed, and a miniature electric cooker still caked, despite Natalie's best efforts, with fragments from what must be a good thousand burnt baked bean dinners. Lucas has got Rod Stewart on at full blast and a series of grunts and crashes and bangs and sploshes from next door signifies that Ernest is embarking on his second bath in forty minutes. And the girl for whom I'm going through all this is now on her way home, putting more and more distance between her and me. No doubt being a real man would mean telling myself to go out and explore every piece of my new home city while I've got the chance, but my feet remain attached to the fading carpet, my bum to the seat of the tea-stained armchair and my head to its cat-pee-stained antimacassar.

The hours of darkness seem to last at least a decade. Rod Stewart makes way on the Bulgarian playlist for Dire Straits, then the Rolling Stones, and, as a grand finale, the subtle and sensitive tones of Ian Dury and the Blockheads. They said it would be a warm and humid night and as I lie there wondering how to rearrange my Pop Hits From Hell chart for the thirteenth time in six hours you would need a Black and Decker to drill your way through the atmosphere. Air is being rationed to two cubic centimetres per person and the Government has stepped in to try and deter the public from panic buying. I splash my way through the sweat-soaked sheets and get up then in preparation for my breakfast conduct an examination of the milk in my mini-fridge. I think I've come out of the night marginally the fresher so I decide to eat in town and Starbucks are awarded the contract. The temperature's already sky-rocketing and by the time I get there sweat is pouring off every part of me. A bacon-filled croissant, lemon muffin and skinny latte get me back on planet Earth, and thanks to the café's gents washroom and the availability of a nearby convenience store with three for the price of two own-brand anti-perspirant and deodorant I can look Marcus in the face when I enter the office and shake hands. Then I sit down with him to discuss working arrangements and sign my soul away.

The good news is that I'm unlikely to suffer again like I did last night, because I can't see I'm going to be in my lodgings any night. Marcus has me rota'ed for 24-hour police station own client duty work four days a week, to include acting for them if they're remanded to next day's court, and then when a few formalities are completed I can expect to do stints on the general 24-hour duty rota plus agency work for other firms when they can't cover. I do wonder if I should ask simply to move my bed into my office and forget Room 23, Belfrage House, 437A Carterbar Road, BS6 3EW with its free disco and sauna facility. I ask Marcus when he can guarantee me some free time. He asks me how between half past seven and twenty to eight every other Tuesday morning sounds, and he doesn't smile when he says it. Then he asks me what I'm waiting for. Apparently there's a Turk in custody who's asked for us. He's been charged with possession of an unlawful firearm and wants to make a bail application. Marcus says the guy's looking at four years if he's convicted. And I feel like asking if he and I can swap places, as he'll be out before I am.

*

It's twenty to six. My Turk is on his way to his remand prison cell, doubtless good news for the victim who according to the prosecution can now once more sleep soundly in his bed and walk free from fear of molestation across our green and pleasant land. But it's not good news for me. Marcus calls me in for an inquest. What went wrong, what were the reasons, and have you asked the Crown Court for an early hearing to get this outrageous decision quashed on appeal. Before you go home, here's a trial for you to do on Wednesday, Ryan Digweed. Oh, and Jake Rodriguez has just been nicked for possession of an offensive weapon, being guilty while drunk of disorderly behaviour and assaulting a police officer and has asked for our services at the police station, and you're not doing anything tonight are you, and no that wasn't a question.

I ring the police and find Rodriguez won't be ready for interview until God knows when, probably the moment I've switched my bedside light off. The custody centre's out in the middle of nowhere but Marcus has managed to get a car sorted for me. It's a pretty crap vehicle and is really only good for local journeys but it's quicker than walking. Until the engine falls out that is. I heat up a cardboard macaroni cheese and read the Digweed file. Then I switch on the laptop and catch up with the weekend's sport, and sure enough, the moment I've dozed off, my phone's going and they're ready to deal with Jake Rodriguez.They charge him and despite my strenuous representations to bail him out, they decide to keep him in custody for court in the morning. I get back to my lodgings at ten past one.

It's too much too soon. At least when I was sitting at home after Louise and Katie left I knew I could be assured of a night's sleep with the promise of another gripping episode of *Checkout* next day, the only thing threatening to disturb my slumbers being the worry as to how soon Cindy from shelf-stacking would find out that her partner Callum from online deliveries was having an affair with Gordon the in-store cup cake decorator. Now I've got the pressures of clients, the uncertainty of when the phone might ring next, which client's gone and got themselves nicked, what for, when I'm going to be needed to go and deal with it. Three a.m, five a.m, whenever. Even though Motorhead upstairs have blown themselves out, I'm still lying there wide awake at twenty past two. I remember something Louise said the night before she and Katie left. 'You've got your wish now, haven't you.' I asked her what she meant and she said I'd always made it clear I'd rather be doing stuff on my own rather than with my daughter. Now, she said, I could do what I want, when I wanted. The irony in her voice was unmistakable but it didn't hit me then like it's doing now. And I'm asking myself if there's something wrong inside my head that I've made the choices that have transported me from family man to bedsit loser. How could this be what I want, what any normal person would want.

So I phone Louise.

Please pick up this time, Louise, please, please pick up. It rings. There seem to be more rings than usual. A good sign. But then it goes on ringing and ringing. I leave it a few minutes then I try again. Two rings this time. Then the voice I want to hear least in the world, "This is the 02 messaging service." For a moment I'm tempted to take the phone, get up, open the window and hurl a short-pitch delivery down Carterbar Road, and if it's a no-ball, who's going to care. Then I've a better idea. I'll ring Marcus now – after all, he's used to being woken at any time of the day or night – and tell him I'm packing it in.

I'm just about to call him when my phone rings. My first thought is that it's another client that's been arrested and I'm about to reject the case and refer them to Marcus instead. Then I look down at the phone.

Natalie.

'You called just now,' she says.

'I didn't. I was trying to ring L … I was trying to ring Marcus.'

'Are you all right?'

I'm dialling my current partner at twenty past two in the morning thinking I'm dialling my ex. And now my current partner to whom I must not appear desperate now knows how desperate I am. Is there anything all right about that.

'I'm not all right.' And again my defences turn to melted butter and I'm sobbing. 'I didn't … really didn't mean to ring you. Natalie, I can't do this. I was mad to think I could. It was stupid, daft … I know you'll hate me but I'm coming home. In the morning. I'll tell Marcus it's not the right time.'

There's silence at the other end.

'I get it, you're ashamed of me, aren't you. Disappointed. I'm sorry, Natalie, I'm sorry I raised your hopes, you thought I was a real man, I'm not, I'm really not, okay. Anyway, I know you won't want me now, not after this, so …' I tail off.

'It's fine,' she says. 'Never thought you could do it. Honestly, it's fine.'

It's fine. Thank God. 'Can I see you? When I get home?'

'Saturday midday in Chichester? The Cross?'

'Perfect.'

'Goodnight, Mike.'

The line goes dead.

I shut my eyes. And next thing I know, the June morning sunshine is filling the room and my radio alarm's announcing the eight o'clock news.

*

I go along to court and ask for bail for Rodriguez, then having failed to get it, I return to the office. Marcus is there. I tell him that with Digweed I'm likely to make it a losing hat trick. I have my pride and I'm anxious that even though I won't be around beyond Friday afternoon he shouldn't think I'm a bum lawyer on the strength of losing an unwinnable case. He seems to read my thoughts. 'I won't think you're a bum lawyer on the strength of losing an unwinnable case,' he says. 'Just be observant. Keep your wits about you. Exploit whatever good fortune comes your way. You never know what might drop into your lap.'

He gives me more good news and more bad news. The good, I can have a free afternoon to familiarise myself with office procedures, forms and so on, and he'll cover any police station work tonight. The bad, he's got to go away tomorrow, Wednesday, for the rest of the week so can I cover any own client police station work Wednesday lunchtime to Friday evening throughout, and oh yes, Fox & Fox have asked us to cover their own client stuff between five on Thursday night and nine on Friday morning so can I do those as well. If I were staying on I'd either be taking him to the European Court in Strasbourg on the grounds of deprivation of basic human rights or bringing a private prosecution for cruelty to dumb animals. But since I'm out the door Friday at five I can afford to be generous. I say it would be a pleasure. His eyes light up. He says he wasn't sure about me at first but now he's calling me a gold nugget and is already talking about a pay rise.

After which the gold nugget goes to his desk and prepares a chart counting down the minutes.

I get away at five and as this is my last guaranteed free time till I go home, I decide to see what Bristol has to offer which Natalie and I didn't cover at the weekend. I walk for miles, first the shops, then the waterfront, then up to Clifton village and the zoo. I decide on a picnic supper and take my sandwiches onto the downs and sit on the grass under a cloudless sky, the evening sun cooled by a gentle westerly breeze, and take a bite of my prawn on granary.

Then for the first time I recall her exact words on the phone this morning. The bit before the bit I was aching to hear.

"Never thought you could do it."

Couldn't be expected to do it, Mike. Not with the worry about where your wife and daughter have gone, how they are, will they come back. Not with the weight of Isabel's loss still hanging heavily upon your head. Not when you've fallen in love and then found you've been ripped away from that love with not a clip or a staple in sight to reattach yourself to that love.

I mean, what else could she mean.

"Never thought you could do it."

Didn't have it in you to do it, Mike. Like you didn't have it in you to fight to keep your wife and daughter from leaving you, or to fight to keep your job, or to fight to last more than forty-eight hours before pressing the panic button while right-thinking people are buried beneath their duvets. I don't need anyone like that in my life, Mike, don't want one, either.

Couldn't have meant that.

*

I get to court in good time on the Wednesday and take my place in the queue to get through the security barrier. There are two police officers in front of me. I see one of them unwrapping a piece of gum and popping it in his mouth. From the conversation he's having it's clear he's the star witness in my trial. More than once he says he's no idea why Digweed's wasting his time running it, better off pleading and asking for credit, probably the only thing that'll stop him going in. My guy's charged with dangerous driving, disqualified driving and drink driving. He's claiming it wasn't him: he maintains that he was a passenger in a car being driven by some other man. The officer who saw him stagger from his vehicle insists that there was nobody else anywhere near it when he caught up with it. My client refuses to say who the driver was. Against the duty solicitor's advice he went no comment in interview, and the court will be bound to draw an adverse inference from his not at least alluding to the existence of another driver at that time. In legalistic parlance, he's stuffed. He's on an eighteen-week suspended sentence and from what I've been able to gather there doesn't seem any real reason not to activate it. I don't always see eye to eye with the police, but the officer's analysis can't be faulted and I more or less repeat this advice to Digweed a few moments later. Trouble is, he doesn't see it that way. He wants his fight.

We're not on at once. There's another trial that's been called in front of ours and with nothing better to do I find myself following the action from the one and nines. It's a charge of handling stolen goods; all the prosecution evidence is accepted, and the issue is whether the defendant knew the goods were stolen. He calls a couple of witnesses to give evidence. It's hardly the kind of fare that fills the public galleries, crams the press boxes with sketchers ready to portray the court scene, and calls for towels to be ready for draping over the defendant's head as he's led away into a waiting prison van. My attention does begin to wander and I'm really only listening with half an ear as the guy's two supporters try and persuade the bench that Sean McSweeney was a perfectly plausible salesman of cut-price iPads. I'm only jerked out of my reverie when the bench chairman, hitherto unruffled and poker-faced, barks 'No eating in court!' to some hapless individual sitting in the back row of the stalls. The culprit's off and away before you can say contempt.

It might not work. It probably won't …

The bench decide to give Mr McSweeney's unsuspecting customer the benefit of the doubt, and moments later my client's being called into court. He confirms his details, sits down, and the prosecutor, a dour middle-aged fellow whose clothes stink of stale sweat and even more stale Right Guard, opens the case. It's clear he thinks the officer's only got to come into court and my man's case is going to crumble so quickly that in no time we'll have the usher coming in with the jug of hot custard. Shortly, in walks Plod. How would you describe your view of the car? Unobstructed at all times. How long did you have him in your sight? For at least three miles. Could you see anybody in the car beside him? Absolutely nobody. Did you lose sight of the vehicle at any time? Not for a second. He may be the only live witness, and his evidence may be uncorroborated, but one thing is certain, I'm on the ropes, no, I'm way beyond that, I'm having a close encounter with the vacuum cleaner in the broom cupboard behind row Q.

But from the way his mouth and his cheeks are moving in between his answers to the prosecutor there's hope. My only hope and it's cobweb thin, but still hope.

'Officer,' I begin. 'Is everything you have told us so far the truth?'

'Yes, sir.'

'Would you describe yourself as a truthful person?'

'Of course, sir.'

'It would never occur to you to tell the court something that wasn't true.'

'Certainly not, never, sir.'

'Or indeed to show disrespect to the court by eating when you were addressing it. Or sucking.' Pause and a slight *diminuendo*. 'Or chewing.'

'Certainly not, sir.'

I pause as long as I dare.

'Officer, are you chewing?'

'No, sir.'

I feel goose pimples on the back of my neck.

'Officer, what have you got in your mouth?'

'It's … er … medicinal. I've had a cold.' I can see his cheeks reddening with every syllable.

'Very good. So what is it that's really in your mouth?'

'I … I don't know.'

'Yes, you do. What is it?'

'It's … it's a mentholated gum.'

'It's not a prescribed drug, is it?'

'No, sir.'

'You were chewing it, weren't you?'

'It was in my mouth, sir.'

'Answer my question please. You were chewing it, weren't you.'

He nods.

'And mentholated gum's not medicinal, is it?'

His voice is barely audible. 'No sir.'

'So when you said on oath you weren't chewing, you lied, didn't you. And when you said on oath it was medicinal, you lied agan, didn't you.'

He looks towards the prosecutor clearly hoping there'll be some objection. And the prosecutor merely shrugs. The ball's hovering in front of an open goal.

'Officer? Hallo. Didn't you?'

He looks down at his pocket book and mumbles an affirmative.

'Officer, you've given evidence against my client. You've sworn on oath to tell the truth. Yet the very first substantive questions I ask you, you've given me answers I know, you know, aren't true. Haven't you.'

Silence.

Some people are on the pitch …

*

I'm not in bedsit land for long. Marcus has made it clear he wants me in peak condition, and I can't be dazzling the courts with my forensic brilliance and then be prevented from such sleep as I am allowed by the overpowering stench of festering socks awaiting a day out at the launderette and Songs For Deaf Sofian Lovers crashing down from room 8A. The novelty of Baby Belling-ed chilli con carne has begun to wear off, as has the need to complete an application form in triplicate supported by three references and criminal records check every time I want to trim my eyebrows. So having received a substantial pay increase, I decide to upsize, and after some window shopping during one of my twenty-minute exercise yard breaks I become the proud tenant of a furnished garden flat close to the city centre. I go to the Major, stand to attention, request immediate discharge and on being granted it I salute him, stand easy and dismiss.

I'm starting to enjoy my work. I'm at the police station most nights and in court most days, keeping convicted clients out of prison, getting innocent clients off, and getting more than a few guilty ones off as well. It started with Ryan Digweed and that gives me the confidence to do it again and again, which in turns breeds enthusiasm for my work that I've never felt in my career before. And I'm doing it without antagonising the Crown advocates and the court staff. I'm attracting work to the firm. People want to instruct me because I'm good. Marcus says business has never been better. It does mean that at least on weekdays I never stop, I'm beginning to forget what an armchair looks like, and my relaxation is sitting at my desk or dining table looking at files and reading online law reports for technicalities and loopholes that can get even more clients off or keep them out of prison.

There are windows of inactivity poking through the madness. With Marcus and myself sharing out the own client duty work, I do find I have some Saturdays and Sundays free. I've used a couple of them to go by train to Buxton and see mum. We talk about Louise and Katie. I'm not even getting voicemail from Louise now, just a recorded message that the number's no longer obtainable. I ask mum if she thinks I could or should be doing any more than I am to ensure they're safe and well and that Katie's happy. She says it's still early days, many fathers don't see or hear anything from their exes or their children for three years, never mind three months. Just make sure she knows you'll be there for them. You've got her solicitor's contact details if you want to get the courts involved. Louise isn't pushing for divorce, that must mean something. I tell her I don't want solicitors, I don't want court orders, I want civilised and adult. I ask mum's advice about what to do about our house which is in our joint names, and again she's being the pragmatic mum, the sensible mum. Leave it for now. You don't know what the future holds, you may need the house again sooner than you think. She says in the meantime I should go out walking again, enjoy the countryside, get to know the area, put things in perspective. So I do start walking again. Money's still tight and long expeditions are out of the question so I'm doing local walks, sometimes in Bristol itself and sometimes in the rolling farmland on the fringes of the city and in the Mendips. It's countryside where walkers are often just tolerated rather than welcomed, where paths that are rights of way aren't as well maintained and signed as they are in more popular walking country, and where paths that aren't rights of way tend to come with signs warning that trespassers will be executed. As a result I find myself experiencing a whole host of situations that are ripe for inclusion in the Walkopedia Hall Of Fame. Arriving at the far end of a patch of woodland after a good couple of hours' careful map reading, only to find the way out of it blocked by impenetrable barbed wire. Finding paths obstructed by invasive vegetation, herds of cattle, heaps of cattle effluent, or an assembly of half-completed luxury homes, more land urgently required. Scratching my head when signage gives out altogether and I find landmarks and path junctions where none should exist, only then discovering I'm 5 miles off course and have missed all the scenic highlights. Grappling with footpath guides whose authors are prepared to sacrifice clarity for brevity, turn right then shortly left through 2 gates, shortly right again over a stile and footbridge and then further stile and along farm track into field, halfway across field bearing half right and across 3 further fields. And even where navigation is straightforward there's no shortage of other cards up the fates' sleeves. Crossing a golf course fairway not sure which way I'm supposed to be looking for maverick balls. Struggling with a farm gate which detaches from its hinges the moment I touch it or which appears specially designed to trap at least one finger during the process of opening it. Experiencing that cruel optical illusion which makes a pub appear to be only a couple of minutes' walk ahead but is found at the very last minute to be separated by a river requiring another two hours walking to cross.

But I wouldn't do it if I didn't enjoy it. The scenery may not boast the charisma of Haystacks, the rugged grandeur of the Brecon Beacons or the aggression of Kinder Scout, but it's worth the route-finding challenges and the occasional rural obstacle course to experience the tops of the hills above the city and their vistas of the Severn and its crossings, the huddles of grey stone cottages beneath elegant green hillsides with the fragrance of rose and sweetpea floating from their gardens, or the banks of the river Avon onto which the sun sprinkles fragments of gleaming silver. My exploration may provide only brief respites from the demands of the work but seems to give me extra strength to find my way through the worst of them. And with my being constantly on the move, I find I'm losing weight and feeling healthier than I've done for years. I'm downloading described walks and find myself with more potential expeditions than I could complete in ten lifetimes. I'm buying walking magazines and using waiting time in the nick and at court to have a regular go at the walkers' crossword. I'm so proud when I complete one that I send it off, not that I'm desperate for the star prize of a year's supply of foot massage oil. And I'm googling long-distance paths, wondering if I might tackle one if I ever get the time, and marvelling at the place names the like of which Gavin has imported into the world of Walkopedia. Sibbertswold, Croglam, Dolanog, Little Tongue, Shakers Furze, Vellan Drang, Friar Biggins, Penycloddiau, Tugnet, Widdop, Wharram Percy. As an alternative to counting sheep, I know nothing that comes anywhere near it.

It doesn't stop me yearning for Natalie. She may be delighted I'm not Mr Quitter but the need to avoid being labelled Mr Desperate is just as acute.

So I have to ration my contact.Of course we do speak on the phone, and we text, and we email, and we chat on Facebook, and I tell her about my walks, and I've sent her flowers on her birthday but none of this is any real substitute for what I need. I need to see her, reach out to touch her, feel her and love her more and hope to make her love me. I've suggested meeting on a couple of my free weekend days, but she's always got something else, usually work-related, and it's never happened. Anyway, we agree it would be great to have a long weekend together and she says she's definitely free for the whole of the fourth weekend in August, so I ask Marcus for some remission for good conduct. It needs more crawling than an Olympic swimmer puts in during a year and my tongue has to do overtime on his brown brogues. But after kicking me in the face a couple of times he gives me the weekend I've asked for, including the Friday, at the same time warning me that I'm not to come back with dirty knees and I mustn't forget my clean PE kit on Monday morning. Then I'm picked up and deposited head first into the canal.

*

The days and weeks hurtle by and our weekend together is here. I've had to spend most of the Thursday afternoon at the nick, but Marcus relieves me as promised and I'm back at the garden flat in time to meet Natalie at seven thirty. She wears a yellow top and denim shorts and Converse boots, there are no worry lines on her face, there seems to be a more effulgent glow in her cheeks and a broader smile on her lips, and as we enjoy these first few minutes together she keeps saying how great I look and how well I look. I want her now and I need her now. The weeks of calls, and missed calls, and messages, and waiting, and longing, and more waiting, explode into a cascade of passion and fury and love and excitement and excruciating pain and excruciating delight.

We go out for dinner and sit in a trattoria on the corner of Alma Road and Whiteladies Road and they bring us plates piled with pasta, red stone jugs full of fruity red wine and deep bowls protesting under the weight of tiramisu, and as the candles flicker and the pianist moves from Rachmaninov to Chopin and the oranges and pinks of the declining sky outside the window give way to soft still darkness, we enter each others' worlds and I love the fact that as she extracts for me the best bits of her life, she's now beginning to look for the best in mine.

We drain the last dregs of our liqueur coffees and the final few drops from the jug, pay our bill and walk out into the Bristol air, the streets even at ten to midnight alive and awake. We're not tired, there's still so much to say and so much love still to offer to each other, and for hours we just walk and talk. Then we come back to my flat and I pull down her denim shorts and peel off her yellow top and scream the flat down as for the second time that evening our togetherness, our empathy and our interdependence spiral upwards into a million fireworks of satisfied wants and fulfilled desires.

*

We've decided to go walking on the Friday. Having cleaned our walking boots the night before and seen the haloes floating above our heads, we choose Cleeve Hill, the summit of Gloucestershire and the Cotswold hills and a few minutes' walk from the 102-mile Cotswold Way long-distance footpath. It's on Toby's list but certainly not one of the toughies; from his notes we ascertain that it's been included because of its easy accessibility, its comparative height above nearby Cheltenham, the magnificence of the grandstand panorama from the top and its links with pre-history. It's not a long walk to the summit from the nearest road so rather than risk getting snarled on the M5 in the rush-hour we set off mid-morning and stop over in Cheltenham for a lazy coffee. Then we drive to the start point, parking near a golf clubhouse and joining a clear track, aiming for three tall transmitter masts. From the leaflet and map we've picked up in Cheltenham we see we're on Cleeve Common, a plateau of about three square miles, abounding in Iron Age earthworks and designated a Grade 1 Site of Special Scientific Interest with a variety of orchids, glow worms and butterflies. It isn't that warm out, but we're not complaining. The chunks of high grey and white cloud, wafted by a capricious westerly wind, are mitigating the impact of the summer sun, and for the time being seem to have no intention of keeping us from seeing for ever and beyond.

We leave the track to speed up our progress to the masts, and on reaching their protective fencing we change direction to walk uphill beside the fence, aiming for the trig point marking the official summit of the Cotswolds at the top of the rise, with a fence and a rather disjointed stone wall to the right. The climb seems almost too easy. We look at each other as if to say, is this all there is to it. Perhaps after our experience of Derbyshire and south Wales we never expect any half-decent hilltop to give up without a fight. If there is a catch, it's that we've moved so far from the edge of the plateau that we've lost the wider views, although Natalie identifies the distinctive Malvern Hills exploding from the surrounding levels. And both of us can pick up a bank of black on the horizon. The trouble is, it's not on the ground but in the sky, and while above us there's a watery blue, black is now on the march and poised to scoop us up in one lethal pincer movement. We return to the masts, but now continue in the same direction and make our way up through lush tufty grass to an isolated tree on the highest ground immediately ahead and look down on the sprawl of Cheltenham, facing south-west. And we watch as the cloud envelops and blots out the town and the surrounding countryside, and the next moment the deluge, the first rain I've seen for three weeks, sweeps onto the common and in turn forces us to run in the hope of shelter. But there's no shelter and in the end we just stand and merge our saturated faces and soaked tops and clam-encrusted hands … and laugh.

But we can't stay welded forever and as the cloud continues to fire its water cannons over us, we force ourselves to move onwards, taking our bearings carefully and hauling ourselves to another trig point, this time at the top corner of the plateau, and known as Cleeve Cloud. Although it's slightly lower than the summit we've just come from, the curtain has lifted to reveal a panorama that's immeasurably superior, encompassing not only Cheltenham and the Malverns but Bredon Hill and the Welsh mountains including the Brecon Beacons. Grandstand really doesn't get near it. But while sunny intervals are breaking out across the Principality it's still throwing it down on Cleeve Hill and despite the fact that the tail of the storm is visible, that tail has bile enough for us both and much more to spare. Our guide, protected from nature's worst by Natalie's transparent map cover, tells us that if we were to detour southwards we'd be able to follow the plateau edge and enjoy the splendid sight of the steep crags of Castle Rock. But our priority is the car. We scramble down a steep embankment then, using an imposing stone ivy-clad house as a marker, we drop down to complete the circuit. And as we charge along the home straight, the rain is no longer just falling, it's banging and clattering, because it isn't just rain, it's hail. It doesn't sit, it bounces upwards before crashing to the ground, and a sword of lightning springs from the blackness above, answered by a furious explosion of thunder and I wonder if the whole plateau is erupting and throwing itself down to the plains below. Natalie gets to the car first and throws open the doors and we've made it and now we can laugh once more.

After we've stopped laughing comes the silence. The silence of bewilderment and perplexity that follows the watching of a film on DVD at triple speed, knowing that the good guy's won the war and won the girl but wondering what on earth the hurry was. And this wonderment multiplies as, in minutes, the hail and the rain disappear and there's clear blue sky through the windscreen and a brace of robins are sunbathing on the bonnet.

'I love you, Natalie.'

She smiles and says nothing. Like she did each time I said it to her last night. And once again I wish I hadn't said it, because I know she thinks I've only said it so she can say it back. I don't need her to tell me that doesn't count.

'Can I ask you something,' she says. 'What would have to happen to make you love Katie?'

It's a question Louise has asked in one form or another possibly fifty times since Katie came into our lives. But I know that Natalie, unlike Louise, won't be satisfied with the muffled grunt, the shake of the head, the switch of topic to the price of cheese at Morrisons.

'I don't think there's a formula,' I say. 'You can't create love where there isn't any. It's like expecting an oak tree to grow where you don't put down the seeds.'

'Supposing someone or something planted a seed.'

'Who would do that?'

'Maybe someone who cares about you both. Maybe someone who doesn't want to see you drown in self-pity, in regret for what might have been.' She places her hand on my knee.

I put my hand over hers. 'It's too late. I blew it and that's that. She's got Louise and she's got Paul. She's fine.'

'Supposing she wasn't.'

The glare of the sun through the windscreen is almost blinding us. 'Come again?'

'Supposing she wasn't. Supposing she fell ill, or worse. Something happened which meant she wasn't there for Katie.'

'It would never happen. Louise is rock solid. Good health, mega-dependable. She'd never let anything happen to Katie. Never let anything come between them. Anyway, I couldn't do it.'

'No, I don't suppose you could. Not on your own.' She reaches into her jacket pocket for her sunglasses and puts them on. 'But with someone who meant more to you than anything else, someone you really loved, someone who learned to love you, someone who grew to love Katie, maybe because she never had a child of her own ...' Her voice tails off. She leans over and kisses me on the lips. 'I just don't want you to rule it out, Mike. I don't want you to shut it out.'

Now I lean forward and kiss her on the lips and the cheeks and her neck and over her jungle blonde hair.

'Mike,' she says in a whisper.

'Yes, Nat?'

'Let's climb that hill again.'

We retrace our steps to the trig point on Cleeve Cloud. The rain seems to have frightened everyone else away. We're on our own, looking out across to Cheltenham and the Malverns and Bredon Hill and the Brecon Beacons and we feel like monarchs of all of it. The landscape is our own, our very own, and nobody's going to take it from us, the small effort involved in our ascent rewarded one hundredfold, rewarded by promotion to ownership of what seems like a whole world. Once again we're in each other's arms and I can feel, just by the way she holds on and the gentleness with which she lets go, how much more love there is in her than when I first left her to come to Bristol. But even as we gaze, and wonder, we can see the next bank of storm clouds lining up for its own direct assault and we decide to head back to the car for the second and final time. And on our way back down the hillside I'm already cherishing those moments when there were crowns on our heads and orbs and sceptres in our hands.

*

She's woken me up at quarter to eight next morning. I'd had visions of sleeping in till ten and enjoying a leisurely coffee and cheese and bacon-filled bagel in Cypriano's in Claremont Avenue then a wander round the galleries near the waterfront. But she's got other ideas and tells me that with warm sunshine forecast all day we're off in the car to High Willhays. It sounds like a stately home and I've never been a great one for probing historic piles. But it turns out that High Willhays is the summit of Dartmoor and together with its neighbour Yes Tor it's on Toby's to-do list. The drive in her car will take a good three hours, she says, so we need to start early. On the map it doesn't look as though it should take half that time but I've reckoned without Bank Holiday Saturday traffic on the M5 and although we never actually grind to a halt, our 15mph procession with most of the population of the Midlands towards the promised land of clotted cream teas, chocolate-box villages, rugged cliff paths and shops crammed with packets of toffee fudge manufactured in Ipswich is so respectful that round each corner I train my binoculars for the coffin and the pall-bearers. Neither of us feel like talking much. It's only once we get past Exeter and are able to leave the motorway and follow the A30 into the heart of the Devon countryside that we relax. We drive through Okehampton and up to a parking area close to Okehampton Camp then change into our boots and head out onto Dartmoor.

I've never been on Dartmoor, not properly on it. I've visited Devon just once before, on a family holiday, but I'm certain we didn't venture into the moors on foot. I remember when I was a teenager some mates of mine had to go to there as part of their Duke Of Edinburgh

Award Scheme and they came back telling of losing their way among featureless heather wildernesses, sinking in blanket bogs and trying to brew alphabet spaghetti in a tent which at the time was being lifted from the ground by a friendly passing hurricane. So it hasn't been high on my travelling bucket list. But while, yes, there's heather, acres and acres of it, our initial encounter with the moor seems more like shaking hands with an eccentric uncle than being pounced upon by a seven-headed dragon. To begin with there's a tarmac track beneath our feet with no danger of disappearing below ground floor level, and even when this veers away left and we're heading straight on along a rougher track, the going is good to firm and we've cleared the water jumps without falling. To our left are Row Tor and its higher neighbour West Mill Tor, two of Dartmoor's trademark tors, granite hills clothed with heather but bare on top, leaving chunks of summit rock exposed to the sun and wind and rain. One reason Natalie was so anxious to come here today was that it being August, the heather is at its best; on Kinder Scout it was, well, just heather, but now I look out onto a concerto of purple, each torside a proud bride dressed for its granite summit husband. We're gaining height and arrive on Black Down, where to our left we can see a col, a dip between West Mill Tor and the still higher Yes Tor which now comes into view beyond. We now have to head for that col, which is still a load higher than we are on Black Down. It's one of those infuriating climbs where with each step you take the ultimate objective seems that much further away. The gradient is intensifying and as we place our feet down, they're sinking lower and lower into the ground with each step, and we can smell the filth on our boots and feel the drops of the liquid mud as they tickle the bottoms of our gaiters.

We reach what is effectively the top of the pass but also the base of the dip between the two tors. I'm all for a rest but Natalie, whose self-confidence seems to have soared since our Brecon Beacons experience, says we need to press on and we can rest when we reach the top of Yes Tor. The summit is visible, albeit white cloud is beginning to lick at its granite cap, and in the absence of a clear path we use the summit as our marker. As we turn ninety degrees to head Yes Tor-wards, the ground is reasonably level to begin with, but we know this is just Nature toying with us, lulling us, playing games, and sure enough, it's not long before it springs a water hazard on us. It's called Red-a-ven Brook, a playful moorland stream dotted with rocks and boulders, a snatch of life and vitality and vigour amidst the timeless solemnity of the heather and granite. We stop and look for a footbridge. Around the brook are bog pools bordered by yellow and pink flowers which Natalie pronounces with authoritative tones to be bog pimpernel and tormentil, and there's also a green-stalked plant with a head of creamy white hair which puffs and dangles and which she declares to be cotton grass. I'm about to award her a nature column in a national Sunday newspaper until she's honest enough to admit she'd done a spot of google homework while I was packing the rucksack this morning. But googling alone can't help us with the brook crossing. There is no bridge. The only way is to ford it. 'Think of it as peeling a plaster off your skin,' Natalie says. 'One quick movement, no pain. If you hesitate and think about it as you do it, fatal.' I then watch with admiration as she leaps from slime-coated rock to slime-coated rock to reach the far side. My instincts prevent me from replicating her gracious leaps but despite a mistake on stone 1 and an initial refusal on stone 3 I've done it. And our reward is the toughest climb yet. The path is clearer and Natalie keeps reassuring me that once we get to the summit the real hard work is done, it being only a slight descent and modest climb to our ultimate objective. I find I'm having to stop every half dozen steps but each batch of steps brings greater and greater payback, as the heather oceans and the chunky granite furniture on each tor top now acquire a backcloth of fields and forests. Natalie points to a bird fluttering above us and identifies it as a skylark. At first I believe its song to be one of welcome but no, it's a song of laughter, not with us but at us, because as the ground levels out, the white cloud blots Yes Tor from the map in one deft move. From the triangulation point there's just swirling, maddening, mocking white.

I remember a tongue-in-cheek piece in one of my walking magazines about walkers' denial, where you refuse to believe that there's nothing to show for all that hard work and by standing there long enough you will, by a process of self-hypnosis, convince yourself that the cloud isn't actually there at all. But Natalie's pragmatism triumphs and far from standing in stupefaction I find myself, after the briefest intermission, walking with her off the summit. We glide down a gentle incline to a col and then up again towards High Willhays, the very top of Dartmoor and the top also of the whole of southern Britain. The terrain is a mixture of rock and heather and unclothed earth and that is all we can see as we make the innocuous ascent. As we get near the spot which my GPS assures me is the highest point, giants begin to emerge, sleeping monsters, boulders and more boulders, and we're no longer in Devon on an August Saturday but part of another civilisation, another timeframe, perhaps even another planet. Through the soup of white I'm expecting an appearance either of alien life forms or David Tennant in a police box. Natalie has gone on ahead and she shouts to me that she's found the precarious heap of stones which is the summit cairn. I scramble up to join her and we sit in silence, our joy at having achieved our objective dulled by the bitter realisation that this could be anywhere. Anywhere at all.

The shared disappointment, like the white sea, can almost be touched as we go back down to the mini col between High Willhays and Yes Tor. Here we're to turn right along a firm track that will lead us by another route back to our starting point.

But ahead of us, Natalie thinks she perceives a break in the cloud. So we retrace our steps to Yes Tor.

And as we arrive back at the triangulation point the veil lifts.

I'm fearful that we're imagining it, that my denial has metamorphosed into a highly dangerous hallucinatory state, but praise God, it's not just our imagination, it's happening. As quickly as the cloud descended, it's vanished and in seconds all Devon is ours. We stand and stare at the hillsides blanketed with heather, we look back across the col to the imperious boulders shooting heavenwards from High Willhays, we watch the sun's rays tumbling onto the brow of West Mill Tor, and beyond the moor, we gaze at the million and one verdant fields, the patches of woodland, the villages and hamlets.

Natalie turns to me and kisses me on my lips, and tears of utter joy and wonderment fill my eyes. Now, as we receive just reward for our endeavours, would be the time for her to say it.

But she says nothing.

Not for the first time today, disappointment sours the thrill of achievement. I place my arm round her shoulder. I need reassurance that whatever it is that's stopping her saying it, it's not me. I tell myself she's obeying Gavin's entreaty. That's it. She's showing her love of the surroundings by giving. Standing, staring, absorbing every detail. It seems like hours before she turns to me, kisses me again and suggests we move on.

We decide to retrace our steps to the mini col and take the different route back rather than walking back to the car the same way. Satisfied that the view from the top of High Willhays can be no better than that we've just enjoyed, we turn left at the mini col and join a clearly defined stony track which descends on a gentle gradient along the slopes of Yes Tor. I demonstrate my limited knowledge of moorland wildlife by pointing out a red grouse, but anything I can do she can do better and, as we find ourselves fording Red-a-ven Brook once again, she indicates to me a pair of Dartmoor ponies. With their long slender legs and rough coats, they look every inch the product of a harsh environment where Nature offers slim pickings indeed for its hapless residents. As I look beyond the tors to the green patchwork beyond, I recall that family holiday, in mid-Devon when I was in my teens, and the unending succession of switchback hills which turned getting from one village to another into a three-day expedition. Now I'm looking down on that same countryside and wonder what all the fuss was about. I'm more conscious than I've been on any of my walks this summer that hilltop walking puts the down below stuff into perspective and allows you to believe that so much more might be possible than you ever used to believe.

I don't want to come down and I hate the fact that as the track descends, keeping West Mill Tor to the left and Row Tor to the right, I'm losing dominance of that green patchwork. I hate that in next to no time we'll be on the road and among the down below stuff again rather than towering above it. I'm holding hands with Natalie but I'm not saying much to her and she's not saying much to me. We're now within sight of the car and from having been on our own throughout our walk, we can see two or three groups of walkers coming towards us. The spell is breaking up before my eyes and I can feel the magic and the wonderment and the joy draining away through the soles of my boots.

Then Natalie stops walking and turns to me.

'I love you, Mike.'

*

Now she's said it once she can't stop saying it. She says it as we sit down together in the car. She says it again as we sit in the Okehampton pub garden over glasses of Devon cider. She says it as we go on to the village of Lustleigh and sit down in a garden bordered with roses and honeysuckle behind a thatched cottage, and break open scones, smothering their insides with clotted cream and gooseberry jam. She says it after we've hauled our bags up the stairs of a bed and breakfast just outside Moretonhampstead and sit at our bedroom window, gazing out at Dartmoor across the emerald green fields and switchback hills. And the last time she says it is the best of all as we lie together under a duvet which might have been made of cream silk, having offered to each other our bodies, our desires, our everything, and shattered the peace of the Devon evening with our pleasure.

At Sunday breakfast we eat scrambled eggs and smoked salmon on home-made granary bread then go for a stroll. We descend a hill so steep we could roll down it and stand on a little packhorse bridge over the stream at the bottom and I ask her to come to Bristol to live with me. 'I'll live with you anywhere,' she says and then she tells me she loves me again.

*

Next day is Bank Holiday Monday and it's back to business as usual, down at the police station at two thirty in the morning with three clients to see, then the magistrates' court for three hopeless bail applications. But it's all money coming in, money that'll help us establish ourselves in the city as a couple, and already in my mind the garden flat is no longer mine but ours.

I may have escaped Marcus' clutches for a single weekend, but he gets his own back over the next three days. It's non-stop. There isn't even time to think about the ridiculous hours I'm working, let alone google local spiritualists to see if there's one who might summon the ghost of William Wilberforce. By Friday morning I'm dead on my feet and I'm told off by the chairman in court 2 for snoring. Thank God it wasn't in the middle of one of my cases. I've developed a great respect for the Bench in the city, but I'd be inclined to lay substantial odds against this particular chairman having been vomited on at ten past two in the morning when trying to take instructions on an allegation of taking of a double decker bus without consent. Or finding himself compelled, as I'd been compelled two hours later, to explain to a man in for dangerous and drunken driving the difference between a tunnel mouth and a black-painted chemical waste transporter. I tell Marcus at lunchtime about my *faux pas* and he lets me take the afternoon off.

I decide to surprise Natalie. She's already told me she'll be at home tonight, and if the trains behave themselves – I don't trust my car outside a radius of five miles – I'll be with her by five thirty. They don't and I'm not. A signal failure just outside Temple Meads station keeps me chewing my nails for forty minutes, and what material I have left on the end of my fingers is eroded even further when we grind to a halt somewhere near Warminster. Meanwhile, conditions inside the carriage offer excellent preparation for all those who having passed from this life are fated to come back next time as a Ritz cracker. And the reward for finally getting to Southampton, where I've to change trains, is the announcement that owing to a lineside fire just outside Eastleigh all services are subject to delay, alteration and short notice cancellation, with tickets being accepted for reasonable alternative journeys operated by Brittany Ferries and the Midland Red Bus Company. The upshot is that I'm knocking on her door three hours later than planned.

She opens it but within a moment of her doing so I realise it's not her. It's just someone who looks like her. As she sees me she turns white, and there's suddenly a crazed, distant look in her eyes, and she's looking down, and shaking, and I'm gripped by a sickening fear.

'You need to go,' is all she says.

All I can do is shake my head and stammer. 'Go? What … what do you mean?'

And at that moment a man about her age appears at the door. He's noticeably taller than she is, with a red face and ginger hair and a rough ginger beard.

'Mike,' Natalie whispers. 'This is Toby.'

12

Allander(n) – Glossy supplement or insert in expensive walking magazine consisting of range of very pricey walking-related products together with technical specifications that look like something from a degree level mathematics paper

'But Toby's dead, sweetheart.' I'm aware of a kind of indulgence in my voice: the voice of denial, of my attempting to lead her gently away from whatever has started this delusional thinking, but not quite knowing where to begin.

'Mike, don't you think I'd recognise my ex-partner.' She turns to the ginger man. 'Listen, babes, I think you'd better disappear for a bit. Okay?'

He says nothing. He nods and walks out into the street, right past me, and as he does so my heartbeat quickens. His whole body shouts outdoors: not only his beard but his deep red cheeks, his tousled hair, a slight underarm whiff and small smears of mud round the bottoms of his trousers. It's just what I would have expected of the genuine article.

She ushers me into her front room.

'I was going to phone you, Mike.'

'I don't understand. You told me he was dead.'

I can see agitation rolling across her face. 'I just don't know where to start. What to say.'

'You said he was dead.' If I say it enough times it'll be true. 'He was killed in a plane crash. He'd gone travelling and his plane crashed and exploded. He was incinerated.'

'He never flew on that plane.'

The six words and seven syllables smash into my head and set off forest fires in my heart.

He'd booked onto a late afternoon flight, she explains. He'd booked it online, a last minute thing, non-refundable. He'd gone and checked in but the flight had been delayed by two hours. So he'd gone for a coffee and while he was waiting for his chosen beverage he'd got chatting to Stella. She was a company executive and had just got back from a business trip. And she was power-dressed to kill. Sharp black jacket and crisp white shirt. Short black skirt and high heels. They'd continued their conversation over their lattes. When he told her that his passion was walking, she'd told him her home was in one of the most scenically stunning parts of Canada.

She'd kept on saying to him, if you love walking, you'll be loving where I live. And all the time he was loving her sharp black jacket and crisp white shirt and short black skirt and high heels.

'He fell for it,' she goes on. 'Fell for her.' She gets up and stands in the centre of the room, folding her arms. 'I think it was mutual. The outdoor walking type obviously appealed to her. Anyway, it saved his life.' I can see the light of love in her eyes and it has an intensity I realise I never saw as we sat in Lustleigh among the roses and honeysuckle, or in our bed at Moretonhampstead, or anywhere else after she'd told me she loved me.

And she explains how it saved his life. The time comes for him to say goodbye to Stella. They exchange mobile numbers. He gives her a kiss. It's not just a kiss on the cheek. It's much more. And she responds. Responds fifty times over. She says she'll be waiting whenever he wants her. He walks away towards security and all the time he just can't keep his eyes off her. As he's about to disappear from her sight, he waves and she waves back and blows him a kiss. He goes through security, he waits air-side, he even gets on the plane. They're hurrying everyone aboard, wanting to get going as soon as possible, make up some of the lost time. As he takes his seat, he's thinking God, what is he doing, walking away from that sharp black jacket and all the rest. He gets up and grabs his bag. And a moment later he's getting back out of the plane. In the confusion of getting everyone on, nobody challenges him and in his rush to get back to Stella before she leaves, he doesn't tell anyone he's gone. The flight isn't full so presumably nobody's bothered to query the empty seat. He's picked his way to the exit, and if anyone's noticed him or missed him, the word obviously hasn't got back to the airline. He's kept all his vital gear as hand luggage so he doesn't give a monkey's about his backpack. Catching Stella means more to him than a sackful of putrid laundry.

He's caught her with seconds to spare. She's previously told him she'll be taking a taxi into town and he dashes down to the taxi rank and she's actually just getting into a vehicle. By now it's eight at night so they go for dinner then to her hotel room, they spend the night together, and the next morning they drive to her house in the mountains. I suggest he must have heard a news bulletin or picked up a paper or glanced at the news online, found out about the crash from that. Apparently not. He's never been a news junkie or a technophile. All he'd ever want to check his technology for would be the weather.

'He had Stella,' she says with a sigh. 'He had the mountains. And all the time he was there, nothing else mattered, nothing at all. By day, out walking. By night, warming her bed.'

She tells me again what she told me in Derbyshire; her trying to phone him three times, calls which she thinks Stella intercepted when he was in the bath, and then her finding out about the air crash on the news. He'd even been named in the press reports, one of three Englishmen who perished in the inferno.

I ask why if Toby's half the man Natalie's made him out to be he hasn't rung her and come clean about his transatlantic paramour. She turns to face the window and for a while the silence can be heard in the Solomon Islands. When she does answer I can tell how she's struggling with this, unable or unwilling to grasp the notion that he wasn't only human but imperfect. And she's defending him. The impressionable, curious guy, being lured, seduced, persuaded by the promise of not only the businesswoman but the snow-clad pine forests, lakes that plunged into the underworld, mountains that stretched into God's back yard. The guy who'll come back to his senses when the bubble's burst and it's time to return home and face the real world once more.

I'm running out of places to go. I ask her about Toby's family. Did he never keep in contact with them even if he didn't have the guts to ring her. She's turning back to face me. A slower ball, this one. She snicks it away for a quick single. They aren't really that sort of family. They've never been that close. Any of them. His parents split up years ago, live miles apart from each other and from him. He goes months without speaking to them. They wouldn't have expected him to keep contacting them from abroad. Natalie explains she rang them and they talked about a memorial service but it's never happened and they were quite happy to leave her in charge of sorting through his affairs. But every time she's opened the drawer with his personal effects and his bank details she's broken down in tears and never did a thing about any of it.

And she tells me she's sitting at home and the phone rings and he's at Heathrow and will be back in Sussex in a couple of hours, and now here he is. He's made full and frank admissions in interview. He's been an idiot. It was great for a while but after the novelty wore off he began to miss his life in England. Stella's constant absences with work left him lonely and unloved. Then she's come back from a business trip and says she's met someone else. Hours later he's on a plane bound for dear old Blighty. He's now returned to Natalie and still loves her and wants her to forgive him and love him all over again.

*

Now she sits down on the arm of a chair and cups her head in her hands. 'I'm so sorry, Mike.'

'So … so that's it, is it?'

'Sorry?'

'Are you back with him?'

She smiles. 'I forgive him.'

'And what does that mean?'

She raises her voice just slightly but there's no defensiveness in her tone. 'I wish it hadn't happened. I wish he'd been stronger, of course I do. But he's a man, isn't he? It's how men are made. Weak, vulnerable, susceptible, call it what you will. Just … men. Yes, of course I wish he'd been stronger. I wish he'd had the guts to ring me, told me he'd met someone else. But now it's happened, I accept it, we can draw a line, go forward.'

'Go forward? You mean go back to him?'

'I … I don't know.'

'Choosing him over me? The lead role now back in place, the understudy now surplus to requirements?'

'I don't know. I'm sorry.'

'Look, Nat, please, just come straight out with it. Tell me. Now. Please.'

'Mike, I don't know, okay. I just don't know. I'm sorry. I'm sorry.'

And as she speaks, I hear footsteps and Toby's come into the room. He just stands there, near to the door leading into the hall, his hands together, looking down at the ground.

'I thought Natalie told you to go,' I say.

I see him turning to Natalie. She glances at me and shrugs.

'Can I speak,' he says.

I move a step closer to him. 'You've got a tongue. I presume you can.'

Natalie throws me an anxious glance. 'Mike.'

'I know I've done something unforgivable.' His eyes remain fixed on her. 'And I'm sorry. Sorry for what I've put Nat through. Sorry for what I've put you through. But I'm also human. I know you're human and you've every right to be angry and upset. I mean, if it were the other way about I'd feel the same. I honestly would, Mike.'

'Don't you patronise me.'

'I'm sorry, I don't mean to patronise.' He shakes his head, retreats a couple of steps, and stands there, no longer the David Livingstone of Canbury Crescent but the schoolboy summoned to the headmaster's study for eating Double Deckers in RE. 'But are you going to tell me you've never messed up?'

'Of course I've messed up,' I say. 'But I've never done to any girl what you've done to Natalie. You made it clear to her through what you did that you wanted nothing more to do with her.'

'I don't deny it.' His voice is feeble and diffident and anxious.

'Just one call. One text. All it would have taken.' I can see him shaking. I've never been feared before and I'm starting to feel fear of myself. 'Do you know something, I wonder if you knew about the crash and you knew people thought you were dead and you were quite happy it stayed that way all the time it suited you. Quite happy that is until you want to go back to your previous model because the new one's run out of steam.'

Natalie cuts in. 'Mike, that's not fair.'

'And what happens the next time some smart businesswoman turns your head? How do you get out of that one? Eaten by a grizzly bear, perhaps?'

Toby shrugs and holds out his hands.

And I realise I can't do the talking bit any more. It's the culmination of everything, the hours of travelling, the absurd overwork, and the days and the weeks of the ecstasy of being in love mingled with the pain and frustration and anger and anguish of being apart. Words now can't do it for me and I find myself drawing back my fist ...

And Natalie's screeching, shrilling my name, a knife through the suffocating atmosphere which hacks my eardrums into tatters.

I stop in my tracks. I withdraw my hand and slump backwards. I look up at Toby and I can see him flinching, backing off in terror, and without another word I walk out of the room and out of the house.

*

I must have walked for an hour and a half at least, laps and more laps of suburban streets in gathering darkness, and as I've paused during the seventh circuit for a tyre change I feel a hundred times less sure how to get Natalie back than I had when the starting horn went.

I'm wasting my time going back there this evening, I reflect as I pass the boarded-up Forever Food Company store at the corner of St John's Terrace for the eighth time. In any case my phone's just rung and surprise surprise, the cops have picked up our client Connor Lahane. He's clocked up so many police station visits they're now charging him rent for his cell, he wants me personally, and they'll be interviewing him in the morning. I decide to go straight back and get a train to Southampton to pick up the Bristol connection only to find that the last one left ages ago. I'm forced to find a hotel in Southampton and stay the night there before getting the first train to Bristol next morning. I make it to Temple Meads by eight thirty and with other clients to see after Lahane I end up in the nick for the rest of the day. They finally charge Lahane at half six that evening, a few trivial matters, armed robbery, grievous bodily harm with intent and attempted arson. Then it's another full day in the police station on Sunday before going down to the magistrates' court on Monday to try to persuade District Judge Naismith to grant Lahane bail pending his appearance at the Crown Court.

The speed of the judge's rejection of my application means I've longer than expected before my next commitment, so after popping back to the office I go to Starbucks in order to regroup. I order the largest Americano and fruit bread with extra butter – the default single pat is never enough – then make my way to the red leather settee in the corner and fall into it. I glance across the coffee table in front of me and there's a young woman in white T-shirt, jeans and white plimsolls, with a teapot and cup in front of her.

I'm too stunned to fold her in my arms. I'm too stunned even to lean towards her. So I just sit there, motionless, unable to even consider making inroads into the mound of shuddering foodstuff I've just purchased.

And Natalie's the one who has to speak first. 'I'm sorry,' she says. 'I'm so sorry.'

I pick up my cup and sip from the tankload of caffeine. 'It's not enough for you to be sorry.'

'I know.' She pushes her cup to one side. 'Mike, I had to come and see you. To tell you ...'

'It's over?'

'Not over.'

'That you don't want to be knocking around with a guy whose first resort when you put him in a corner is to threaten physical violence.'

'No.'

'That all that stuff with me has just been one big fat stupid mistake.'

It's stock defence advocacy training. I've seen some solicitors get slaughtered because they underplay and gloss over the things that go against them, only for the court to pick up on all of them after the silver-tongued peroration has ended.

'I still love you, Mike.'

Now I do get out of my seat and come round and sit beside her and place a kiss on her lips.

'You mean ...'

'Mike, this is so difficult.'

'If that's code for you want to finish, please just say now. Get it over.'

'I don't want to finish.'

At that moment two women come up with two children and plonk themselves on the settee I've just vacated.

'Let's go for a walk, Mike,' Natalie says.

*

We walk arm in arm alongside the canal then away from the city centre, finding ourselves in a part of Bristol I've not explored before, a section of old railway line converted into a footpath. The council appear to have made an effort to spruce it up, providing some information boards and boxes of leaflets with details of wildlife and plant life to be found in the area, but there's still a very urban feel, cigarette ends competing with the thistles for undergrowth space, and it's not far from the first information board to the first discarded Smirnoff bottle. We're not alone. There's two elderly gents enjoying a morning stroll, a young couple walking hand in smartphone, teenagers on bikes with more bits of wire coming out of them than out of Sellafield, and tracksuit-clad joggers heaving their sweat-lined bodies past us, basking in their virtuosity and their stupidity. We follow the sunlit path in silence for a while then she speaks.

'Toby's got a new job in Canada. A really good one.'

'More of Stella's own work?'

'I think she may have helped, put it like that. But it's what he really wants. He so loved Canada, he's dying to go back. It's with a company based in the UK but he'll be posted in Canada to begin with and when he starts they want him to go straight out there. Thing is ...' – and I feel her hand tightening in mine – ' ... he wants me to go with him this time.'

For a minute it doesn't actually hit me. A flying bomb whose engine has cut out, and me, frozen and immobile, on its downward path. No means of escape yet daring to believe it might somehow be diverted off course.

'And?'

Then having uttered this syllable I wait for the explosion, the dust, the debris and the paralysing pain.

But the explosive seems to be suspended in mid-air. She appears not to have heard me. She shakes her head. 'God, it's such an amazing deal for him. Big salary, lots of time off to go walking and climbing, an offer he couldn't refuse.'

'Lucky guy.'

'I'll say. We really had ... he really had to pinch himself.'

The power of the blast almost throws me off my feet. 'We. You said we.'

'I mean he.'

'Too late.' The shock waves are shaking my body to bits. 'You've made up your mind, haven't you. You're going.'

She stops and looks into my eye. 'I've not made up my mind.'

'I think you have.' I'm flat on my back, waiting for the brickwork around me to disintegrate and bury me alive. 'I mean, let's be rational here. Canada with your first love, your best love, the one you said you could

148

forgive anything just to see him. Then there's me. Mr Loser. Mr Nothing In Particular. Nothing in particular to offer you now or ever.'

'You know that's not true, Mike. If it was I wouldn't be here now. Anyone would have reacted as you did. He's the weak one. He's the harder to forgive.'

'And yet.'

'And yet nothing. He knows I'd be taking a huge risk with him. He's got his eyes open, Mike. So have I.'

'I love you.' The three words of one with nothing in particular else to say, nothing in particular that might influence her decision.

'I know, Mike.' She kisses me on my lips. 'I just don't know what the hell to do. It's unbelievable. When I was fifteen, before I started seeing Toby, I cried myself to sleep night after night because I didn't think anyone would love me, certainly not love me enough to spend the rest of my life with me. And now ...' She smiles and shakes her head. 'I'm sorry.'

I fold her into my arms. I see the freshness and softness of her face set against the severity of the grey high-rise block immediately behind her and the tiredness of the cracked dirt track beneath our feet. The fear of losing her doubling and redoubling by the second.

'When have you got to decide by?'

'Toby needs an answer day after tomorrow latest.' She smiles but I can see the worry lines on her forehead. 'I wish it was longer. So much longer.'

'Ask him for longer then.'

'Don't think I haven't.' Now she disentangles herself from me. 'I need to go. Get home. Think.'

'Think with him, you mean.'

'No, Mike. He's not with me. Not living with me. He's with friends in London.'

And a moment later I'm walking back down the old railway path. Alone.

She may not be living with him but I don't trust him not to be round there every spare moment. I need to be there too.

*

I wander back to the office and Marcus is sitting at his desk.

'What's up with you?' he demands. 'You look a mess.'

'No, I'm not. Honestly. I'm ... fine.'

'You're not. I think you could do with some more time off.'

Either I've not heard him properly or I've walked into somebody else's office altogether.

'I ... I'm sorry?'

'You're down to do the Cobb trial tomorrow and Wednesday, aren't you.'
'Yes.'
'I've managed to get counsel to cover it. Take the next two days, I'll see you on Thursday. '

I finish what I need to do and at four o'clock I'm on my way to the station.

*

I ring Natalie and ask if I can come straight round to see her. But she says she won't be there. She's gone to stay with her sister in Salisbury, to talk it over with her, and she won't be home till tomorrow. In the meantime, the phone lines will be closed, so don't call because your vote won't count but you may still be charged. We agree to meet tomorrow evening in Chichester at Luciano's. My final chance to impress the court, and I'm reckoning that if award-winning cuisine and wines, followed by coffees and liqueurs at 87 Park Drive, fail to swing the jury my way, nothing will. I'd thought about going back to the garden flat tonight and travelling tomorrow but I can't risk the trains being mucked up again and it's a good opportunity to do something about making our house fit for human habitation once more. I can picture it now. Cobwebs decorating every corner. A layer of dust of about the height of an average Christmas cake sitting on every skirting board. A smell which incorporates the alluring aroma of sour yogurt with the sensuous scent of damp underpants. The garden now officially designated an extension of the Amazon rain forest. The floor knee-deep in letters I've never got round to having redirected, from congratulations on getting the once in a lifetime opportunity to win a foam rubber car washing sponge, to opportunities for tripling my expenditure on car insurance in one easy lesson.

I get back to Chichester just before nine. I walk home from the station, go up to the front door and dip into my pocket for the key. And as I do so, the door opens.

It's Louise.

13

Kilmacfadzean(n) – Desire, as you walk through heavy and persistent rain, to exact bloody revenge on weather forecasters who promised "a dry day with long spells of sunshine"

She doesn't look straight into my face. She seems to look beyond me. Then she stands aside to let me come in and closes the door behind us.

She looks washed out. There's a redness round her eyes. Her hair is damp and wispy. She wears a fawn jumper and baggy black jeans. She leans forward and places her arms round me and plants kisses on both my cheeks. And the next moment we're in an embrace and I'm kissing her as well. Kisses of relief, kisses of gratefulness that she's safe, that the wall of uncertainty has been blown apart at last.

'I'm sorry, Mike,' she whispers. 'Tell me to shove off if you want.'

'How long have you been here?'

'A little while.'

We walk together into the front room. Every surface is a mirror, unsullied by dust or dirt. You can see out of the windows without having to shovel away six inches of muck first. There's a neat pile of unopened letters for me on the mantelpiece. The only smell comes from the vase of roses on the windowsill.

I gesture around me. 'Thank you,' I say.

'It wasn't a pleasure,' she says. But she smiles as she says it.

I sit down but she doesn't. She offers me a mug of tea and I accept. She disappears and comes back in a few minutes with my tea. She hands it to me then stays standing in the centre of the room.

'I wanted to tell you I was coming,' she says. 'I couldn't get hold of you.'

'You couldn't get hold of me.' I find myself shaking my head in incredulity. 'If I've tried to phone you once I've tried a hundred times. And how many times have you picked up?'

'I know.' She looks down at the floor. 'But you get why, don't you.'

'Do I?'

'Mike, I needed to get us out of that situation. And to stay out of it. I couldn't be doing with you bending my ear, trying to get us back. We were starting again, Paul, Katie and me. I contacted you to let us know we were safe. Then I contacted you again with my solicitor's details. There was nothing else to say.'

'Not even just the odd message from time to time? To say you were okay?'

'Mike, I needed to put that space between us. I thought you'd understand that. But what do you do. Keep ringing and ringing. Half two in the morning on one occasion. I had to change my number after that.'

'So when did you eventually try ringing me?'

'The other day. But I had a new phone and found I'd lost all the numbers on my old one. Honestly couldn't remember yours.'

'Could have emailed. Or gone on Facebook.'

'I needed to talk to you,' she says. 'I got back here, no sign of you. I asked Gwen opposite, Les Abercrombie, everyone round here, no idea where you were, how to contact you.' She sighs and gazes out of the window, her arms folded. 'I expect you want to know what I'm doing here.'

'It's your house as well,' I remind her. 'So what has happened? You broken up? Has he chucked you out?'

She turns to face me. 'God, no,' she says. 'No, quite the opp ... I decided to come.'

'Where's Katie? With him?'

She shakes her head. 'He's had to go off on business for a week or two. She's back at school this week so I've left her with friends. Really good friends. I just thought it would be nice to get back to Sussex. Some sea air. Catch up with a few people. Hoped you might be here.'

'You're lucky to find me here. I've been in Bristol. I told you, remember. What about you? Where have you been?'

'Nottinghamshire.'

'Okay.'

'Say it,' she says. She wanders up and down the room. '"You poor bitch, ending up in the north Midlands, miles from Sussex you love, miles from your home, your proper home, the sands, the sea, the Downs. Whatever possessed you." Go on.'

I couldn't have put it better myself. 'No. Not at all.'

'I mean, God, it's not my first choice of county,' she says. 'Yes, I do miss the hills, and the countryside, and the sunshine, and the warmth, and the beach, and ... well, everything. But it's got its compensations. We've rented a great little cottage, pretty village about ten miles from Nottingham. It's lovely, Mike. Really close-knit. Everyone knows everyone. Nice neighbours. Katie's so happy. They've a community centre with a pre-teen club which she loves. Free newspaper. Thriving shop, Nice pub. Even a café.'

'You'll make an estate agent yet.' Maybe it's the length and tedium of the journey, maybe it's the fear of losing Natalie, but the initial joy and relief of seeing my wife is wearing off and bitterness is taking its place.

'Anyway, why did you disappear so quickly? Drag Katie out of school without telling me? Not a word to me. Didn't you owe me that?'

I incline my head down towards my still full mug of tea. I expect her to meet fire with fire. First cast the beam out of your own eye. People who live in glass houses. Don't you owe me for the years you were too lazy to pick your own nose.

There isn't. There's silence. I look up. She's rocking a little on her feet. Her cheeks are a kind of cold grey, blown along by a rain-bearing breeze.

'Let's not, hey, Mike,' she murmurs.

I point to the settee. 'Why don't you sit down.'

'I'm still stiff after the coach.' She smiles. 'I won some coach tickets off our local paper. Didn't want to waste them.' She goes over to the sideboard where there's a third-full bottle of Riesling and a quarter-full glass. She points to the bottle. 'On special offer today. Treated myself. Do you want some?'

'Tea's fine.'

I watch as she gazes out of the window. Her smile gives way to a frown.

'Something out there bothering you?' I ask.

She doesn't answer. She doesn't move her head.

'What is it?'

She jerks her head round to face me. 'Kids. It was kids. Those ones from 81. They've been running up and down the street all evening. Last evening too. Playing football. Kicking it against cars. And houses. Ours once or twice. Gwen's house mostly. I'm ... I'm frightened they're upsetting her. Keep on thinking should I go out and say something.'

'I'll go if you like.'

'No, it's fine. I think they've gone now anyway. Stupid. Stupid to ... to make such a fuss.' A schoolgirl giggle. 'Have you eaten?'

I point to a plastic bag containing a pack of a dozen bacon rashers and a couple of bread rolls, plus a four-can pack of lager and some chocolate. 'I'll do something in a minute. Have you?'

She nods. 'I think I'm going to turn in now.' She heads for the door. 'Hell, all my stuff's in our old room. I'll go in Katie's.'

'There's no bed in Katie's. It's empty. Stay where you are.'

'You sure?'

'Positive. I'll go and find a B & B or something.'

She turns to me and frown lines appear on her face. 'What's wrong with the settee?'

'What's right with it,' I mutter. 'Listen, sweetheart, I've been on the go all day. I need a decent night's sleep. I don't get many nowadays. I need a bed.'

153

'I don't want you to go,' she says. 'It's your house, for God's sake.' She points towards the stairs. 'Why don't you sleep with me. I don't mean ... I mean sleep as in, you know, really sleep ...' She imitates a snore and then breaks out into another juvenile guffaw. Then she seems to collect herself. 'Mike, I'm sorry. I'm not doing this very well. Come to bed. When you're ready.'

'Deal.'

She bids me good night and disappears off upstairs.

When she's gone I give Natalie a ring, tell her I'm back in Chichester. I guess I'm fishing, hoping for some indication as to what she's decided. But she's giving nothing away. We confirm our meeting arrangements, then she says she's off to bed and thanks me for calling and says she'll let me know her decision at Luciano's tomorrow.

And just the thought that she might decide against me puts a lump in my throat the size of the Rock of Gibraltar.

*

I may have had the use of my own bed and been spared the prospect of a defence solicitor call centre alarm bell but my subconscious is still ignorant of the fact. These days, whether I'm officially on call or not, I always seem to be listening out for the phone, daytime or night time, wondering which of my clients has got himself arrested. Now I've this precious time off, having taken steps to ensure the call centre won't be able to get me, I should be shoving work routine into the back of my mind and trying to relax. But as I lie there, I realise I'm more awake than if I'm covering not only our firm's own-client duty work but six other firms' own-client duty work and the general twenty-four hour duty rota as well. It's my own stupid fault I suppose. I doubt if among the standard list of insomnia remedies you'll find the downing of two three-slice-of-bacon butties, two king-size Mars Bars, a coffee and a can of Carlsberg in front of *The Stepford Wives* immediately before retiring. Not that Louise is helping. I've heard her get up at least twice in the night and if she's shifted position in her bed once, she's shifted it a hundred and sixty times, and the covers have moved this way, then that, then this again, then away from my side of the bed altogether and as she shifts for the 161st time they've parted company from the bed completely and are expected in approximately six minutes at Terminal 7, JFK Airport, New York. Then of course sometime after five thirty I do get off, and next thing I know, Louise, fully dressed, is dragging me out of bed at nine.

Notwithstanding my excesses of the previous evening I fancy a fry-up using the rest of the bacon but it's not in the fridge and I can't remember where else I might have put it. So after I've dressed I suggest to Louise that we go and treat ourselves to brunch in town.

'Better idea,' she says. 'Let's go walking. I don't want to blob around in town all day.'

'Where? The harbour?'

'Ditchling Beacon.'

*

Old times' sake. Louise reminds me that it was still quite early in our relationship. We'd met in Brighton and it was a cloudless sunny day. We just fancied a change from the Lanes and the Pier and the beach. At her suggestion we hopped on the train and in ten minutes we were in Hassocks, about to start a half-day ramble on the South Downs. I may not have liked walking but we were in love so anything we did together was going to be good. A steady but not over-demanding climb had brought us onto the top of the escarpment and a brisk march had got us to the Beacon itself, the highest point on the Downs and the summit of East Sussex. I loved it. We loved it. And we're repeating it today and Louise assures me I won't need the map I've got because having stepped off the station platform I'll remember all of it.

Conditions are even better today than they were then. There are bits of cloud about but only bits, and none of those bits are daring to threaten the sun's supremacy over this early September morning. Yet at the same time there's a generous breeze which forecasters assure us will moderate the heat. I know the visibility is good if from our converted loft I can peep through the dormer window and see the tops of the hills above Chichester. Today I think I can even see people on those tops.

All the outdoor gear Gavin sold me back in May is stuck in Bristol, and apart from my trainers I've brought nothing else back with me that's suitable for walking in. I still have some clothes in the house which have never made it to Bristol in the first place, but none of these are suitable for outdoor exercise save a loose-fitting T-shirt with a rip down the back, and tight blue polyester shorts that would make me look like an extra in *Gregory's Girl*. I decide I'd rather risk muddying my one decent pair of chinos than go viral on You Tube. Louise wears a rugby top and jeans. I offer her one of my T-shirts and say that if it's sunburn she's worried about we could remortgage the house and buy some half-decent sunblock. But I've barely got the words out before she's saying if it's all the same to her she'd rather stick with her own clothes, in every sense. At least the rucksack I brought back from Bristol, my small day backpack, is good for carrying liquid, energy bars and mobile phone.

A Brighton-bound train comes in immediately. There's the odd free seat, but Louise says she's happy to stand in the lobby area by the doors. I tell her we'll be on our feet much of the day but she says another forty-five minutes won't make any difference, and when I put my head into the adjacent seating area and smell the sweat and stale cigarette smoke on our fellow travellers I see the wisdom of her choice. Each station stop brings the slithering open of the doors and a welcome lungful of fresh Sussex morning air. We change trains at Brighton, we're soon at the start of our walk at Hassocks, and as we begin our walk up towards Clayton at the very foot of the escarpment, we're talking. Talking about us. The things that have bound us, the things that are common to us, the things that we'll each understand about us. I don't mention Natalie. I sense Louise didn't want to come all the way to Sussex to hear about my new love life, such as it is. I may have messed up the family bit, but I've pride, and if I tell Louise all about Natalie today and Natalie's gone from my life tomorrow then who can blame Louise for thinking it's another reflection on me. Of course we discuss Katie. I ask her the things every self-respecting dad should ask, is she enjoying school, what does she like doing outside. She's doing great, Louise says, loving school, getting excellent reports from her teachers. I think back to what Natalie said on Cleeve Hill, try to tell myself that if other things were right, Katie and I would be right. But I can't help wondering if Louise thinks I've become irrelevant in our daughter's eyes. This man who once had something to do with her life, now traded in to make way for a much more reliable and effective Paul-shaped model, one who'll compensate for the substandard fathering she's had to put up with most of her existence.

So we carry on talking about us, not talking about now but about then, before Isabel and Katie came along, when everything we did together and for each other was an adventure. Our days and weekends away, our holidays, meals out, fun, laughter, silly, crazy. Young. So young. I think back to one of the things Gavin had said as we'd walked back down off Shining Tor. You don't remember the blisters, the mud, the thirst, the peatbogs, the getting lost. You remember the view stretching out forever, the play of the golden sun on the purple moorland, the bowl of apple crumble and custard and pint of Charles Wells' Bombardier. Your subconscious does the editing, the deleting, the perfecting. As Louise says, we can't look forward together but we can look back together, and the view back seems to get better and better with every memory that we share.

We arrive in the village of Clayton and find ourselves by the church of St John the Baptist. Louise suggests we have a look round it. We go inside, and though I've no interest in historic places of worship this one's a bit special. It boasts a chancel arch that pre-dates the Norman Conquest and wall paintings that go back to the middle of the 12th century. I study one of them, trying to work out what it's trying to depict. And as I look round I see Louise is kneeling before the altar at the chancel arch. There's a real power in the stillness. I get my phone out, put it on silent and return it to my backpack, fearful of smashing to pieces the spiritual spell that has seemingly woven itself around Louise, as it has done around countless worshippers in this place across countless centuries and no doubt will still be doing all the time these walls continue to reach up towards heaven. And as she kneels I stand and watch and wait. She rises to her feet and we set off again.

We walk on for a few yards along Underhill Lane, and looking up we see the green whaleback South Downs escarpment overshadowing us, as if poised to swallow any latter-day Devil foolish enough to cut a new Dyke across its path. After a brief piece of taxi-ing, it's time to saddle the whale. We bear right up a signed bridleway, and begin the ascent, the views to the Weald beneath us improving with each step. We pass two windmills, known as Jack and Jill; Jill is the more attractive and photogenic with its sails and bright white clothing, while the darker sail-less Jack, to the left, is something of a poor relation. The prodigal son hoping for forgiveness but not daring to expect the feast. Beyond the mills, we bear left onto a clear track heading south-eastwards and gaining more height. A signpost announces the South Downs Way long-distance route coming in from the right, a wide unerring band of chalk, once a Bronze Age trading route used for the transport of jet and gold, and a key line of communication for the Romans during their occupancy. The workaday route of yesteryear has now become a walker's paradise, a firm straight imperious course, sweeping eastwards along the escarpment top, haughtily oblivious of cares below. We continue to climb, but soon reach the top of the escarpment, passing a sturdy wooden direction indicator known as Keymer Post. As we walk, we taste the legacy of the recent late summer heat: the tired languor of the pockets of vegetation, the crunch of the dry grass beneath our feet, the dewpond now reduced to an embarrassed puddle. But with the arrival of fresher air has come the jaw-dropping clarity. We look out across Wealden woodland and farmsteads and mellow flint-built villages to the one side, even their proud churches and mansions becoming insignificant stone blobs on a giant unending canvas, while to our right the sea and the cliffs and the South Downs come together in a cacophonous riot of blue and green and cream. As we walk, I watch the butterflies. The air just shimmers with them. Louise can remember all their names from her childhood. Dancing blue. Adonis. Chalkhill. Cabbage white. Meadow brown. Fritillary. She seems to know her birds as well, better than on that April morning in Norfolk at any rate. She identifies one lemon-headed flier as a yellowhammer and says if we listen carefully we might hear the male's trademark song "A little bit of bread and no cheese." Even though no song is forthcoming it's good to have an excuse to slow down and in any case we need to pace ourselves so we can manage the last climb. I know the summit is near, I feel the passion of the composer coming to the climax of the final movement of his *magnum opus*, and I hear the clash of cymbals as I see the triangulation point marking the Beacon itself. We haul ourselves up to the stone stump and we've done it. It was on this spot that in 1588 one of a chain of fires was lit to warn of the approach of the Spanish Armada and now I want to light one in celebration that we've done it. Louise crumples to the ground but she's smiling and then she's laughing. Having risen to her feet she reaches for her phone and moments later the selfie she's taken of the two of us is on my phone as well. We look at the selfie, and laugh and joke. And as we laugh I see, for the first time since Isabel was taken from us, the girl I fell in love with, the girl I knew before the isn't came along.

*

Ten minutes, perhaps fifteen, have passed. We haven't spoken. We've stood there, side by side, watching, waiting, enjoying.

I turn slightly and look into her eyes. A smile plays on her lips.

'Happy?' I ask.

'What's not to like,' she murmurs. 'The sun, the countryside, the sea … it's … well, it's perfect.'

'So why leave it all, then.'

She draws back from the trig point and sits on the grass. She motions to me to join her and I sit down beside her.

'I never wanted to leave it,' she says. 'But right from when I first met Paul, he told me he might need to move offices if he wanted promotion. He was very fair. Told me he'd quite understand if I didn't want to commit to that. A few days before you came round that time, he said something had come up in Nottinghamshire and he was likely to be wanted up there almost immediately. And then the very day after you came round he got a phone call. We literally just got in the car and went.'

'You could have followed later. You could have stayed just a little while longer and told me what was going on.'

'I know.' She turns to me and pain splashes across her face. 'But I saw the terror in Katie's eyes when she saw us fighting. Later on, after you'd gone, I went and talked to her. She told me something I never knew, we never knew.'

'What?'

'Her natural parents. She's never really talked about them before. She said they used to fight. Hit, punch each other, push each other. Lots of shouting, lots of screaming, lots of crying. To begin with she never saw it. She just heard it. Then one day she was in the same room with them and they started. Right in front of her eyes. She said it was the most frightening thing she'd ever seen. After that, they used to do it all the time, didn't seem to care if she was there or not.'

It's as if the sky above me has turned grey and the grass beneath our feet has turned to ash. 'Oh, God,' I whisper.

'So you can see what she must have felt when she saw us. My only thought was, get her out of harm's way, like, at once. I went round to her school next morning and saw the Head. Told her what was happening. It was ... it was fine. Katie was bemused, bewildered, but I think she understood. Said she didn't mind all that much. Wasn't getting on with some of her classmates. Didn't like Gemma, her form teacher. She was okay with it. Okay to go. We got in the car and left early afternoon. Spent a couple of nights in a hotel, then stayed as guests of one of Paul's workmates till we were able to get our own place.'

'Katie never told me she didn't like Gemma.'

'You probably never asked, did you.' There's not a trace of accusation or resentment in her voice. 'But don't you get why I didn't want you knowing where we were? Why I had to keep you out of the equation when changing Kates' school? I've made this big decision, huge decision, to go, and go quickly. And there's you, bending my ear, trying to drag me back home because you couldn't find the right button to wash your underpants. I mean, can't you see how difficult this was for me? You wouldn't have been helping. You do get that, Mike, don't you.'

I sigh. 'Suppose.'

She runs her hand through her hair. 'I'm not going to lie,' she says. 'It's taken a long time to adjust. I've missed Sussex, I'll be honest. Missed my old friends, my ties, my work. And the countryside, of course. Been easier for Katie. But, I mean, okay, I don't expect you to want to hear this, but it's working. We're working as a new family. Paul's got away from Pamela, thank heaven, and that's certainly helped. Nothing's been too much trouble

159

for him. Lovely home, lots of love and laughter and … yeah. It's worked.'

'Good. Great.'

She reaches into her bag and produces three photographs which she hands to me. 'First one's Katie and me outside our new house,' she says. 'Second one's at a car rally. Paul's got a passion for fast cars. His one vice he says. He's a brilliant driver. And there's one of us on a shopping trip. Kates with her new iPad.'

I look at the pictures and I'm struck not so much by the prettiness of the cottage, or the hatefulness of the out-of-town shopping complex, or how much Katie's shooting up, as what Louise is wearing on her feet.

'Good God,' I blurt out. 'Don't you suffer from altitude sickness in those?'

'People change, Mike. Okay, they felt weird at first. I thought I was going to fall off the edge of the world. But it's kind of, well, exhilarating, I suppose. Katie loves them. Thinks I look great in them. I think she wants them when she's a bit older.'

I hand the pics back and watch as she puts them away, then gaze up at a snowstorm of cabbage white butterflies against the clear sky.

'So how do you fill your days? I mean, when you're not strutting your stuff in stilettos? Have you found work?'

She shakes her head. 'I've tried for loads of jobs,' she says. 'I've made the shortlist almost every time. Once they as good as told me I had the job. But no. Not to be.' She grins. 'It's fine. Anyway, money's not a problem. Paul's doing very well. He's sensible too. Hates waste. Anything Katie or I no longer need, he finds use for. Reckons he's saved us a Lottery jackpot since we got together.' She smiles. 'No, as I say, it's fine. Gives me more time to myself, to read, to garden, to cook. Paul loves good food. I've grown to love it too. Every night we sit down, seven o'clock, all three of us, no telly, no technology, just us. Sharing a proper meal. Then we might watch something, and Katie goes off to bed and … just us. A glass of wine, Chopin or Satie, the sunset and the night sky …'

'You'll have me crying in a minute,' I tell her.

'I recommend it, Mike,' she says. 'New love.' Then she turns to me and places an arm round me. And she whispers. 'To old love.' She kisses me on the cheek.

And we sit there, lording it over the Sussex downs and Weald and cliffs, her arm still round me, while the cabbage whites dance above our heads.

*

160

We've mixed it up a bit coming back. We've dropped down into Ditchling village; we've had a brief but well-earned coffee stop, we've wandered round the Norman church, and we've admired the ancient timber beams of Wings Place, the brand new museum of art and craft, the charming Conds Cottage, and the former home of Eric Gill the sculptor. I'd have been happy to catch the bus back to Hassocks but Louise wants to walk. And as we walk, and then head back on the train, we're talking more than we've talked since those days when we loved, and not only can I see why I loved her but how I could, just could, love her again. And I'm cursing Paul because he seems to have done for her what I long ago lost the ability to do for her.

It's gone half past five when we get back to Chichester. We get home, change out of our sweat-caked clothes and have a shower each, then I open another Carlsberg while she pours herself most of the rest of the Riesling. I sit on the settee and she kneels on the mat and as I sip I notice her staring into my eyes. She's wearing a starchy white top and black trousers and there's more colour and life and vigour in her face than I've seen since our earliest days together.

'I … I really wanted to say thank you,' she says. 'It's … it's just been lovely.'

I lean forward and kiss her. I kiss her cheek. Then she kisses my neck and all round my face and on my lips. And I'm thinking of her in those heels and whether it's the drink or not I don't know but first our lips are meeting and then our tongues are meeting. For a few crazy seconds Natalie doesn't exist, Luciano's tonight isn't happening. Even as we're kissing I'm thinking, this is ridiculous, it's going to spoil everything, ruin the fun and the laughter and the memories, and I wait for us both to come to our senses and remember we're a couple that's breaking up. She's the one who pulls free but I see no look of disgust on her face and she's still kneeling on the mat.

She looks into my eyes.

'There's stuff I haven't told you,' she says. 'Didn't know if I should tell you or not. Didn't know how you'd take it.'

'Try me.'

'I mean, one part of me was saying, none of your business, we've moved on, you've stopped caring about me, about us. But Mike, I realise I owe it to you.'

'You're pregnant.'

And immediately I wish to goodness I'd not said it because the warmth and joy in her face has been extinguished in a moment.

'No, Mike. Where to start, God, where to start. Look, here it is straight.

Okay, first off, I'm not well. I've a rare medical condition.'

'What condition?'

'It could kill me. Very soon.'

I look at her without moving, without reacting. Then I reach out and fold her in my arms and wait to feel the heat of her tears.

There are no tears. She breaks free from my grip. 'It's fine, Mike, honestly. I don't need your sympathy. Just needed to tell you. So glad you were around so I could tell you. So glad we had today.'

'Do you want to tell me about it?'

'You may as well know. Started with these really bad pains in my head a month or two ago. I went to see my GP. He couldn't explain it, said he'd refer me on. I heard nothing for ages. But in the meantime, Paul told me one of his best friends was a specialist. Said he'd see me. Turns out I've developed a rare blood disorder. Not sure why me, but why not, hey. I can't remember what it's called but anyway I've started on a course of medication. It may work, it may not.'

'So it's terminal?'

'They can't say. It affects different people differently. I could live normally for another twenty or thirty years, I could collapse tomorrow and be dead by next Friday.'

'And Katie knows, I take it?'

'We both sat down and told her straight away,' she says. She gets up and wanders to the window, taking her half-empty glass with her. 'It was the worst moment of my life. I just dried up. Couldn't think what to say. But Paul was fantastic. I mean, brilliant. He always has been with Katie. They adore each other. I think his Quaker faith helps. Got it spot on. I think he missed his vocation. He'd be a great counsellor.'

I walk over to the window and stand there beside her, gazing out as the kids from 81 smash a football against Gwen's garage door. 'Nothing's certain, sweetheart,' I say. 'You've said it yourself. You could live for years and years yet.'

'Or not,' she says, gulping another mouthful from her glass. 'Paul and I have these conversations, night after night. What's best. To know I'm going to go in say five years and do all the things I want to do, or to stay in ignorance, hope I'll get longer, all the time, thinking I might get less … I'm …' And now she begins to pant, and rock on her feet, and she's taking another swig from her glass and I find my hand reaching out to steady her, to keep her from crumpling to the floor.

And having steadied her, I place my arms round her.

As we're standing there, she's facing the window. I'm about to kiss her on the cheek when I see an expression of alarm on her face.

'What's the matter?'

'Someone looking in the window,' she says.

'Wretched kids. I'll go and sort them out in a sec.'

'It was a woman. Youngish. Blonde. Gone now.'

I release myself from her arms and turn to the window. There's nobody there.

I start to shake.

I pull my phone out from my backpack. And I remember it's still on silent.

I go to messages. A text from Natalie. An hour ago.

HI MIKE, RUNNING EARLY WILL COME ROUND 2U, NOT GOING 2 CANADA, CALL ME ALL LOVE N XXXXX

14

Navax(n) – congregation of cheesed-off walkers wandering round outdoor goods shop in Keswick on wet morning in August with no decent walks or other open-air activity possible and the only indoor attraction being the pencil museum

I put my phone away and turn and Louise is right there behind me.

'I'd go after her if I were you,' she says with a smile. But her lips are quivering.

'How did you know?'

'It's fine. Go after her.'

'I … I can't. Not while we've still stuff to talk about.'

'It isn't important, Mike,' she whispers. 'Not to you, anyway. It's fine. Really. Fine. I'm glad you've found someone. You and me both. Good. It's good. Go on. Push off.' Each syllable flat, and lazy, the words of one reeling under the blow of a damp sponge to the eyeballs.

'We need to talk. Talk more.'

'Not now, Mike.'

I look down at my shoes. 'I don't know what to say.'

'I think goodbye is normal.'

I shake my head. 'I can't leave you like this. I owe you more than that.'

'Oh, rubbish, Mike, you don't owe me anything.' A smile plays on her lips once more.

'What are you going to do?'

She permits herself a light laugh. 'I don't know. I really don't know. I may live, I may die. I expect I'll die. Most people do, don't they.'

'I mean, now. Are you going back tonight? Will you stay?'

She holds her hands out. 'Who knows. If I get going soon I might make the overnight coach.'

'No. Stay another night. Stay with me.'

'I just hope she'll make you happier than I did.'

'Please, sweetheart. I'll try not to be too long. Then I'll come back and we'll talk, really talk. About us. About Katie. Okay.'

She reaches out and runs her fingers over my arms, but she's shaking her head. 'There's nothing more to say, Mike. Is there.'

I pull an old Tesco receipt from my wallet, write my mobile number down on the back and hand it to her. 'That's if you need me,' I say. 'But you're not to go.'

'I think I'll go and lie down.' She crunches the paper in her hand.

*

I go outside but I can't see Natalie there. I walk up and down the street, looking at the parked cars, hoping, praying that her car's there and that she's inside it. Nothing. I try phoning her and there's no answer. So I text her. Need to see you, explain who she is, why I was with her, what I was doing with her. I look at the time and there's still a good hour before we'd originally planned to meet. What to do. Go back inside, or go in search of her. I try phoning her again, try texting her again, still nothing coming back. I decide to go after her using the most direct route to the city centre, and if I can't find her, to go to Luciano's and wait for her there.

There's no sign of her en route for the centre so Luciano's it is. The sun which played upon the tops of the Downs has exited stage right with a final defiant beam of orange fire, and the light chill of dusk is giving way to the barren coldness of night.

At exactly the agreed time she appears. She wears a deep green dress and strappy high-heeled sandals. But she's not wearing a smile. Her face bears a heavy frown and in the glow of the street light directly above us I can see her eyes are reddened and damp and her whole body seems to be shuddering.

She comes up to me and stands in front of me.

'I need to explain, Nat. Please let me explain.'

She says nothing. She just remains standing, with tightly folded arms.

'She's not well. I thought she was going to pass out. That's why I was holding her.'

'Her.' She's looking to the ground. 'Who's her.' Every syllable is a lead weight from her trembling mouth.

'Louise. My ex-wife. Well, soon to be ex-wife. I found her here when I got back yesterday. She's ill, Nat. Got a death sentence hanging over her. Could be next week, could be anytime. I couldn't just dismiss her. I'm not that shallow. She's got a new life now, new partner, better guy than I could ever be. She doesn't want me round her any more. She literally came down just to tell me. I don't suppose she'll ever bother me again.'

'Where did you sleep last night?'

'In our … my house. My bed.'

'What about her?'

'Look, it was just convenient. Nothing was ever going to happen. I couldn't shove her onto the settee. And I needed a decent sleep, couldn't face kipping on the floor.'

'Okay. Okay.' She unfolds her arms. 'What else?'

'Sorry?'

'What else did you and she do?'

'Nothing.'

She looks straight into my eyes. 'What about the snogging.'

'Snogging?'

'That's what I said.'

'It was nothing. I mean it. Nothing. We'd had a bit to drink. I was anxious, anxious about you, what you'd decided. She was emotional. She's upset. I've told you, she could die any time. Imagine. What was I meant to do, push her away?' From nowhere a fresh confidence bubbles up into me that somehow I can beat a path through the gorse bushes and the bear traps that have been thrown between us. 'I can't just pretend we had nothing. What sort of man does that make me when she's really up to her neck in it? If I walk away, I'm the heartless one. Let her in, I'm the unfaithful one. You've got to understand, Nat. See my difficulty.'

'Of course I do.' She smiles.

'I'm just sorry you had to see us like that. I know what it must have looked like.'

'Mike, I didn't see anything. I never came round.'

For a second my tongue turns to stone. 'What … what do you mean?'

'I never came round. I've been nowhere near your house.'

'Louise said you were at the window.'

'She doesn't even know me, does she. No, I was waiting for you to call me. Was going to come round then. I guessed you'd be out. I didn't want to be waiting ages for you. Then I got your texts.'

'Natalie. Please. Please. I …' My forehead starting to melt.

'Mike, calm down.' She places her right hand on my brow. 'I'm just glad you were honest enough to confirm it. Didn't try to pretend none of it happened.'

'You get it, then.'

'Of course I get it.' I lean forward to kiss her, only she's shaking her head. 'But Mike, I can't go on with you.'

It's a thousand volt charge through my heart. 'What?'

'I can't … can't do it, Mike. I'm sorry. Changed my mind. I've just rung Toby, told him I'm going to Canada with him. It's all fixed.'

'But I've explained. Can't you ring him and unfix it?'

'I'm not saying I don't believe you. But you've got to see it from where I'm standing. You and Louise, you've unfinished business. I'm not saying that's a bad thing. Not condemning you for it. But it doesn't give us the new start I want. That I want for us. I mean, you've said yourself, could be years yet, and if each time she thinks it's coming she's rushing into your arms … and you're getting out the booze … just … just see it my way.'

'I've told you she won't be coming back. She's got Paul.'

'Has she told you that? She's never coming back?'

'Oh, God, yes … I mean, not in so many words … but she made it clear by what she said …' But looking at the frown of disappointment and disbelief and distraction on her face I realise with every word I utter I've not only lost the argument but the match and am crashing out of the Premiership. So I decide to bring in a new striker during the transfer window and put him straight into the team. 'Anyway, is this worse than Toby picking up a new girlfriend in Canada and not having the guts to breathe a word about it to you until it had gone down the khazi?'

'Yes … no … I don't know.' She sighs. Her voice becomes quieter. 'Perhaps I should be a lawyer like you. Decide everything on a strict intellectual basis. Weigh up who's got the strongest case. Trouble is, I'm not like that. I don't do intellectual. I suppose I do emotional. Trust myself to know what's right. And what I do know is I was ready to put my faith in you, and now you've owned up to all this and after what Toby had done to me I so hoped I could absolutely rely on you that we could just give to each other and nobody else …' Her voice isn't getting louder but the words are piling up and jostling with each other in their desperation to get out first. And then her face disappears into her hands and I hear a succession of choking sobs.

'I'm sorry,' I reply. 'What more can I say. I'm sorry.' And I place my arms around her.

She doesn't fight me off but nor does she put her arms round me. She reaches into her pocket for a tissue. 'I'm sorry too, Mike. You're a great bloke and I'll always feel something for you, always feel loads for you, but … but …'

'Please.' I kiss the side of her cheek and feel the saltiness of her tears on my tongue. 'Just let me do something. Anything to show you can trust me … anything at all …'

'It's too late. I've made up my mind.' An evenness reappears in her voice and I can sense a revival in her self-confidence and composure. 'And I'm really sorry, Mike, and I know you won't want to hear this, but now I've thought about it again, it suddenly seems right. I've suddenly got a good feeling about it.'

I can't hack hearing the next few sentences from her. So I do the job for her, churning out the lines, the amdram enthusiast putting in for a part he doesn't want. '"You'll regret it if you don't go. Chance of a lifetime. You only live once. Such a great country." Right?'

167

She smiles through the sobs. 'If you say so.'

'Just please don't say it's meant to be. Please spare me that.' I rub some maverick tears from the corner of her face. 'And you'll be happy to go? Even though he could fall straight into Stella's arms the moment you touch down? Or if she's had a better offer, some other smart tycooness who flutters her eyelashes at him across the airport Café Rene?' The pangs of jealousy are linking arms and dancing round and round my mind. Visions of this man she's never really stopped worshipping. Sinking his snout into his family-size portion of fettuccine. Planning his latest 3000-mile pre-breakfast hike or sponsored charity hop up the Matterhorn. Looking forward to his forthcoming mention in the Queen's Birthday Honours List and beatification by His Holiness the Pope. Saint Toby. Mr Peter Perfect. Come on, Natalie. Remember what he's really like. Not human but actually inhuman. Recall his battle with cocaine addiction, his nightly round of ritual Satanism, his collection of Little Jimmy Osmond vinyl LP's.

'Don't,' she murmurs. 'Please don't, Mike.'

'I think you're trying to convince yourself.'

She shakes her head. 'No, Mike. Please. I think you'd better go.'

'When are you going?'

'Monday teatime. Flying out to Toronto from Heathrow at half five. And before you ask, we made all the arrangements in case.' Her face softens. 'Mike, it didn't mean anything. Was never a done deal.'

'Nat, you can't do this.'

'Please, Mike, you'll just make it worse.'

'You're upset. You need to think about this properly.'

But I know they're just words, evaporating into the September night.

And ten seconds later so is she.

*

I wander home. The house is in darkness.

I go inside. The bottle of Riesling has gone. The glass is upside down on the wiping-up area of the draining board. The floors and carpets are clean and uncluttered.

I go upstairs to the bedroom. The bed is empty. All traces of Louise have disappeared.

I look around for a note from her. Something to tell me where she's vanished to, where I can contact her. I do see two bits of paper but Louise's writing isn't on either.

One is from someone called Tamara who says she's staying with Gwen opposite, wanting to know if as a lawyer I can help do something about the kids kicking a ball against her great aunt's house and apologising for calling at a bad moment earlier.

The other is on the arm of the settee and it's the Tesco receipt with my mobile number on it.

*

Next day's unusually warm for September, twenty-six degrees in the shade, the train to Bristol is delayed, and as I sit on the platform for an hour and then on the floor in Coach A I feel as though there are great strands of treacle on my fingers. All I can think about as I stagger off the train and crawl into a bus is a hot bath.But the water had to turn cold sometime and as I clamber out and wrap a towel round me, my inside still feels dirty and rotten and decayed. The feeling isn't assuaged in the least by the prospect of a full day in court tomorrow, Thursday; five hours of my life asking magistrates to let offenders walk out onto the streets where every bone in your body is telling you they ought to be behind bars until they're too old and feeble to walk.

I'm in work by half past seven, hoping to get a bit of office time to myself, but I've barely switched on the computer to check my emails when Marcus pokes his head round the door.

'I'd like a word about next week.'

Good morning, Mike. Nice to see you back. Did you have a pleasant couple of days. We've missed you. Not too many in custody today, weekend will soon be here. No: the pleasantries may have been there once, but like mist patches in the Sahara, they've been burnt off by the relentless heat of the demands of the daily round.

As always, I try not to sink to his level. 'Yes, Marc, what did you have in mind?'

'I need you to do this two-day trial. Four-handed affray, throwing a carton of tea across a railway carriage into a train guard's eye. We've got three of them, conflict on the other one, Braithwaites have picked him up. Still, should keep you out of mischief for most of the weekend.'

'What days are the trial next week, Marc?'

'Monday and Tuesday. That a problem?'

'Marc, I'm really sorry, I need to ask if you can let me have some more time off. I was really hoping to have Monday. Well, Monday afternoon anyway.'

'You've just had two days. If I'd wanted a part-time worker I'd have hired one.'

'It's ...' For a moment a sick auntie comes to my lips, but the look on his face warns me against allowing it to travel any further. 'It's someone

169

very special to me. Emigrating. I'm really anxious to see her before she leaves.'

'So how do you suggest we cover it? Fritter yet more of our precious funds on counsel? Let the poor beggars do it on their own and drop themselves in it the moment they open their mouths? Eh?'

He doesn't give me time to answer. He's slammed the door behind him.

*

Of course I try phoning and texting Natalie on Thursday night and into Friday, but it doesn't surprise me that she won't pick up or respond to my messages

The Friday's quiet, thank God, and there's time to formulate a plan. I've gone through the witness statements. Of the five witnesses the prosecution are seeking to call, I reckon with a bit of discreet editing, we can dispense with three. We should only need the passenger who ended up with a slice of railway beverage all over his shirtfront, and the guard who's now in the running for Best Long John Silver Impersonation award at the local railwaymen's social club's *Treasure Island* theme night. The two passengers nearby were too absorbed in their technology to give any meaningful account of what went on, and they really say nothing contentious. Then we can I'm sure edit out one or two bits of the police interview as well and that'll mean PC Plum will be off the hook. If we can get through the two remaining Crown witnesses by Monday lunchtime, there's just a chance that the bench will then be prepared to adjourn the rest of the trial till Tuesday first thing. I manage to speak to Tim Braithwaite for the defendant we've had to ditch, and he's fine with all of that. I call Marcus late on Friday afternoon and tell him I won't need to offload the trial onto anybody else. He says well done, many thanks, and here's your reward. Damien Richardson, just been arrested for sixteen counts of unlawful sexual activity with minors. Two separate police interviews of three hours each. Bang goes my Saturday. Then it's Claire Goodbody on Sunday morning, bladed article and handling, and most of the rest of the day goes on preparing not only Monday's trial but other cases for the coming week.

And there's still nothing from Natalie.

*

I go down to court on the Monday morning and begin by offering my opponent a half-hearted section 5 Public Order Act, the least serious type of public order offence. I don't hold out much hope of success: it's a long way down from affray. The prosecutor says he'd love to help, but given that two of my guys allegedly had pieces of broken-off train fittings in their hands which could have slashed the hapless guard's face to ribbons, he'd rather stick with the original charges, thank you all the same. I can live with that, but he goes on, almost as an afterthought, to tell me that unfortunately we won't be able to start the trial till lunchtime; one of his witnesses is stuck in a traffic jam on the wrong side of Birmingham caused by a lorry shedding its load of Maris Piper potatoes across the M42.

The clerk of the court's one of the more sensible ones. I tell him I've got a personal difficulty, and ask him if we can start the trial tomorrow. And he too says he'd love to help, but he points out there's no chance of getting through this trial in only one day, not with bad character applications in respect of two of our clients still to be resolved, and evidence to hear from two live prosecution witnesses and four defendants, three of whom blame the other and vice versa with all the legal ramifications that that will generate. He points out it's already been listed four times for trial and if it has to go over again we'll be lucky, with trial delays as they are, to get it relisted before Christmas. 2036.

So it's Plan C. Blind them with science, or to be more precise, late and unserved disclosure. The last resort of the advocate up to his neck in the brown stuff.

'Your worships, I regret I must ask for a further adjournment of this trial. I've been through the schedule of unused material and I'm still missing the disciplinary record of the train guard. You'll be aware that my clients' case is that they were assaulted, in the first place by one of the co-accused, and in the second place by the train guard. We understand that the guard has previously been warned for abusive behaviour towards train passengers. This is a key aspect of the case against my client. We didn't receive the schedule till last Tuesday and have the right to file a defence case statement formally requesting the further material. The statutory time limit for that has not yet expired and I seek an adjournment in order to file one. Once I've filed such a statement I have the power to seek an order under section 8 of the Criminal Procedure and Investigations Act 1996 that the Crown discloses this further material if they refuse to do so voluntarily. I am aware of the previous history of this matter but it is clearly not in the interests of justice for this trial to proceed today.'

It's a pile of horse dung, I know that. The guard's disciplinary record would be helpful but we've already managed to get in a previous conviction against him for assault so in reality it adds nothing of any significance. Tim Braithwaite diplomatically adopts a neutral stance.

Of course the prosecutor objects, justice delayed, difficulties in keeping witnesses onside, fading memories, no prejudice to the defence by not having the chance to file a defence case statement. It's no surprise when my application is rejected and the bench direct that the case shall proceed starting promptly at 2.15pm.

Plan D. 'Your Worships, in view of your rejection of my application I consider myself obligated to withdraw from the case.' I gather my papers up and walk out.

Half an hour later I'm on the train.

*

The call comes through as we steam through Chippenham.

'Mike, where the hell are you.'

'I'm … I'm sorry, Marc. You're breaking up.'

'What in God's name is going on?'

'Sorry?'

'The court's been on the phone. Demanding that you return and explain properly why you're having to pull out of the trial.'

'Missing disclosure, Marc. I can't act.'

'You can't act? Or just don't fancy it?'

'I've … I've had to go somewhere.'

'This is neglect, Mike. Serious neglect. Breach of discipline. Gross misconduct. Are you getting me?'

'Yes, of course, but …'

'I'm going down there now and telling them you'll be back in time to start the trial this afternoon. And if you're not there then you'll be …'

'Sorry Marc. Breaking up again.'

*

The flight's up there: 1730 Toronto. I'm there by two o'clock and sit for what seems like the length of the flight to Toronto, watching, watching, watching. I've ascertained the check-in and bag drop points but there's no sign of Natalie anywhere near them. Two o'clock becomes three o'clock becomes three thirty and I'm sure I've missed her, then as I wonder if I've actually got the right airport let alone the right terminal building I see her.

She's dressed in a plain green T-shirt and tight three-quarter length leggings and chunky trainers. She's got no luggage, just a small shoulder bag.

She's alone.

I throw my arms round her and kiss her on the lips. 'Thank God,' I whisper.

She says nothing. She just smiles.

Then out of the corner of my eye, as I keep her enfolded in my arms, I see him. He holds two suitcases in his hands and a bulging red pack on his back.

'Need to make a move, hun,' he says.

She turns to him. 'Just give me a sec, babes, I'll be with you.'

'I'll be waiting at bag drop.' He merges back into the crowd.

She turns back to me and gives me a watery smile.

'You shouldn't have come,' she says.

'I wouldn't have come if I didn't think I was going to take you back with me.' I tighten my hold on her. 'It's not too late.'

'This is horrible, Mike.' Now she puts her arms round me. 'We've had great times, you've been amazing, I can't blame you for hating me, hating what I've done to you, but ... I need to think about what's right for me, not for us, and I owe it to myself to put my life first. Oh, hell, that sounds so cruel. I'm sorry ... I'm sorry ...'

She bursts into tears. She releases herself and kisses me on the cheek.

A moment later she's disappeared.

*

I shuffle towards the exit and my phone rings.

'Hi, Marc.'

'Is there any point in asking where you are? What you're doing?'

'I'm ... I'm ...'

'Let me finish the sentence for you, Mike. Fired.'

15

Cookham(n) – any edible recognition at celebration in honour of someone who has a penchant for walking, eg cake made to look like a walking boot or shaped and iced like a snow-capped mountain range

I go to the first junk food restaurant on the concourse I can find and get a regular white coffee and strawberry ice cream and I'm still sitting there with them, my head slumped in my hands, an hour and a half later. And by then the coffee's cold and the ice cream's running along the floor and threatening to engulf the car park.

It's gone eight at night when I get back to the garden flat. The next morning I return the car, contact the letting agents, cancel the tenancy and start packing to leave. Then I go back to the office to say goodbye to the secretaries and hand back my keys. Finally I thank Marcus for having me, wish him all the best for his forthcoming sailing trip, and tell him to keep an extra careful eye out for marauding Somali kidnappers.

*

I'm sitting at home next day counting the hours to *Checkout*. My phone bleeps.

Dear Mike,
Give Steve Coombs a ring. He's waiting for your call.
You'll be fine.
Much luv Natalie x

He may be appointing me the new Director of Public Prosecutions. He could be about to tell me how I can recoup thousands of pounds in compensation from a mortgage-related product missold to me in 1997. Or he might be an astrologer who from his observations of the planet Jupiter in conjunction with the recent movements of Mercury can tell me that my long-term interests are best served by taking up beetroot farming on the banks of the Limpopo.

Then I remember Natalie mentioning a Steve. Steve the editor. It turns out he's the chief commissioning editor of a London publisher, Allanson Harvey. Unless it's about the Gunners, reading and book browsing for pleasure have never been among my principal interests, and I've not heard of the publisher in question, but anyway, he says their firm are publishing the book Toby started, he's a proposition to put to me and asks if he can discuss it with me face to face. So we meet for coffee in London. For some reason I'm expecting him to be a middle-aged man in a dark suit; on the contrary, he looks about thirty and sports a red shirt and royal blue bow tie. If he'd gone for white trousers instead of light brown I think I'd be standing up for the National Anthem.

'You'll be aware Natalie took over the writing from Toby,' he says. He ladles half a hundredweight of sugar into his cup then burrows in his briefcase and withdraws a sheaf of papers. 'And now they've done their grand disappearing act, we're left knee deep in the threepenny bits. This title's been advertised for months. Toby's a very well-respected writer. One of our staples. And anything by him is going to be good news for us.'

'So how can I help?'

'I need you to finish the book.'

I nearly choke on my coffee. 'Me?'

'We tried to persuade Toby to come back and finish it but he says he's too busy with work. He and Natalie told me they thought you were the man for the job. You may not be the world's most experienced walker but you've come a long way in a short time. If you'll pardon the pun.' He grinds out a self-satisfied chuckle. 'Toby actually said ... .'

I don't need to hear what he said. I know what he said, my partner's got to work on him, smoothed some of the rough corners, turned a couch potato into a pan of red hot couch fries. And he's the one who helped her to conquer the heights of Derbyshire and the Brecon Beacons, battling with peat bogs and natural trip hazards on mountainsides. So give the boy the job, and don't worry, he'll create at first and make out that he's dead upset at the insensitivity of it but vanity never fails and he's that strapped for cash so he'll be glad of the spondulicks and he'll deliver in the end.

And the guy's still talking.

'I know what you're going to say. You've never written a book before in your life. Have you.'

'That'll do for starters. But that's not the ...'

'We can help you.' He bites into a thickly iced apple doughnut and I watch as a chunk of stewed apple drops onto the plate below with a squelchy plop. 'We're not looking for purple prose. I mean, obviously it needs to be your own work, your impressions, not cribbed from existing stuff. But we're not talking William Wandsworth. We simply want you to do the fieldwork, prepare the descriptions, take some decent pictures, send them to us, and we'll sort out the grammar and the editing.'

'Look, that's all fine. But …'

He picks up his cup and holds it in mid-smirk. 'Obviously we'll give you a fairly decent advance once you've sent the stuff to us. And you'll get your share of the royalties. You could do very well out of it. Could be the gateway to other projects. Other ventures.' His smirk fades a little. 'There is just one thing that I should mention. One condition of the deal. Your name won't appear on the front cover as the author. I mean, you'll obviously be credited in an inside page. But the book needs to be seen to be one of Toby's.'

I just sit there and say nothing.

'You see, Mike, Toby is an established authority on walking. His name alone will sell copies. I'm afraid with the greatest respect to you, as with Natalie, your reputation as an author is shall we say rather less than overwhelming, and I fear we might struggle to do as well financially on the project. Fewer orders, fewer sales …' He taps the side of his pocket. 'Fewer pounds to recoup your advance. *Prego,* lower advance.' And now he does put his cup down. 'So. You up for it, then?'

I sit back in my chair. 'Is this a wind-up or what?'

I can see him flinching. Another blob of apple from his iced doughnut loses the will to live and falls away. 'Of course not.'

'Mr Coombs, are you aware of what's just happened between Natalie and me?'

'Some.'

'Only some.' I push my cup across the table. Even though I've drunk most of the contents, there's still enough liquid there to splash onto the surrounding table top. 'She's just broken my heart. She's gone off to Canada. Not on her own. No, she's chosen the very man who you want me to do this big favour for.'

'Mike, I was aware.'

'I doubt you know the half of it. This Toby, the doyen of the walking world, keeping your business afloat. Saint Toby. He cheats on her, breaks her heart, hurts her so much she's screaming, leaves her thinking he's dead, been killed in a plane crash. She and I became partners. She gave her heart to me, told me she loved me. And then he bludgeons his way back into her life and feeds her a load of utter tosh about what a silly boy he's been. And she swallows every last mouthful. And now the two of them, not content with that, want me to give up my time and my energy to pick up the pieces they've left behind. Doesn't get much better.'

He pushes the cup back in my direction. 'Mike, don't upset yourself.'

'Each time I study the map, plan the coach or train journey, blow the dust off the rucksack, head for the heights, I'll be back there, back in a place I never ever want to be in again. And once it's all done, this guy who's supposed to have been burnt to a cinder on the side of a Canadian mountain is allowed to get all the flaming credit.'

He lets me sink back in my chair. He lets me fume and pant for a few moments. He puts the last chunk of iced apple doughnut into his mouth and licks around his lips. He taps his fingers over the papers he's produced from his case. Then he smiles. 'Natalie's given me a list of all of them with stars against the ones they never got to. There are only a handful.' He pushes the pages across. 'Mike, you're angry, you're bitter, you're offended, you're everything any sane man would expect you to be. But I think you'll do it.'

'I won't, so help me God.'

He gets up from the table. 'We'll need the script by the thirty-first of December. I'm afraid that's non-negotiable. My email and mobile number are on the top sheet there. We'll be in touch soon.' He ruffles my hair. 'Cheers.' Next thing we're shaking hands and he's gone.

He's ruffled my hair. People don't ruffle my hair. My mum stopped ruffling my hair when I was ten. My dad was never a ruffler in the first place. Nor was Louise, and if she wasn't going to start, nor was Katie either. And if Marcus started ruffling my hair when wanting me to get some toerag out on bail I'd have been on to Meadowbridge Hospital seeking a secure bed for him within thirty seconds.

The train home crawls from Clapham Junction to East Croydon at a steady minus three miles an hour and I keep on expecting the trainer to be hurrying to its aid with a bucket and sponge. Had I a calorie more energy in my body I'd get up from my seat, tear every page of Steve Coombs' package into small strips and throw the lot out of the window, creating my very own amber snow warning somewhere just outside Thornton Heath. But the buffet trolley pusher has now become a registered missing person and the September heat has taken by surprise those rail officials who automatically switch default settings to winter mode as soon as the schools go back after the summer holidays. So I doze my way home and the papers are still sitting inside my bag as I get in.

I'm beginning to slip back again, I can tell. The pounds are beginning to pile on once more and my trouser belt, having been re-engaged after its long layoff, is now staring at compulsory redundancy. There's clutter everywhere and it's only a matter of time before I once more forget the colour of my carpets. My vacuum cleaner, having been startled by its recent sequence of engagements and gained in confidence, stage presence and aptitude with each performance, is now once again resting and if I'm not careful will be seeking the services of a new agent. The bit of paper with my mobile on it is still sitting on the arm of the settee where Louise left it; of course I've tried ringing her new number but I'm now thinking of adding her voicemail messenger to my Christmas card list because it's always her I end up talking to. My bank and mortgage statements, which I can hardly bear to look at, are decorating the window sill where they've been sitting since I opened them six days ago. I've a more fundamental difficulty which is that I've nowhere actually to sit down and I'm going to have to move something from one of the chairs. The comfiest chair is playing host to only one item – my large backpack – and so that gets the vote. As I get hold of it I detect a foul smell inside it, and on closer investigation I deduce that the cause of the stench is a pair of walking socks. I remove them from the backpack and see that mixed up with them is a yellowy blacky gadget which, as the socks savour their first few seconds of release on parole, is shot across the room.

It's the GPS navigator.

I gaze around at the fruits of my new attempt to re-enact AD 79 Pompeii in a peaceful corner of Sussex. I smell the layers of dirt and can almost hear the march of the council hygiene battalions. Then I think of when I used the navigator for the first time, and the confidence that has given me to face the mountains and the moors. I'm striding onto Pen-y-fan, lingering on the banks of the Noe and looking down on Buttermere. Then I'm thinking of my bank and mortgage statements and the sixty-three thousand uses for the advance, and the prospect of more where that came from, and I know he's got me, and I know he knows he's got me.

*

It's clear that Toby's done almost all the legwork for the book. He's not only polished off pretty much all the ones on his list in Great Britain, he's also gone and done everything in Ireland, stopping off in the Isle of Man to pick up a couple there. There are only five starred entries denoting walks to be done as at 1st August, the date on top of Natalie's list. One of those is Haystacks. Done. Another is High Willhays. Done. There's also Cleeve Hill. Also done. Three down, two to go.

Both the remaining two walks are in England. One is the highest point of Lancashire, to be included, according to Toby's pre-written introductory notes, for its remoteness and difficulty of ascent; the twin summits of Gragareth and Green Hill take the walker off the well-beaten Three Peaks track and into a bolder and more intriguing landscape, the summit of Gragareth protected by an almost sheer hillside. Moreover there's no proper mapped footpath linking the summits, so it'll be a case of trial and error and there's no guarantee of success. The other walk is the peak of County Durham, Mickle Fell, one of Toby's top "five star remote heights" in England. Used by the military for firing practice, it's a logistical nightmare which it seems can only be walked on certain days of the year and even then you need a permit. Given what I've accomplished in the last few months I appear at least on paper to have the credentials to undertake the two expeditions. But I still wouldn't wish to attempt to tackle them on my own. I need a companion. There's always the possibility of chancing on another walker and teaming up with them but it's a risky strategy particularly if the only available candidate is someone you'd want to avoid having to wait behind in the queue for the self-service checkouts at M & S.

As I put the paperwork away, reflecting on this difficulty, the phone goes and it's Andy Frost, inviting me to meet him for a drink. We get together two nights later and over our Budweisers he says it's on his conscience that we've lost touch following my quizzing exploits. I'm mindful he's good friends with Marcus Kenton and we tiptoe round that until he congratulates me for having lasted with him as long as I did. Apparently most of his assistants don't manage more than two days never mind two months. I tell him about my assignment and he puts me in touch with some geezer called Martin Laycock who lives in Lancaster, loves walking and knows the way to the tops of Gragareth and Green Hill. We agree we'll meet to do them on Saturday week, the last Saturday in September. He'll meet me at Ingleton, the base village for the start of the walk, at 8.30 sharp that morning.

And, encouraged by that, I go through the necessary application process to climb Mickle Fell. In due course I receive authorisation, the last weekend before Christmas apparently being the only time I can walk it without precipitating World War 3. I go out and celebrate by buying a thick jumper you need a map to avoid losing your way inside. It's all crazy and it's all ridiculous, and with Louise the way she is I wonder if it's decent to be motivated or positive about anything, anything at all, but I know I have it in me to do it, and in a send-for-the- men-in-white-coats kind of a way, I'm looking forward to it.

*

Unable to face another overnight coach journey, and with the help of some money from a bit of consultancy work for a defence firm in Brighton, I've shopped online and travelled to Settle by train. I catch a bus from Settle to Ingleton and here I am; it's three o'clock and it's Friday afternoon and the sun is shining. The rain which has apparently been falling in this part of the country for much of the past three weeks has caused the river running through the village to boil and fume and toss and provide an even more percussive accompaniment to the ensemble of stone cottages and colour-washed gardens and its backcloth of grey-green hills and fells including the Three Peaks, Ingleborough, Pen-y-ghent and Whernside. Day trippers keep their technology poised for the next especially photogenic shopfront or street corner. Coach parties squeal for joy at displays of trinkets and North Country souvenirs in the village gift and craft shop. And ramblers in shorts and T-shirts, weighed down with backpacks, sit at tables outside cafes having earned their clotted cream teas, chunky cheese scones and acre-sized ploughmans from their conquests of the nearby mountains. Save for fighting my way through three coaches of the Leeds-bound train to find a non-overflowing toilet, I've not exercised significantly since leaving home this morning, but I'm relaxed, and I feel in some ways I've done the hard part. Accordingly I order a pot of tea, a double slab of thickly-iced tangy lemon drizzle cake and a jugful of clotted cream and sit down at my table and shut my eyes and for a few moments I'm in heaven.

Then my mobile goes. 'Martin Laycock,' he says. 'I've had to fly out to China on business this weekend. Sorry, mate.'

*

Green Hill and Gragareth. I might as well have delivered a rendition of *King Lear* in ancient Urdu judging by the reactions I get from the townsfolk when enquiring about a guide, preferably human, but otherwise written, to conquering the twin peaks. Without the guide, the task may be beyond me. I think back to Steve's words, that there should be no cribbing, that it must be my own work. But this is responsible research, not cheating, and the impressions and description will still be in my own words. The tourist information office, which I believed to be my trump card, can't help and suggests the newsagent. The newsagent suggests the outdoor gear shop. The outdoor gear shop people suggest Pattersons; apparently the Pattersons, although purveyors of quality cheeses, are known to be fanatical walkers and any summit they don't know within a radius of 45 miles from here isn't worth a single blob of mud on the sole of the boot. Unfortunately the fellow in charge today, while anxious to offer free samples of extra-crumbly Wensleydale, professes to know nothing of the great outdoors beyond the beer garden of his local pub and in the absence of his more knowledgeable colleagues he suggests the best bet is … the tourist information office.

But before passing Go and collecting £200 – if only – I notice a bookshop just next door to Pattersons and the very first book I see in the window –

well, after *Round Hartlepool On A Unicycle* – is a volume entitled *Walks On Lancashire's Tops* by Rufus Cheeseley. The name doesn't quite have the same ring as Alfred Wainwright, and it's one out of ten for imagination of title, but as I leaf through the book I find, on page 36, a guided walk to Gragareth. It's only one of the two summits I've got to do tomorrow, but Cheeseley gives a brief summary of how to reach Green Hill from Gragareth so this guidebook will be a massive help. A few moments later I'm delving further into the recesses of my bank manager's patience. And barely has the debit card receipt disappeared into my pocket than I'm being asked by the sales assistant for an assurance that I'm not going to be so stupid, am I, as to attempt any walk on any Lancashire top tomorrow when the north-west of England is going to see more rain than the whole of the last six weeks put together.

He's exaggerating, he must be exaggerating, he'd better be exaggerating. And indeed all 23 forecasts I hear, watch and read over the next couple of hours say different things. Trouble is, there's a kind of pattern emerging. "Continuous rain." "Wet and miserable." "Cloud cover of 500 feet making visibility extremely difficult especially on the hills." "Prolonged rain, heavy at times." "Persistent rain." "Met office early advice. Localised flooding likely." The only forecast that begs to differ is that in yesterday's *Yorkshire Post*, on the table in the lounge of my B & B, which just provides a black cloud symbol for Saturday's outlook and no little drops falling out of it. Yes, I'll take that one, thank you.

But the warning signs are there from early evening onwards. As I return to the village for an early evening meal, a bank of thick white cloud is competing with the distant mountains for its share of the horizon. The wind, which had been barely perceptible as I let the clotted-cream coated tangy lemon drizzle cake fall into my mouth, is now defying leaves to stick to the trees and is sending showers of fading green and yellow hastening to the ground. And as I lie in bed at half past eleven, the rain is crashing against the side of the house so hard I wonder if I should move the bed a few feet away from the window for fear of being assailed by breaking glass.

I can't sleep for hours then when I do sleep I wake at six thirty and don't want to get up. Last night Mrs Reynolds agreed to do breakfast for me at seven thirty which means rising at seven fifteen and it's worse than getting up for work. At least when I got into work I had a roof and a ceiling separating me from the rain-soaked skies and I didn't have to walk through a field topped with Sainsbury's festive special extra-thick mud to get the day's business properly started. I look out of the window. It's still not properly light, and it's left to the street lamps to show how flooded the roads are below while more of the wet stuff continues to crash down from the sky. As I slump back into the bed, pull the duvet over me and once more sink as deeply as I can beneath its soothing fabric I can hear cars negotiating the highway and each splash feels like one more reason for staying put, not only for the next forty minutes but forever.

I hear Mrs Reynolds up and about. I know it's her because I've never heard anyone, nor am I likely to hear anyone, whistle *Arrival Of The Queen Of Sheba* like she can. I've not got the heart to tell her that I've decided to cancel my swim up Gragareth and breakfast can wait till midday as far as I'm concerned. But I needn't have worried. Her first words to me are 'You're not thinking of going out in that, are you' and I know I've made the right decision, especially when I see the breakfast that's waiting for me. There's porridge of such thickness and depth I expect to see National Rivers Authority warning signs on its banks. The profusion of slices of bacon and fried bread would appear to satisfy the needs of at least fifty African townships. And with toast coming in from the kitchen at three-minute intervals I wonder if there's been some kind of latter-day re-enactment of the feeding of the five thousand but with the additional twist whereby all but one of the five thousand have been called away just as they were about to say grace.

I pay my bill, gather together my things and stagger down the road, soaking every inch of my person in the two hundred yards it takes to walk to the bus stop, and find that I've missed a bus by three minutes with the next one due in two and a half hours.

I've had as much of Ingleton as I can take. I'm already as wet as it's possible to get and I've ten thousand calories to burn. Minutes later I'm setting off towards Gragareth and Green Hill.

*

I've worked out that I can accomplish most of the early part of the walk by doing nothing more intellectually or physically demanding than following roads. As I proceed I'm heartened by the fact that I can still see some patches of unmolested concrete between the pools of floodwater that attend my every step. There is apparently a footpath which would have cut a substantial corner off my exit from the village, but for now, all generous donations of tarmac surfaces are gratefully accepted, gift-aided if possible please, thank you very much. I have a steep climb to begin with, but then the ground levels out and I've a double blessing in the assurance of a firm and reliable highway and the absence of traffic. Plus Kingsdale Beck to my right, now busy completing its online application to out-superior Lake

Superior. The rain's still emptying from the sky; the last forecast I heard last night prophesied "organised rain" and indeed it's being dumped on me with the efficiency of a crack SAS unit and each time I believe I can't get any wetter I get a hundred times wetter.

At a gate with a sign which announces the land beyond to be open access land, the guide directs me to leave the road and, passing through the gate, walk up to the edge of a clump of trees. Here I reach another gate which Cheeseley says provides access to the 30 foot high Yorda's Cave. I'd read about Yorda last night, a giant from Norse mythology, apparently with a penchant for stamping about and swallowing local infants. Tempting though it is to linger in the wooded shelter in the hope of catching a sighting of the beast, and asking him if he could get to work on Gwen's tormentors from number 81 without delay, I need to keep going.

But now that I'm away from the sanctuary of the road, the engine that was keeping my ship moving has been ripped away from its fittings. If I read Cheeseley's directions once I read them a hundred times but it's as if a blip in his PC has suddenly wiped them off the page. There's a path through the clump of trees and according to his directions I think I should be following it. But twenty minutes and three stumbles later I'm back where I started. Another couple of circuits and if I'm not very much mistaken I've spotted Yorda himself, spewing juvenile bones onto the sodden tree roots. So I try something else. I come out of the woods and using the grid reference for Gragareth on the GPS navigator which I input last night, I decide to follow the arrow. All is well initially: I'm able to follow rough but easily negotiated grass immediately beside the trees, keeping them to my left. This feels good, and my sense of optimism increases when I refer to Cheeseley who I see talks about a gate and through the swirling white I can see a gate. The mist relents for a second and ahead of me in that precious second I get a glimpse of the steep hillside which I know guards my objectives. The long reedy grass clings and teases and slithers around my ankles and my gaiters but never imprisons and its soft cushion contrasts with the road-pounding and the bash of boot upon metal. It feels good and it feels right.

Until I reach the beck, that is.

I think back to the river Noe in Derbyshire in May: a benign flow, which I recall wouldn't have been difficult to wade in a crisis situation. Today there may be little more than five yards or so between me and the other side, but this is no benign flow. It's a rush of angry brown water, its ire redoubled when it hits the rocks and the boulders and sends spume high into the soaking air, joining the million droplets that heaven is sending down to earth and crashing back into the swollen depths. I'd never thought water could be so violent, so brutal, so ruthless, a *sine qua non* for man's survival and at once a potential instrument of his doom.

Until we lost Isabel, that is.

And even though I wasn't there, I can see her murder by torrent being played out before my very eyes and with each action replay I see the terror and the helplessness on her face, and I have to turn my eyes away.

I try walking beside the beck upstream in the hope of being able to ford it where it's narrower. I can't see what lies beyond, or where I might be heading. As the rain intensifies, water now being hurled onto my cheeks and invading my personal nostril space, so does the mist become a fog. And the ground beside the beck is rising vertically. There's no way forward, and as I look back I can't even see the way I've come.

I need a grid reference for the clump of trees. At least I can use my navigator to steer me to those. I reach for the single sheet map I've printed off Google. But what I pull out of my rucksack is a piece of paper which instantly disintegrates into a soggy illegible mess.

I read somewhere that if you find yourself in this situation, stop, sit down, have a drink from your thermos and take a few bites of chocolate, and this will allow the brain to recharge and devise some positive and rational solutions. So I do all these things. I'm still full of Mrs Reynolds' breakfast but I sit down and unzip my backpack and have some sips of tea and two squares of Bournville. I think I've enough strength to get myself out of here and struggle back to Ingleton, and hopefully make the bus home within a few hours. Better, I might wake up in my bed at Ingleton and realise all this never happened. The tea tastes of balsamic vinegar, but as my teeth grind through the dark chocolate I feel a new impetus to get out of this with my dignity and my limbs intact. As for the book, though, Steve will just have to find someone else to take on the mantle of the new King Toby.

I rise to my feet, haul my rucksack onto my back and move off. Then immediately I trip on a loose rock and crash to the ground, spilling the entire contents of my unzipped rucksack across the grass.

*

I'm still lying there what must be a full hour later. I don't think I'm hurt but I'm shaken, and I'm shaking, and I want to be somewhere else, no matter where. Anywhere, any place I thought I would never wish to be again, in Howard's office being given another kicking, in Bristol's custody centre at two thirty in the morning, at the Emirates where Chelsea have taken a three goal lead with only five minutes left, or in the shopping streets of Manchester with a good four hours to kill before my tr ...

His number is still locked in my phone.

'Gavin? Remember me? The poor so-and-so you sold all that walking gear and GPS navigator to?'

He's done Gragareth before.

*

Transparent and glib may be his middle names but he knows his stuff. He says if he didn't have to work today he'd have come out to walk with me. He uses his own technology to provide a grid reference for the bottom edge of the clump of trees, I set the GPS and once again I'm on the move. The grass cushions the soles of my boots but then starts to tease in a different way, the moisture now turning the tufts into miniature ice rinks which send feet and limbs splaying with every step. But then the trees come into view and Gavin sends me round the left-hand end of them and then directs me to veer right, and keep the trees to my right. There's more than a touch of the *Golden Shot* about it. Right a bit, left a bit, right a bit, and with the mist thickening again and the trees ceasing to be visible when I get more than 20 yards away from them I could be on a Lancashire hillside or in the Lidl customer car park, Hemel Hempstead. Then Gavin tells me a customer's waiting, and suddenly it's just me and Cheeseley.

The good news is that Cheeseley's directions now make sense. The bad news is the rain's not letting up at all and now that Gavin's no longer yelling instructions into my ear, my confidence is draining from me once again, draining a great deal better than the water that's lapping round the tangly grass beneath my feet. I keep plodding uphill, passing through a gate in a crossing wall; ahead of me, according to Cheeseley, is the ridge on which both Gragareth and Green Hill are situated. I'll take the guy's word for it. The mist and low cloud are now thicker than the big print works of Dostoevsky and I'm just determined to avoid drifting from the straight line I've resolved to follow. Beyond the gate I'm directed to head diagonally left, aiming for another wall rising up the hillside, but, Cheeseley warns, I need to "tread carefully and patiently, for the going is extremely soggy and there is no path as such." Well, he's spot on and I've got Manchester's entire water supply for the month of November inside my boots to prove it.

At length the wall comes into view through the mist, and apparently it is now, to quote Cheeseley, "a simple matter of following parallel with and to the right of it." But it was never going to be as easy as he's made it sound, and the magnitude of the task becomes clear when a gap emerges in the swirl to reveal the nigh vertical hillside ahead. Cheeseley's advice is to "Take your time, pausing every so often to admire the magnificent views down to Kingsdale and beyond." I hate the man. Hate him. "You may well need to resort to hands as well as feet in places, but you're helped by footholds in the ground, and patience is rewarded when, after a gentler finale, you reach the very top of the ridge, crossing the Lancashire/ Cumbria boundary wall via a gate and stile." It may be just a couple of lines of print, but in reality it's a half hour doggy paddle, my hands having to dig what seems like ten fathoms for each yard of progress. The rain relents and the visibility improves a bit and I tell myself not to look up, to keep scrabbling and digging and then scrabble and dig some more, and I'll get there. And as I'm being elevated to World Scrabble Champion I tell myself I must be nearly there now and permit myself a look up, and there seems even more hill ahead of me than there was when I started. I want to cry out, cry out to my mum who won't hear me, to whatever God may be the basis of my non-belief in non-belief, but my only audience is whatever unseen creatures may populate this bare, unlovely, loveless ridge of filth. It's the stupidest thing I've ever done in my life.

And then after the half hour of madness there is something I can see ahead: the top of the ridge and the boundary wall along it. Now there seems to be some point in getting the navigator out, especially when I spot the grassy path which Cheeseley says leads straight to the summit of Gragareth. As the mist closes in once more, with soupiness that has me reaching for the salt cellar and extra croutons, I follow the clear green path from the wall. Cheeseley's warning that after wet weather this can be "very spongy" is an understatement. With each step I'm sinking ever closer to the tower of Melbourne Cathedral. But the navigator confirms I'm getting closer all the time. A hundred and twenty feet from the trig point, 116, 112, 102, 98, and I look up and … no, it can't be. But yes it can. Oh yes it can.

The mist has disappeared.

It's vanished, exited, quit the scene of the crime without leaving a name and address. And it's as if my eyes, tight shut, have suddenly opened. As I reach the trig point there's light in the sky, the rain has stopped, the clouds are parting and I see flecks of blue above me. There ahead of and around me is land; miles and miles and miles of land including the town of Kirkby Lonsdale, the Forest of Bowland, the Howgill Fells, and, in the other direction, the near-at-hand summit of Ingleborough. Cheeseley suggests even the Lake District and Morecambe Bay may be visible on a good day. So why can't I see them. Because today is a good day. It's the best day.

There's still work to do and in any case I'm too cold and wet to linger.

I go back to the boundary wall, and I find I just need to walk alongside it and I'll be at Green Hill very shortly. Green Hill is fractionally higher than Gragareth but right on the border between Lancashire and Cumbria; because of that, some people apparently assert that it's not the true summit of Lancashire at all. There's no path shown on the map, just a green carpet immediately to the left of and parallel with the boundary wall, and that's what I need to stick to. Again it sounds more straightforward than it is; it's not the easiest walk along the carpet, and I keep needing to step round or over a thousand watery or boggy channels that decorate the ridge top. But that's as much of a fight as the invisible gods guarding the summit of Green Hill seem prepared to put up. The summit comes almost before I expect it. It's all a bit of an anti-climax; the next hill beyond, Great Coum, is a great deal higher, but it's in Cumbria. All I've got to show for reaching this slightly dubious Lancashire summit is a modest cairn with views no better than those I've been enjoying throughout my walk along the ridge. But who cares. I've made it, and I've done it all by myself, and two and a half hours later I'm back at Ingleton and even though someone's munched the last slice of tangy lemon drizzle the orange and blueberry is just as good.

The sun is shining from a cloudless blue sky as the bus pulls away from Ingleton, and I don't want to leave. I could stay for a lifetime and if I had more money to my name I probably would. I see walkers heading off down the street, anticipation and excitement lighting their brows, and I want to be them. I love the freshness, the stillness, the innocence, and I love the imperiousness, the arrogance, the grandeur. I remember what Natalie said to me once. She said Toby found the outdoors like a drug: at first it excited curiosity and suspicion, then slowly became utterly addictive, where being away from it for any length of time could be dangerous. I see what the man means. I want more. I need more.

*

There are no delays on the journey home which is just as well as I'm still not back till gone half past ten. As soon as I get in I stoop to pick up the mail. Among the rubbish is a white handwritten envelope with an ordinary stamp. I don't recognise the handwriting and for a moment I assume it's yet another attempt by junk mail merchants to induce you to open a package that would otherwise be heading straight for the recycling bin.

Then I see the Nottingham postmark.

I open the envelope and pull out the letter. It's on headed paper with the name Paul Faraday but there's no contact details. Just the words

Nottingham, Friday, handwritten below the name.

Dear Michael,

I'm really sorry to tell you that Louise is most unwell. As I think she mentioned when she saw you, she had been diagnosed with a serious illness quite recently. We hoped for a generous period of remission but sadly it appears this has been denied us. We think it may only be a matter of weeks or possibly even days now. I'm afraid she isn't up to seeing anybody just now but obviously if that changes or if there are any further developments I will let you know. Please keep her in your thoughts. Katie sends her love.

With our best love and prayers Paul, Louise and Katie xx

16

Chinley Churn(n) – lingering feeling of disappointment you get when having splashed out on buying expensive walking gear for your new partner you see it years later, having been used only once, being heaped onto a pile of stuff for the weekend car boot sale

I need to see her before she goes. That is, assuming there really is no way back. And just as important, if there is no way back, I need to re-establish contact with Katie, however happy and settled she is with her stepfather. I know Louise has good reason for not wanting me to know where they are, but I'm stifled by the sheer disempowerment. It's back to the same treadmill as before. I even consider travelling to Nottingham and scouring all the villages within a ten-mile radius to see if there's a house which matches the one I saw in the picture Louise showed me. I then realise I can't remember what the wretched house looks like. I speak to one or two people who might have kept in touch with Louise and whose details I've still got, and they're as baffled as they were when I spoke to them in the spring. As a last resort, I go onto the Internet and see if it's feasible to engage a private detective. I get a call from one later but I'm given the same response I got from enquiry agents: before he'll even open a file on it he wants money, lots of money, and I can't afford to give him lots of money. I can't afford to give him any money. I ask if he's prepared to act for me on a no-win no-fee basis. I think I hear a guffaw and the line goes dead.

As I fiddle with my phone, wondering whom to try next, I discover the selfie of Louise and me up on Ditchling Beacon. I print it and put it in the centre of the collage on the mantelpiece. Then I sit and sit and gaze and gaze at that picture.

And as I gaze, I know I'm falling in love with her and wanting her all over again.

*

It's a week after the letter from Paul. I've sent Steve some draft material from my Gragareth and Green Hill walk but also told him about Louise and asked him to forgive me if in all the circumstances there's a slight delay in completing the project. And he's gone into compassion overdrive, my

God, you poor thing, how awful, and next thing he's invited himself down to Chichester to meet me for coffee. Least he could do, he says, lifting a spoonful of chocolate-covered froth from the top of his latte and emptying it into his mouth. Don't worry about the book, you've done well to do what you have, perhaps it was a mad crazy idea but we wouldn't have asked you if we didn't think you were the right guy for the job. We'll get our best man onto it, never fear, he can do Mickle Fell and tidy things up, you'll still get credit for what you have done and BTW your impressions of the Gragareth walk are just what was needed and and your pictures almost professional so keep at it, you never know …

'You're missing the point,' I tell him.

'What do you mean?'

I ease a portion of pastry from my lemon tart. 'I want to do this now. I know what I said when we met before but things have changed. I want to get up Mickle Fell. Don't you get that. If I can make Green Hill and Gragareth, I can do Mickle Fell, I know I can. I want to. And I don't just want Mickle Fell either. I want more. To do more. If I can't get to her, can't stand in the way, can't derail the express that's squashing her flat, for God's sake, let me do something. Anything. Anything that might make her look down on me afterwards and say, actually, this guy wasn't such a ruddy waste of space after all. '

He takes a moment to digest this. Then he narrows his eyes.

'You're sure?'

'Quite sure.'

'Well, if you're sure … I was going to … I don't think … no. No. Maybe not.'

'Go on.'

'I won't be offended if you don't want to do it. I really won't. There's others I could ask.'

'Do what?'

'You heard of the Walk Half Your Age event?'

'Nope.'

'Been quite well publicised. Basis of it is that on a particular day, everybody who enters is sponsored to walk half their age in miles. There's a prize for the greatest distance walked within twenty-four hours. I think originally they thought about everyone walking their whole age but that's a bit tough on those over about thirty.'

'Will still be a bit tough on anyone who's over ninety.'

He doesn't flinch. 'It's excited a lot of interest. I know plenty of people in their sixties who are capable of doing thirty miles. It's not just the prizes. Great vehicle for charity fund raising. And promoting walking as a leisure

190

activity. So, question is, are you up for it? Having a go yourself? Subject obviously to how things develop with Louise?'

'S'pose so,' I reply. 'Can't promise how much sponsorship I'll get.'

'Don't worry too much about that,' he says. 'As publishers we're very interested in this. We're bringing out another walking title in a year's time. Shortly after the one you're doing now. *Walking For Pleasure And Reward*. There's a fairly substantial section on walking for charity. That's why I want you to take part. I want you to help write it.'

*

It's late October and the leaves are still on the trees but the air today has the promise of mid-winter. There's no rain to speak of, rather a sullen cloud cover and a moody, mercurial wind, a random, unfocussed wind that storms in from all directions and none. The strict rules devised by the Walk Half Your Age organisers say that the half must be rounded up so for me it's twenty miles and Steve's suggested I do mine along the south coast, starting above Brighton and aiming to finish on Beachy Head. As a return favour I ask if the section of the walk from Cuckmere Haven to Beachy Head via the Seven Sisters could be added to my book. Of course Toby will object. Like an ascetic in some far corner of Wales frowning on the excesses of the material world he will dismiss my activity as frivolous, unworthy and an abomination in the sight of the Lord. Steve's made it clear that he, not Toby, has the last word, but I've not met Toby in a business context and have no idea whether he will be as amiable and conciliatory as he was when I first saw him or whether he will seek to visit bloody retribution on those who have displeased him, retribution in which scalpels, rusty meathooks and testicles play a large part and general anaesthetics do not. But for now, it's in. I've been so preoccupied with trying to locate Louise I've had no time to get sponsorship from anybody other than from Steve and Andy, nor any time to persuade anyone to walk with me. But at least Steve has promised he'll meet me at the trig point on Beachy Head at four and says I mustn't be late.

The walking's been routine enough as far as Seaford. Virtually all the way from Brighton to Newhaven I've been following good clifftop paths but to the accompaniment of the constant noise of the A259 coast road and then the sprawling villages of Telscombe Cliffs and Peacehaven on the inland side. With the mouth of the river Ouse to negotiate and the cliffs giving way to a length of beach I decide to stick to the A259 from Newhaven to Seaford; although it means leaving the coast, I've checked and I'll still have completed twenty miles by the end of the day. At Seaford, however,

I return to the sea, walking the short distance from the town centre to the promenade. The promenade leads past a Martello Tower, one of a line of defensive structures built in the 19th century when the threat of French invasion was a very real one, and almost at once I'm ascending towards Seaford Head. After the easy road walking it's a shock to face such a sharp climb but the pain is soon over and I'm following a level green road over the headland, looking back to Seaford, the mouth of the Ouse and the cliffs behind. Not that it's a day for admiring the clarity of the views and boasting you can pick out the clock tower on the Arndale Centre in Eastbourne. It's a day for moving forward, forgetting what's behind and straining towards what is ahead. The ground falls away and I'm dropping to Hope Gap, a secluded spot in a valley between rising cliffs, and rocky pavements dating back nearly a hundred million years. From here I pass a line of coastguard cottages and drop to Cuckmere Haven, the valley between Seaford Head and the Seven Sisters through which the Cuckmere River flows. It's a virgin estuarine landscape, unsullied by clusters of chalets and caravans or the stink of frying doughnuts. There's meadow, and there's water, and behind there's white-faced chalk cliffs, and downland views, and there's solitude, acres of solitude. My guidebook tells me that on a hot summer's day there's no better place to linger and watch for peregrine falcon, curlew, hen harrier and grey heron, at the same time admiring the course of the original river as it wanders and loops and frolics as if wishing to delay its inevitable collapse into the sea. But with today's grey and wind, and the number of miles still to walk, there's no temptation to linger.

The mouth of the Cuckmere's only a few feet wide but it might as well be ten miles wide because there's no way across it. Instead I have to follow a muddy path inland, on and on, returning to the A259 and following it over the estuary. Then I begin the walk back towards the sea. The diversion from the coast feels like an imposition, a punishment, rather than the pleasure the guidebooks say it should be. Without Louise or Natalie to provide their ornithological observations I'm not sure if the white winged creatures waddling along beside me are Canada geese, dabchicks or wood pigeons, but today my thoughts are on getting through the exercise and if I think too much about Louise or Natalie I may just crumple. And on this grey day where every bluster of the wind seems to catch me unawares there's no guarantee there'll be anyone around to mop me up. I'd thought I was joking when I said to Steve I hoped there might be a minibus touring the country to pick up the Walk Half Your Age participants who failed to last the course. It doesn't seem so funny now.

At length I'm signposted away from the estuary and begin to climb. As I gain height I see the full layout of the Haven and its watercourses, not only the twists and turns of the original Cuckmere but the straight cut which was added over a century and a half ago to speed the flow and spoil the fun. I continue along what is an undemanding but steady green-carpeted incline, and reach the Seven Sisters. Despite the name there's nothing especially feminine about them. They're a succession of chalk clifftops interspersed with depressions, which are actually the valleys of ancient rivers. The grass beneath my feet is firm and the way forward clear and unobstructed but it's tough, no, it's brutal. It's the ultimate in rollercoaster rides, back-breaking climbs alternating with knee-jarring descents. There are consolations in the form of views forward to Beachy Head and back to Seaford Head, and there's always the chance, so my book says, of the sighting of fulmars and cormorants, but all the time I'm having to watch to check my ascents have not been so diagonal as to threaten to hurl me from the chalk edges to the Channel abyss below. It's galling, no, it's infuriating, not once but seven times, to win the height and then to lose it again, and I'm wondering why I didn't just stick to the A259. Or better still just walk up and down my back garden 900 times, or whatever the equivalent of 20 miles is. I've not measured it recently. At any rate the maths provide a distraction of sorts and I complete the seventh Sister and negotiate the drop down to Birling Gap, a freak cleft in the South Downs with steep steps to the sea that were used by smugglers. I pause to note the assembly of cliff-edge buildings here, frightened, tense, vulnerable to every high sea and every blast of the wind, and to see from an information board how recent stormy winters have redrawn the maps of the coastline and reduced still further the size of our Island home. Global warming, some say. Nature must have its way, others contend. We've borrowed this land from the sea, and nobody's in a position to argue when it seeks repayment. I allow myself an Americano at the café there, and now I have to pay for the height lost with yet another climb which takes me to the 19th century Belle Tout lighthouse. This itself has had to be moved more than once because of the advances of the sea; it now stands on what was once an Iron Age camp and is surrounded by downland that's rich in orchids. Once more I lose height, dropping to the coast road from East Dean before the ascent of Beachy Head proper begins.

It's a killer, this one: the loftiest point on the whole of the Sussex coast at 535 feet high. And as I slog, and pant, I feel not only the exertions of my walk to this point but also the pressure to make it by the time Steve has stated. The wind is swirling, sometimes helping, sometimes pushing me along, then smashing into my face, defying me to travel a step further, then deciding to blow in from the land and try and topple me over the cliff edge, and then calming and pretending it's done its worst before reinvigorating. Now it's upping the ante, sending pockets of rain from the heavy skies above, and I can almost hear its laughter at my weakness and my frailty. But as with so many of my other walks, the greatest pain offers the greatest reward: the sight of the 125ft tall lighthouse, the diversity of colours of plants on the hillside, and the views which extend back to Brighton and beyond and on to Eastbourne and beyond. Rumour has it that on a clear day you can see France. And though the first letter of Toby to the Corinthians chapter 1 beginning at the 13th verse would probably have him pouring scorn on every last step up the hillside, you can be forgiven for thinking that there can be nothing higher than this and everything is below. Reaching the highest ground, I stand on the edge of the cliffs and gaze up at the grey of the sky and down at the water that has claimed so many lives, lives of those who felt there was nothing left for them except more of the same: same despair, same isolation, same sorrow. The meeting place of the gods at their most benevolent and indulgent, bestowing on their subjects a windswept pageant of ethereal colours and placing in their hands the glorious illusion of invincibility, and the gods at their most mocking and contemptuous, calling those consumed by awareness of the futility of existence to bring down the curtain on the final act of the farce.

I turn and head for the trig point, set some way back from the cliff edge, and I'm only ten yards or so short of it when I hear someone behind me calling my name. But it's not Steve calling. It's a woman's voice. It isn't one I recognise; it's lower pitched and more gravelly than those of Louise or Natalie. I look round and see a young woman approaching me. She's roughly late twenties and wears a bright green jumper and light blue jeans. Her cheeks are smooth bronze carpets and there's a bounce in her stride. Her curly auburn hair is familiar and I just know I've seen her somewhere before.

She extends her hand to me. 'Michael,' she says again. 'Good to meet you.'

'Er – should I know you?'

'You might,' she says with a smile. 'Jodie Carteret.'

*

She's a down-to-earth girl with a down-to-earth laugh and mud on her trainers. Full of admiration for my walking exploits and congratulations on my fund raising and good wishes for the future and we must do this again sometime and it'd be a pleasure to do the foreword for Toby's book, just remind me when you need it. A very ordinary girl really.

Except she isn't. While she goes off to the restaurant complex for a pee Steve comes up and explains he'd apparently had to pull so many strings to get her onto Beachy Head that rumour has it he's being headhunted by the *Andy Pandy* production team. He'd not told me she was coming because he was convinced she'd cancel at the last moment and didn't want to raise my hopes. He says Jodie's now agreed to lend her endorsement to *Walking For Pleasure And Reward*. Not that she'll write any of it, of course, she can barely write her name, but just the mention of her on the front cover will guarantee sufficient sales of the book to keep him in apple doughnuts for the next three decades. He's also somehow managed to assemble a press conference and photo shoot with buffet in an Eastbourne hotel the same evening, together with some other walkers who got to Beachy Head earlier or trekked over the inland section of the South Downs Way from Alfriston, and Jodie will be there as special guest. I tell him I'll only come along if he can guarantee that any news feature coming out of it doesn't carry the headline BEST FOOT FORWARD which makes me want to throw our local paper across the room every time they use it. A car's waiting to take us the short distance into the town, and there I am, being photographed with her, being paraded as an ex-lazybones who's now answered the call of the wild and has embraced it with both feet. And one of the reporters Steve's invited has found an angle, heralding me as the Arsenal obsessive who may have eaten all the pies, but is walking them all off. He enquires if I knew that it takes 2 hours 9 minutes to burn off the calories consumed when downing a standard-sized steak and kidney. He also asks me a few Gunners questions but as I expect they're of the What Every Schoolboy Should Know variety. All very easily answered. But he beams, and gushes, and it's clear he thinks I'm God. He asks me what's next, and I tell him about my book and about Mickle Fell and he writes it in his diary and wishes me luck. The pressmen are ambling homewards now, and I seek out Jodie to say goodbye to her, hoping for a congratulatory peck, but she's long gone. Nibbled on half a hot sausage then buzzed off.

*

But Jodie's Jodie. As Steve reminded me, she may have broken my heart but I won't have been the first and I won't be the last. And she's the only one to have brought a light to my face since that letter from Paul. Even if smiles were being rationed I'd still have a shedload of coupons to spare and now, a Sunday in early December, I'd find myself in danger of being charged with hoarding them. It's not just that I've lost Natalie and now Louise is slipping away. It's my financial situation as well. With my dad's legacy having gone there's been no money available for the mortgage and I've already accumulated a box file's worth of emails and letters from the building society. So far, so polite and civilised, may we respectfully remind you, do let us know if we can help, don't hesitate to go the CAB, you may be eligible for free legal advice, so forth. It might get nastier once I'm into the second week of arrears.

I've sought employment with defence solicitors locally, but none can offer me a full-time post. The best they can offer is to let me attach to them as a kind of freelance which would at least enable me to get myself on the next January to July court and police duty rotas. In the meantime I'd been hoping there might be some consultancy or agency work available. But there isn't any. Everybody's cutting back, having to do twice as much for no more money, chasing whatever work they can find. So in desperation I'd got some employment in the drive-thru' section of a nearby fast food restaurant. I'd been lured by the glossy recruitment posters that jumped out at me when I was in there sipping at my regular latte and chewing on my hot apple pie. Trouble was, the posters said nothing about the less glamorous aspects. More specifically, being threatened, as I had been, with a punch to the mouth at twenty past three in the morning because of the deficiency of gherkin content in the quarter-pounder with cheese I'd just served an overweight boiler fitter on his way to a clowns' convention in Colwyn Bay. The subsequent hearing had been a travesty of justice, the penalty meted out for the crime being inappropriate and leaving me feeling disappointed and embittered. The guidelines weren't followed and I suspect if challenged on appeal the sentencers would have been castigated by the reviewing court.

But if I hadn't been sacked I think I'd have resigned anyway.

Mum can't help. Or rather I won't let her. I've been to see her a few times and she's clearly not herself. The new extension's letting in water and she explains that when she called someone in to look at it they discovered more work that needs doing urgently. It's going to cost her thousands. I know if I told her what my circumstances were really like she'd insist on putting me first but I couldn't live with the possible consequences to her. Instead I have to pretend. I've pretended enough about Louise and Katie. Now I'm pretending about money. Pretending there's lots more consultancy work lined up, several firms interested in taking me on, was never that happy in Bristol, it's all fine. I don't know what puts a sharper knife through me, lying to her or having to remind myself later what the truth is. Even without knowing that truth, she's suggested I contact Louise's solicitors and get her agreement to sell up. It's crossed my mind too. But the fact is that once everyone's had their share, from the conveyancing lawyers right down to the estate agents' in-house cat, there won't be enough left for a roll of past-its-best-before-date charity shop toilet paper.

So the next step's the dole queue. That is, unless pride forces me to offer to fill one of the vacancies shown on the *Law Society Gazette* website. But I don't feel a thrill of guilty pleasure at the prospect of joining Macclesfield District Council's procurement department. And joining a "constantly busy" criminal legal aid firm somewhere in the outer suburbs of Liverpool has less appeal than synchronised creosote gargling in Kirkwhelpington.

*

As is the case most Sundays, there's not much to occupy me till the Sky footie starts. I tend to put the local radio on in bed while the God slot's on Radio 2, though frankly the fare offered on Rustic FM isn't much more exciting. It certainly isn't today, the breaking news this morning being the arrest of a 60-year-old for turning his window box into a mini cannabis factory, a major police initiative against speeding motorists on and around the Chichester bypass, and North Selsey United's shock 2nd round Sussex Refrigeration Trophy exit to the Findon Valley Warriors. I get up and get dressed and after breakfast watch a couple of You Tube videos, then have a wanderette down the road mid-morning to buy a paper. I emerge from the shop to see no less than three superstore delivery lorries passing by, adding their own carbon size 12 bootprints in their hurry to offload their frozen turkeys and Christmas puddings. So much for the day of rest.

I've never been a huge sucker for Christmas. I don't know if it would have made any difference if I went in for the religious side but as an adult I never have done. I suppose I had a faith of sorts when I was very young. But then it started to be tested and I got a lot of stick for it and I wanted to believe it all so much and lay awake at night thinking it all must be true and there must be some sense in it, the message having been inculcated into me over so many years. Then rationality and the relentless march of existential logic took over and I had to concede what my subconscious had been telling me for so long. That it was dad who'd been eating the mince pie and the carrot left by the fireplace.

But I guess that throughout my adult life I've found something warming and reassuring about the festive smells, sounds and lights, be it hearing *Santa Claus Is Coming To Town* on every visit to Superdrug from the 12th October onwards or reading six pages of letters in the local paper from outraged correspondents following the announcement that there'll be no illuminations down Pauncefoot Street this year. Or else, buying a double pack of six luxury mince pies in Marks & Spencer at lunchtime and realising at the end of the afternoon's work that I've scoffed every one of them.

This year, though, I can't do it. Any of it.

So I wonder what to do instead. It must be possible to google NO CHRISTMAS THIS YEAR THANK YOU and find a suitable way of non-celebrating the festive season. I switch on the computer and the screen saver's just coming up when there's a knock on the door.

I can't think who could want me at quarter past two on a Sunday afternoon. The Jehovah's Witnesses came round this morning so it's probably not them again yet. Well, not after I told them where they could stick their *Watchtower*. It could be carol singers. There's a local group that come down our street most years and they're pretty good. But they tend to pop up a bit later in December and a bit later in the afternoon. It's more likely to be the kids from number 73 to whom you give fifty pence just to stop them recycling their 18-rated version of *While Shepherds Watched*. I rummage in my pocket and find a coin of that value, place it on the table beside the front door, then open up.

There's a man standing there. I've seen him before somewhere but I can't place him straight away. He's dressed in a black sports jacket with shiny buttons, a white shirt and a green and red striped tie. He's holding a stout Waitrose carrier bag.

'Hallo. Good to see you again,' he says.

'Can I help?'

'I hope so.' He extends his right hand towards me and offers an affable smile. 'I think we've a few things to talk about. May I come in?'

I take his hand. 'Forgive me.' I retreat a couple of steps. 'I don't think …'

'You may not remember me. Paul Faraday.'

17

Stony Turgate(n) – first serious rift between you and new partner when s/he agrees to join you for a walk then after 200 yards finds spurious pretext for packing it in

I usher him into the living room, invite him to sit down on the settee, and make him a coffee. Then having given it to him I sit in the armchair. I'm only grateful I'd cleaned and tidied the place yesterday. It's not fit for a royal visit even now – that bit of paper with my mobile number on it remains on the arm of the settee – but it's an improvement. Twenty-five hours earlier and he'd have been competing for settee space with at least six brown sauce-stained dinner plates and two thirds of the contents of my cutlery cabinet.

'I'm so glad you're here,' he says. 'I didn't want to have to write.'

'About what? Louise?'

He nods. 'I'm very sorry to tell you she passed away about three weeks ago.'

I knew it was coming. But I still find myself gripping the arm of the chair for support.

'Did she suffer?'

He shakes his head. 'Thank God, it was very peaceful.' There's a soothing reassurance in his voice.

'I was kind of expecting it,' I say.

'I'm sorry about the letter. I'm very sorry you had to find out like that.'

'I ... I already knew she wasn't right. Knew she had this ... this ... she came to see me. Told me then.'

'I gathered she had seen you,' he says. The words continue to flow from his mouth with the mellifluousness of a woodland stream in summer. 'I'm pleased she did tell you. I'm pleased she had the courage to face up to it.'

'Just wish ... just wish I could have done more.'

'There's nothing you could have done,' he says.

Through his serenity I think I detect a profound sadness. 'God, I'm sorry,' I say. 'Me, me, me. What about you. Are you okay.'

'I think so. Yes, I really think so. I try to remember how I managed when my mother passed away. My fellow Quakers have really helped. But they've warned me, told me to prepare for that time when everyone's exhausted their supplies of sympathy, they're going about their business again, and all the formalities are over and you get this horrible realisation that the world's carrying on quite nicely without her and you've got to get up every morning and deal with it.'

'You know if you ever need a hand ...'

'That's kind. Thank you.'

'How's Katie?'

'As you might expect. My dad and I had done our best to prepare her. She accepted the inevitable before it happened. Of course she's still very upset. But she's a very bright intelligent little girl. Her thought processes are very advanced for someone of her years. My dad's been great with her. They get on so well. I actually brought her with me today. We arranged for her to go and see one of her old school friends from down here. We'll be going home straight after this.'

'Can I see her?'

'It's been a long day for her, Michael. Long journey down. Long journey home.'

'We need to talk about her.'

He takes a sip from his coffee. 'You know, Michael, I'm a great believer in not creating problems where none exist.'

'I'm sorry?'

'Katie's settled. She's getting on very well at school. She's made some great friends. At her half-term consultation, her teachers were glowing about her. English outstanding. Maths, streets ahead of the rest of the class. She's becoming a very proficient pianist. I think she could go a long way, with tuition and practice.'

'So?'

'As I say, she's settled, Michael. This is a special and difficult time for her, where she greatly needs continuity and stability. As a lawyer, you'll appreciate that, I know. Later on, when things have calmed down a bit, we can perhaps look at it again.' Now he slurps from his coffee and slides his tongue round his lips. 'So. You'll probably wonder. Why I've not told you sooner.'

'Well?'

'This isn't easy to tell you, Michael. You'll want to know at some stage. May as well know now. Louise wanted it that way. To go very quietly, seamlessly, without fuss, without outsiders. I have to say that exercised me. I tried to persuade her. That you as her husband, still her husband, should have been there, to say your goodbye to her, to be present for her laying to rest. But she was insistent. She said it was more for Katie's benefit than anything. Avoid fuss. Keep it simple. Of course, she said, once she had gone, once the formalities had been completed, you should be told, and given the chance to pay your respects. So that's why I've come. I couldn't put all this in a letter. I didn't have your phone number either.'

I sit back in my chair. 'God, she must have hated me. Really hated me.'

'What makes you say that, Michael?'

'I mean, I get – you know – not wanting me to know where she's moved to. Not after the way I was as a husband, as a dad. Give her, give Katie, give you all a chance to settle down, new family, all that. But not to let me near her ...' And now the realisation of the depth of her hatred is beginning to hit me, I find myself trembling and my cheeks are melting. 'Not to let me near her even when she knew I'd want to ... I loved her. I really loved her. I know I screwed up, I know I let her, let Katie down ... did she need to punish me, punish me like this. And you know what really hurts. That when she came to see me she was ... she was really opening up, sharing about her illness, and then I desert her. Desert her for someone who goes and dumps me the same evening. So he's got nothing, the boy's got nothing.'

Paul dips into his carrier bag. Firstly he produces and passes to me the service sheet for her memorial ceremony. A glance at the paper confirms they'd kept that simple too. Then he removes a brown paper package and hands it to me. 'She asked me to give this to you,' he says.

I drop the service sheet and tear at the wrapping. There's tons of the stuff. My hands are shaking and my eyes are watering and I've always been pretty crap at doing anything fiddly with my fingers so it takes ages. But Paul shows no irritability or impatience. He watches and smiles.

After thirty-three years I get through the final layer of brown paper. It's Louise's orange jug. She'd bought it on our honeymoon. We'd been for a swim in the sea late one afternoon and I realised I was with the sexiest woman in the world. Then we'd gone back to our hotel and never even made it into our bed, but just crashed to the floor the moment we got into our room and it had been unbelievable, truly unbelievable. Then we'd showered together and changed and gone into the old town and sat with plates of linguine in the shade of a cluster of orange trees. We'd wandered arm in arm along the cobbled main street with its tavernas and its cafés and craft shops bursting with trinkets and pottery, and I was scared, petrified, because I thought it could never ever get this good again. And this shopowner had seen the love in our eyes and invited us in and showed Louise the jug, not just a plain orange but a mosaic, a clumsy mosaic of light orange and gentle orange and deep orange and almost intense orange. Unique, he kept saying. You can go to the ends of the world, you'll never see one like it. Louise fell for it all. She kept it as hand luggage on the flight home, hugging it as she would her own child. "I'll never part with this," she'd once said to me. "Never till my dying day." And now I'm holding it, and seeing it again is like watching Louise die in front of me. And as she dies I'm in love with her again, more than I loved her that evening among the orange trees or in the shade of the olive groves with cicadas chirping above us, or in the soft salt water of the Mediterranean. More than our first walk on Ditchling Beacon watching for the fritillaries and cabbage whites, more than when we tasted the doughnuts crammed with runny strawberry jam, or scones that came with vats of clotted cream and lemon curd, or brick-sized slabs of tangy, sticky grapefruit cake.

Now Paul's coming up to me and offering me a handkerchief. And he's sitting on the arm of the chair and putting his arm round me and I find myself weeping into the arm of the man who took my family away.

'I'm sure, quite sure she never hated you,' he says. 'If she did, why would she have wanted you to have that jug. You can't torture yourself. You can't dwell on the past.'

The tears dry and Paul places his other arm round me and we find ourselves in embrace.

'I'm sorry,' I keep on saying. 'I'm sorry.'

'God grant me the courage …'

And this non-believer in non-belief, this septic sceptic, is joining in prayer with the man who took his family away.

*

After we've prayed we just continue to embrace in silence. It's Paul who finally pulls away and lets me sit back in the armchair and dry my eyes.

'I need to be getting off soon,' he says. 'It's a long drive for us. You need to collect your thoughts and have some time to yourself.'

'Don't worry about that. I've more than enough. Do you want another coffee before you go?'

'No, thanks. We'll … in fact, come to think of it, yes. That would be very kind.'

He passes his coffee mug over to me.

'I suppose we ought to talk about Louise's affairs before you go,' I say.

'There's not much to talk about,' he says. 'She made a new will not long before she died. I've a copy if you want to see it. I'm one of the executors. In the long run all her stuff will go to Katie. Though to be honest, she didn't have a great deal anyway. I know she was particularly anxious for you to have the jug. If anything else comes up that you need to be involved in I'm sure my solicitors will contact you. Or your own solicitor. Whatever you prefer. We can exchange details before I go.'

I rise and pick up the orange jug which is beside me on the chair where I'd left it as I'd disintegrated. And as I take Paul's mug with my other hand and walk out into the kitchen I can barely remain on my feet. I put the kettle on again and I look at the orange jug again and pick it up and run my fingers round and round it, tracing every shade, every texture, every mood of orange. And as my fingers run round it I chance to look inside it.

There's something there. A folded piece of paper. It's wedged at the bottom so has made no sound. I fish the paper out and unfold it.

Dear Dad, Paul doesn't know I'm writing this. Please don't tell him. I've always loved you and I'll always love you. Take care, love Katie xxxxx

And suddenly the whole room is filled, engulfed, with images of the little girl who came, albeit belatedly, albeit indirectly, out of my love for Louise and her love for me. The little girl who invented games I couldn't be bothered to play, read to me stories it was too great an intellectual effort to listen to, drew me pictures I was twenty seconds later using as a coaster for my mug of Nescafé instant. The little girl whom it was too much trouble to love, too much trouble to be loved by.

I want her now. I want to start to learn to love her now.

*

I go back into the front room with the coffee. 'Paul, I need to see her. Need to see Katie. Before you go back.'

He smiles but says nothing.

'Paul?'

'As I said. She'll have had a long day. It's not straightforward. She's not seen you for months. These things need handling with huge care. I suggest we leave it for the moment. All right?'

'Can I have your address?'

'Sure.' He brings out his wallet, removes a card from it and hands it across to me. 'My solicitors.'

I shove the card into my pocket. 'Isn't it just a lot easier if I contact you direct?'

'I don't think so, Michael. I really don't, all right.' And for the first time I detect a slight brusqueness in his tone. 'Now, please forgive me, but I, we, really ought to be going.' He rises to his feet and picks up his bag.

'What about your coffee?'

'It's all right. We'll find a café.' The harshness in his voice seems to melt away once more. 'Michael, I'm sorry. I don't mean to sound terse. Please understand. It's a hard time for all of us. She was a very special person, Louise. A very special person. Let's celebrate that.' And I detect a trace of a tear in his eye.

His words bring back memories of our last day together. Of Ditchling Beacon. I want a more tangible reminder of it now. I cross the room and glance again at the centre of my collage of photos on the mantelpiece.

It isn't there. There is a picture where the selfie of Louise and me was, but it isn't the selfie. It's a picture of my dad. Moved to where the picture of Louise was.

And I look at Paul, then I look at the collage again, and then I look at Paul again, and we're just standing there, and again I'm thinking back to the day that picture was taken. And virtually without warning comes the crash of the collapse of scales from my eyes and at the same time a charge of adrenalin with the noise of a million horses and chariots.

'Will you excuse me for a second, Paul.'

'Sure.'

I go back out into the kitchen. In minutes he'll be gone. I've minutes to do what I'd be needing a full day to do if I were doing it professionally. I've not the benefit of the tools that assist someone doing this for a living: statements, CCTV, unused material. All I have is my ability to retain facts and details in my memory, combined with a good dose of experience and a generous tablespoonful of instinct. Then having prepared and mixed the ingredients I go back to the living room.

And I look straight into Paul's eye and I say it.

'You killed her.'

He says nothing. His expression doesn't change. The colour of his face doesn't change. He doesn't move.

'I don't expect you to buy it,' I say. 'But it's true, isn't it. From the moment she came to live with you, you subjected her to constant domestic abuse. And when she ceased to be of any use to you, you wasted her. Got rid of her.'

Now a smile flickers around the corners of his mouth. 'Explain,' he says.

'She'd never have wanted to move away so quickly. Not without telling me. But no, she had to go, didn't she. Out of my life, just like that. The very day after I went round. Katie, yanked out of school. They refused to tell me where she'd gone. Made me feel like a criminal. God knows what poison you invented about me to stop them, stop her new school, consulting, involving me. You forced them away. Katie and Louise. My family. Fair?'

He doesn't say a word.

'And once Louise had gone, you isolated her. You wanted her all to yourself. She may have been able to text me a couple of times, but you confiscated her phone so she couldn't do it any more. I guess you trashed it. And I don't suppose you ever let her have a phone after that. Or access to a computer so she could email me or contact me on Facebook. You wouldn't have wanted her contacting me or any of her friends. Would you.'

Still nothing from him.

'I saw three photos of her. High heels. Stiletto heels. She hates them. Always has done. I never saw her in anything but trainers and pumps. She'd have hated it. Loathed it.'

'What else?' His lips barely moving.

'Well, that was just the start, wasn't it. Objectify her first, get her used to being a chattel, a plaything of yours. Strip her of her independence. I mean, you'd sold her car before you even left. Didn't you. As for work, she's not to go out to work, is she. Got to stay and keep a nice house and cook for you. She told me she kept on being turned down for jobs, once when she was more or less told it was hers. How was that, eh?'

He moves a couple of inches towards me and now I can feel the warmth of his breath. 'Go on.'

'And on the subject of food, cooking, what godawful diet were you forcing on her which made her crave meat so much? There she is scoffing half a packet of bacon on the quiet in my house, my bacon for God's sake. As for booze, when I knew her, a glass a day, tops. That day, guzzled the Riesling like it was being banned from the supermarkets next morning.'

He nods. He nods.

'Then you start to hit her. Hit her to the head, so hard she has to go to the doctor. Hit her where nobody can see if she covers up. Arms, legs. So she has to cover up. Beat her so hard that she can't even sit down on her backside. God knows how she survived that coach journey. She hated coaches. But it was all she could afford, wasn't it. She must have been that desperate to get away from you that she got on the thing in the first place.'

He looks at his watch but says nothing.

It's what I know, what I've been trained for, and I need to press on while the focus is there, while my audacity is still holding my nerves at bay. 'She'd changed. Changed in every respect. When she lived with me, she was assertive, single minded, couldn't suffer fools. Then when she came back, she was jelly. She was petrified. Kept looking out. For you. Convinced you knew where she was. Convinced she was going to be murdered in her own home. Did you know, when we saw each other that day, we visited a church. And I looked, and she was praying. Practically a card-carrying atheist. On her knees. And she had good reason to be praying, didn't she. Praying to be spared the fate she knew was coming her way.'

Now he's looking into my eyes. 'Keep going.'

'And of course she's not going to breathe a word to me about what you've done to her because she knows if I go to the police with it, she's signing her own death warrant. '

He nods again. 'Is that everything?'

'And then you got a friend to invent some fictitious garbage about a rare blood disease. Win win, isn't it. Whether she decides she can't cope any more, or you decide you've no more use for her, you've got it to hide behind. That, and her prescribed medication. Whatever that may have been. God, I bet you were so plausible to the paramedics when they came round. And to the police. And the coroner. And now to me. No wonder you didn't want me up there these past weeks. No ruddy wonder.'

'Mmm hmmm.' Now he strokes the modest stubble on his chin.

'And if you'd not stolen that picture from the collage I guess I might still be believing you. Don't worry, I don't need it. You keep it. I've got it saved on my phone. It's probably the only one you have of her looking happy. Properly happy.'

He reaches out and places a hand on my arm just below my elbow. I mustn't flinch. I don't flinch. 'Michael,' he says. The briskness has gone. 'I don't blame you one iota for reacting in this way. It's your grief. I can put you in touch with some excellent organisations that can enable you to grieve appropriately. But this isn't helping you, it isn't helping me, and it's just upsetting you more. I really need to be on my way. Katie will be wondering where I am.'

And now he's striding past me and going out of the house. And I call after him. 'I'm going to the police tonight. Tell them everything.'

I follow him out of the front door. I try to run to catch up with him but I'm in my slippers and I'm not fast enough. I see him walking to his Merc and getting in. And I look towards the front passenger seat and she's sitting there, wearing that red coat with the white dots, head in a magazine, Katie, my own daughter Katie.

I need to speak to her now.

But he's already started the engine and is driving off.

I go after them but again my footwear lets me down. I've not even got the car number. So I go back in and kick off my slippers and run upstairs to the loft from which I can see the end of my road and its T-junction with Bishops Avenue. At least then I can tell the police which way they went.

And from the loft I see the car, having negotiated the junction, blast its way onto the far side of Bishops Avenue. Then it hurtles off along that road. Travelling at what must be sixty miles an hour, it overtakes a line of slower vehicles by swerving into the opposite carriageway, forcing a cyclist onto the pavement. It careers round the corner by the primary school and disappears from sight.

18

Tilly Whim(n) – one of a number of lovingly composed captions to be found in photo album of past walking exploits which seem naff and cheesy when revisited years later, eg "Making it to the roof of Great Britain: forget Ben Affleck, Ben Nevis for us every time!"

O f course it's pointless to go to the cops. The fact is I've not got a shred of evidence. It's all supposition. He may have ridden out of town in a cloud of guilt-laden smoke but as far as my interrogation's gone, he's just stood there as though I've read him Arsenal's results during the month of September 1979. If the police were indeed involved in the investigation into Louise's death and he's been able to outwit them, what chance have I got, an unemployed lawyer whose transferable skills in the twenty-first century market place don't even extend to getting the gherkins right.

I go back into the front room. I go to the settee to straighten the cushions, determined to erase all reminders of his visit. And I see that the piece of paper with my mobile number on it is no longer on the arm.

Then my phone bleeps. A text message.

I don't recognise the sender's number.

GOOD 2 MEET U SEE YOU V SOON P

*

After reading the text I try to pretend that nothing's different. So I get a mug of tea and put Sky Sports on. But this particular game might involve Rochdale coming back from four down against Liverpool at Anfield to equalise in the ninth minute of added time and it would still excite me about as much as a late-night Channel 5 documentary on the lobster fishermen of the Galapagos Islands. I make myself a bacon sandwich and it comes back up within an hour. I'm cold, there's a draught coming from somewhere, but I can't be bothered to get up again. I decide to have an early night, but I'm still lying on my bed at half past one in the morning feeling more wide awake than I did in any of my law lectures.

Then I hear a bang on my front door.

To begin with I try and kid myself that it's no more than a sound inside my head, and that the fear of it has translated it into apparent reality. But then there's another bang, twice as loud as before.

My knees primitive percussion instruments, I walk to the window and look down. I see a figure shuffling around by the door. It may not be Paul Faraday. But the light isn't good enough to say for definite and the vague belief that it might be Paul Faraday or someone he's hired to do the job for him mushrooms into overwhelming conviction and I collapse back onto my bed with oceans of sweat pouring from my forehead and I'm crying out in panic and helplessness.

I stop crying out and for five minutes all is quiet. Then I hear footsteps. It's someone coming up the stairs.

My stairs.

There's nowhere to hide. Nowhere.

I'm dead.

I'm not ready to die. Please, God, I'm not.

'Are you all right there, Michael? Can I help?'

I recognise the Glaswegian accent. I look up and see the owner of the voice in the doorway. It's not Paul Faraday. And if it is a hired hitman, Paul's made a strange choice. It's Colin from number ninety-five, our neighbourhood watch co-ordinator and the favourite to win the *Today* programme's Busybody Of The Year award for the thirty-sixth year running.

'Your front door was wide open,' he says. 'I was concerned.' He always has been a bore and a pillock. But I want to throw my arms round him and kiss him.

I thank him, ask him to shut the door on his way out, and watch him walk downstairs. The dress rehearsal is over and I flop back down on my bed, my nerves yanked from their moorings and crushed to sawdust.

*

It's a third-floor furnished bedsit in a grey-brick terrace in Littlehampton, on a road whose name I remember well from the days I practised in Sussex as a defence advocate. There's been some serious stuff here: aggravated burglary, armed robbery, and even attempted murder. And any thought that the quality of life in the neighbourhood has improved is dispelled the moment I walk through the door into the communal hallway, to be greeted by three smoking teenagers with their bicycles, and the fragrance of stale pee and fresh sick.

But given the resources available to me I suppose I should be grateful

209

it's a roof that'll be over my head and not the lid of an empty Winalot box in front of the Oxfam shop.

I don't know how long I'll have to stay. Maybe a week or two. Maybe forever. I've brought with me everything I can, and I'm arranging for the rest to go into storage. I'd thought about going to mum's but there's every chance Paul could find her address. I've no idea what the guy might be capable of so I'm taking no chances. Nobody must know where I am. I've told mum I've moved away, haven't said any more than that, told her I'll be in touch again before Christmas and we'll fix up when to meet during the festive period. I've told Gwen and Les Abercrombie and Colin that I've gone and that's all they or anyone else will need to know.

I'd tried to prepare myself for the very worst as I took delivery of the keys from the landlords but my worst has got nowhere near it. As I enter my new abode the stench on the landing is replaced by the odour of days-old excrement that wafts from every corner. The loo looks and smells as though it was last flushed in 1956, the frosted glass in the loo window is broken, the kitchen sink appears to be supporting its very own nature reserve, and the settee in the lounge shows off more springs than Alice. The boiler control panel offers three settings, Cold, Colder and Colder Still. And hearing the sounds up above, I'm guessing that one of my fellow tenants is building a life-size model of the Titanic.

But I'm no longer in Park Drive and although the crashing of hammer and the squealing of chisel and the roar of the Black and Decker continue at regular intervals through day and night, I'm safe. For the moment.

*

Bereavement. All things to all people. Some doing their best to shrug it off and get on with life, perhaps seeing it as part of a cosmic grand plan. Some angry, moving into denial and trying to fight it. With me it's neither. I've no real concept of any God, no sense of there being any grand plan, and no ability to put it all behind me and embrace what's to come. But nor have I any fight in me. Now I just get this sense that with no wife, no natural child, an adopted child I won't see again, no partner, no job and no home, nothing matters any more, and that the world can do as it likes as long as it doesn't do any more to me. I switched my mobile off right after the text came through, and kept it off till I was able to change the number. It's not only the fears for my safety. It's wanting the world, just for a while, to shut up, go away, and get on somebody else's case. I don't have the radio or TV on much. I can't bear to listen to the news. I can't cope with my own problems so how can I be expected to take on those of others. Most of the time I just sit there, gazing up towards the window, and thinking ahead to Mickle Fell.

I know I could put Mickle Fell off. I know Steve would understand. But I don't want to put it off. I want to do it. I need to do it. I need to do it now. Louise rejoiced in describing me as the definitive guy who never mind starting something but failing to finish it, couldn't even get started. The thought of her being up there willing me on to both start and actually complete the task doesn't enjoy huge compatibility with my belief system. But I can believe, I must believe, that her words have made a difference and therefore her being has made a difference.

It's as I squeeze my buttocks between the fragments of exposed rust-encrusted metal on my sofa and look again at the Mickle Fell paperwork that the true cost of proving that Louise has made a difference becomes clear. To start with, the summit of the fell is a long walk from the nearest road; even if my travel arrangements go to plan, and I'm able to get all the way to base camp by motorised transport, I'll be battling against the clock to complete the walk in daylight. Next problem, my research reveals that the walk itself, although posing no real navigational difficulties, is the definitive Pennine obstacle course, with numerous streams to ford, peat hags to negotiate and, close to the summit plateau, a virtually sheer hillside, a hell of a sight steeper than Gragareth ever claimed to be. What's more, there's no guarantee of a mobile phone signal, so I can't necessarily expect to get any assistance in the event of an accident. And lastly according to pretty much every website and every newspaper I pick up, the forecast for the weekend of my visit is for the north of England to be engulfed in a snow superstorm straight out of Chapter 16 of the book of Daniel which will commence the moment I slam the door of my cab having handed over the rest of my life savings to the driver. I've tried to engage a walking companion but Gavin's having to work, and as for Martin Laycock, I would never have thought it possible for anyone to speak with such red-blooded zeal about a pre-Christmas team-building energiser weekend in Market Harborough. It's crazy, no, it's insane, and I bet Toby's got wind of it all and as he slips on his jacket ready for another permit-free mountain expedition in Canada, with generously-State-subsidised buses from city to resort every thirty seconds, he's loving it, and loving the fact that he's taken me for such a mug I'll soon be on a Diamond Jubilee rack in Windsor Castle souvenir shop.

On top of all that, there's the little matter of the journey up North in the first place. I've made some enquiries of hire car companies but they all want a sizeable deposit and there's no money for one. So it's a train ride to London, a night on the coach from Victoria to Darlington, and a bus to Barnard Castle from where I'll need a taxi. A Google search reveals three firms that are based in that town. I try Fast Cab first, but none out of the chief executive, managing director, company secretary, practice manager and principal driver of the firm can assist as on that day he'll be holidaying with his mum in Llandudno. Quickride operates an excellent service from the town at remarkably reasonable prices, and the drivers are no strangers to adverse conditions, including snowstorm, forest fire, earthquake, tornado and hurricane, and it's only a pity that the service in question operates out of a town in South Australia with a similar name. Which just leaves Door2Door and its sole practitioner, Mr McMurdo. He does hail from the genuine Barnard Castle and says he can do it, but he's got other jobs on straight after mine and if I'm not there at the time agreed, there's no possibility he'll be able to fulfil my booking. And it doesn't take the brain of Stephen Hawking to mentally list the number of things which could delay my arrival at our rendezvous point, from police assistance being sought to eject secret coach toilet meths drinkers, to a slice of burning toast precipitating an emergency evacuation of Darlington central bus depot. I tell him I'll think about it and will call back.

I consider other possibilities, including hitch-hiking, robbing a bank to pay for a private helicopter, and the much more straightforward option of just slitting my throat. And as I contemplate, Mr Fast Cab is on the phone again. 'If you're desperate, my mate Bazza and his friend Yazza will be passing that way leaving Barnard Castle at around half nine,' he says. 'As long as you've no objection to walking the last five miles and sharing with half a dozen dead chickens and ten buckets of cow poo.'

McMurdo gets the job.

*

It's the afternoon before my planned Saturday ascent of Mickle Fell. As I walk from my new abode to the station my rucksack's too heavy, way too heavy. Granted, there's lots to take. Change of clothes, change of footwear, map, mobile, guide notes, GPS, toiletries … the list of essentials seems endless. But it still shouldn't feel like this and it's only when I examine the backpack after my train's got moving that I realise I've stuff left in my backpack from my Lancashire trip. It's annoying, it's infuriating, but there's nothing I can do – I can't afford to chuck any of it away – and as we make our way in and out of Worthing and on along the coastway route towards Hove I find myself quite enjoying the reliving of my Gragareth antics, courtesy of the descriptive genius of Rufus Cheeseley, and improving the photographic appearance of the man himself. I do believe he looks more distinguished for the glasses and moustache that now adorn his image on the back cover.

Between strokes of the pen I gaze out across the South Downs, bathed in the afternoon sunlight; indeed the sky has been cloudless since dawn, and for the past three days. But I'm not fooled. The promised belt of snow, one of many forecast to hit the country during the last few days before Christmas, is expected to sweep in off the North Sea overnight. Its exact course is as yet unclear and even in the mid-morning forecast they couldn't be certain whether it will march straight across central England and out towards Ireland, buy a kilt and set of bagpipes and take up residence in Scotland, or plunge down into the soft South for afternoon tea at Fortnum & Mason. But wherever it does its worst, we can according to the media expect an above-average sized ration of chaos, commuter misery, transport meltdown and crippling of local infrastructures, with gritters unable to cope and salt supplies running out after the first tentative flurries. Having finished with Cheeseley I'm looking out of the window pretty much all the time, willing every snow forecast to be as Michael Fish-type-accurate as possible, unable to turn my mind to anything else, because it matters, really matters. As I was waiting for the train earlier I'd found a free local newspaper on the station concourse and I'd thought that might while away a few minutes' travelling time, but I've not even got past the headline on the front page. Then again since the headline in question is RESIDENTS ANGER OVER NOISY DUSTCARTS I guess I'm probably not the only one. Walking to Victoria coach station from the railway station after my evening meal, I look up and there's now an ominous absence of stars in the sky. Then I feel wet stuff of some description brushing my hair and my cheeks.

I get into the coach station and it seems that on this Friday night Christmas starts here for the entire coach-travelling population of southern England. You can see it not only in the crowds of people and suitcases and backpacks, but bags and bags and more bags of wrapped presents, and anxious looks on the faces of every intended passenger, terrified of missing the last call for the 2300 to Huddersfield. I find the right gate for my coach and take my place on a bench between a slight Asian woman and a much larger and considerably hairier man whose chin is on a collision course for the belt of his trousers.

At length we're called forward and invited to form an orderly queue. Within seconds the orderly queue has become a giant python, coiling itself round and round the gate 16 waiting area, and round again once more on a lap of honour. Unless some of them don't have tickets, there has to be more people here than even a triple-decker stretch coach could

213

accommodate. It's not till gone half past eleven, when we should have been gliding out of the coach station, that I climb the steps into the vehicle, the driver welcoming me aboard with the warmth of a frozen lemon sorbet in Lapland's new Asda store. There's still a good forty or fifty people behind me in the line and I grab one of only a couple of seats that are left. And then of course the driver's coming through the coach, demanding to see everybody's ticket, summarily ejecting those who've somehow crept on without. It threatens to get nasty. Men are thumping the seat tops, women are bursting into tears. You can't make me get off, I hear in between the rants and sniffs and f-words and c-words and snivels, what about my kids, am I supposed to kip down here all night, and I feel every last drop of the emotion and angst and sheer terror of the ticketless ones, left standing with their suitcases, their backpacks and their bags of gifts. It's quarter past midnight when we at last appear to have a coachload of legitimate passengers and the driver manoeuvres the vehicle away from its stand.

By quarter to one, we're on the motorway.

By two o'clock, it's whiteout.

*

It's now six thirty in the morning. We've not moved since crawling into Tibshelf Services somewhere in the Midlands at about two forty-five. This was a scheduled stop anyway, the driver told us, as if to try and import some normality into the situation. So we'd got out and I'd bought a small tea and packet of two shortcake biscuits. With each bite I could see my bank manager's face turn an ever deeper shade of puce at the thought of such irresponsible and wild living. On return to the coach at the appointed time, I'd heard the driver announce a delay and it was clear from the tenor of his address to us that he had no idea what to do: whether to risk forging on, and possibly getting stuck in an extra-thick jam with extra fruit pieces from which we might just extricate ourselves by next Shrove Tuesday, or to sit here and hope that the promised lull, before the next megafall, gave the gritters time to do a Moses act and part the white sea. Anyway, at four fifteen he'd made the decision which was to wait for the snow to clear and in the meantime if we wanted to leave the coach and throw a further twenty pound note each at another shot of espresso, just don't send the bill to National Express. Despite the reading material I'd brought, I've not been able to bring myself to do a single thing other than just sit there. There's no chance now of arriving by half nine so I've lost the chance of a ride even on the cowdung express. McMurdo's confirmed that he can't now assist me, but, he says, by way of consolation, there's only been a dusting of snow in County Durham and it's sunny and crisp and a perfect morning for walking. And I overhear the driver saying if we'd left Victoria on time we might have beaten the snow altogether; the heaviest snow was in a narrow belt and we just happened to have caught the worst of it at the wrong time. Thanks, just keep rubbing my nose in it, add a sharp object and I might get that third nostril I always wanted. The frustration redoubles as I reflect that in normal conditions a delay of a few hours wouldn't be a problem; after all, the permission to climb the fell is valid for the whole weekend. But these aren't normal conditions. From what I've been able to gather the snow is forecast to be even worse tomorrow. And there'll be the additional aggravation of changing my return coach booking, that is, if the coaches are still running …

It would take one phone call, one piddling phone call, to Steve to ask him to delay publication so I could have another crack at this walk in more congenial conditions. But I can hear his response now as clear as if he were yelling it at three million decibels. It's too much, too much for you to handle Mike, you're still grieving your loss, we really shouldn't have troubled you in the first place, we've got deadlines, we need this book out for the start of the walking season if it's to stand a chance, we'll get someone else on the job right away. And, yes, surprise, I'll have failed again, like I've failed Louise, and Katie, and Natalie, and everything else in my stupid existence. Some are born failures, some achieve failure, and some have failure thrust upon them, but, what neither the Bard nor anyone else said, some thrust it magnificently upon themselves. I remember Louise telling me a bit of stress in one's life was a good thing. I guess that was prompted by my failure to rise from the settee at all between eleven thirty in the morning and ten to twelve at night one FA Cup sixth round day. Only now can I see her point. We do need stress in our lives. The stress involved in this is vast and it's frightening but what's the alternative. Sitting in that black hole that's my new home watching rubbish and eating sandwiches full of rubbish because I can't afford anything apart from rubbish, pleased and relieved that nobody knows where I am, not daring to set foot in the neighbourhood because I'm too flaming petrified of anyone getting to know where I am.

But the fact remains that the shuddering, quaking frustration at our imprisonment within freezing white walls in the middle of nowhere, and with it the paralysing fear that Mickle Fell might be taken away from me, makes me want to retch for England.

We begin to move at seven. There are cheers of delight and relief. And, in his delight or relief or both, the Nigerian man beside me speaks to me for the first time and as we creep along the motorway at a snappy six miles an hour I'm hearing all about his collection of antique toast racks, his cousin's unlawful imprisonment in Namibia, and the reason for the onion-shaped boil on his left earlobe. The motorway is down to one lane and although no snow is actually coming down, there's enough still lying to cause the coach to slither and skid. I think I'd feel safer if we were being pulled by a pack of Siberian huskies. But we're moving in the right direction. Then I notice the snow thinning and we've two lanes at our disposal. The Nigerian is moving on to his brother-in-law's mercenary activity in Togo. At length the snow clears and we arrive at Darlington.

The hands of the town hall clock stand at ten forty-five.

*

I'm left with one hope: that I can negotiate an affordable fixed price fare for a taxi all the way from Darlington to base camp. Even then I'm going to struggle to get back off the fell in the daylight but I've no other options. It's tempting to head straight for the nearest taxi rank but I need some food. I certainly had next to no appetite during the journey but it would be little short of suicidal to attempt Mickle Fell on an empty stomach. I ought to be grateful that I've made it this far, but I feel no more relaxed or positive than I did at ten past five this morning when a couple at the front of the coach tried to initiate a sing-song. I'd heard better versions of the *Skye Boat Song* in the hospital wing of our local cat and rabbit rescue centre. Thank God for the *Yellow Submarine* which had torpedoed it so everyone could get back to sleep.

Perhaps it wouldn't seem so bad if I felt that others were sharing my discomfort. But as I walk through Darlington's main street in search of sustenance on this, the last Saturday before Christmas, it seems I'm the only one not looking happy, relaxed and excited. A crowd of rosy-cheeked children line up to be received by Santa Claus, the width of his avuncular grin more than matched by the length not only of his false beard but also his very genuine ear hair. *Silent Night* is being belted out *fortissimo* by the massed bands of the Bishop Auckland Chorus, in front of a Christmas tree that groans under the weight of a thousand baubles and fairy lights and parcels and stretches high enough to split the ozone layer. Bouncers stand outside Marks & Spencer to prevent excessive overcrowding in the mince pie, chocolate yule log and luxury cracker departments. A trio of teenage girls with denim belts, sorry, skirts, exit screaming with delight from an accessory store, as eager to show off their newly-purchased reindeer antlers with gold and silver sparkles as they are to flaunt their exposed knees and thighs. An elderly cloth-capped gent in a fading red coat with a cigarette hanging from the corner of his mouth stands drooling over his roast chestnuts. The sunshine, coming from a perfect blue sky, has made the thin layer of white covering the adjacent park almost blinding, while the flecks of snow on the bushes and shrubs have turned them into huge chunks of Stollen cake. It's like every silly romantic dream of Christmas come to life, but I feel as though it's a club, a special society for special people, and I've not even got a temporary pass.

There's a bakery doing hot pies and teas and coffees in the main precinct but the queue's stretching out of the door. I ask the guy at the end of the line if there's anything similar nearby and he gives me directions to a place three minutes' walk away. I locate it and take a look inside. The walls have been thoughtfully plastered in a passable impression of sheep vomit. The fried doughnuts are swimming in fat so deep that I wonder they're not equipped with snorkelling devices and flippers. And the accumulation of dog ends immediately outside the door reminds me of a film I once saw depicting an explosion in Battersea. I need to make a move soon and I can't face trudging around in search of other food shops or cafes so settle for a bargain bunch of eight extra-large bananas at the fruit market just outside. They're cheap as well as nutritious so they'll do me. I stuff all but one of them into my backpack, keeping the biggest one out for consumption in the taxi. I decide to get some chocolate as well. There's a newsagents nearby and after I've bought and packed two King Size Mars Bars I check out the weather forecast in the local daily paper. For much of the day it's supposed to stay dry with some good spells of sunshine, but another, much more vigorous belt of snow is forecast to spread across all areas of northern England later this afternoon, with some drifting possible especially in the east of the region. Newspaper forecasts often get it wrong. Perhaps this one is. But then the local weather comes over the shop radio. And this not only confirms the newspaper's tidings of great joy about today, but promises that the snow will intensify tonight to produce the worst blizzards for twenty years across the whole of northern England, persisting into Sunday. In fact there's a severe weather warning in force for the whole of Northumberland, County Durham and Cumbria from five tonight till midday tomorrow. The snow will clear gradually during tomorrow afternoon but the main feature will be the cold; we can look forward to basking in maximum temperatures of minus six Celsius, and with the windchill it'll feel more like minus twenty-six. And if that wasn't enough to have us running for our swimsuits and suntan oil, there's to be a further period of heavy snow starting in the early hours of Monday, bringing significant disruption to the morning commute.

Even as I emerge from the shop I see the sun has become more watery. Then I look up and see a layer of white cloud is now making inroads into the blue of the sky and I also notice a darker band of cloud approaching from the direction of the North Sea.

For a moment I panic. It's madness. It's ridiculous. Buzz off home now. It so happens that to get to the town's main taxi rank, which is outside the railway station, I have to go back past the coach station and there's a coach to London waiting. There's a long queue for it and by the time I've clambered aboard I'm certain that the chances of the driver finding a seat for me are as great as Pope Gregory the Forty-Ninth being elected Vice President of the Virginia Water Ladies' Sailing Club. But the driver says he's a couple of seats spare and although he's not supposed to sell or swap tickets he tells me I look a sorry mess and anybody with an ounce of common sense who doesn't need to be up North tonight will want to separate themselves from it as soon as possible. I produce my ticket and he says he's prepared to be flexible. He points at an empty seat just behind him, and no sooner have I plonked my backpack onto it than I see a hot drinks trolley working its way down the aisle with sixteen different types of coffee and Danish pastries the size of rugby balls.

Thirty seconds later I'm walking off towards the taxi rank.

There are three cars waiting and I go up to the one at the front. It takes a moment to engage the attention of the driver, a heavily-built woman with a shiny black puffa jacket and messy ginger beard, her conversation with a gum-chewing bystander evidently far more important than driving passengers. Finally she deigns to glance round in my direction and in answer to my enquiry produces a typed tariff list. She's asking for about four times more than the combined bus and taxi would have been, and I'm conscious I will need that extra simply to survive over the coming days and weeks. I just mutter 'Sorry' and walk to the next vehicle. The driver of this one shakes his head as soon as I've got the words 'just beyond Middleton-in-Teesdale' out of my gob. So I go to the third. He's rather less amply constructed than Madam Puffa and sports a brown leather jacket, white shirt and green tie. He gives me a smile as I approach, but there's a certain diffidence written on his face and again I fear the worst.

'Before you ask,' he says in broad Scots, 'I'm afraid I've just got a job.' I hear a crackle and fuzz of sound somewhere inside his vehicle. 'Excuse me a wee sec.' He speaks into a microphone. 'Aye, got it. Travis Gardens to Romaldkirk. Single passenger. I'm on my way.'

I watch as he begins to manoeuvre out of the rank.

218

Romaldkirk. Why is that name familiar. Romaldkirk, Romaldkirk, Romaldkirk. I pull my map from the outer pocket of my backpack and open it. There it is. It's just short of Middleton-in-Teesdale.

The guy's on his way. And a second later, I'm after him.

*

It's clear that if and when he can get up any speed at all, I can say goodnight Vienna. But he can't. He moves at a crawl down the street away from the station, and I'm running faster than I've run since as an acne-ridden schoolkid I was conscripted to compete in the 200 metres handicap, but he seems to be accelerating a bit, and I know that if he goes straight through those lights at the end of the street, I'm knackered. They are green and I'm shouting and yelling at them to change. A van ahead of him seems to take time to exit the street and although my man's moving, he's had to slow and I'm making up ground, but then he's come up to the lights, and they're still green, and he goes through them, and bears round to the left. And I'm about to throw myself to the ground in despair and defeat but then I see his brake lights coming on and he's slowing down again and I'm gaining on him, gaining on him, gaining on him. But he's now moving and although I've never run like this as an adult before, certainly not with a million ton backpack, so that I'm panting and gasping and wheezing and I'm feeling glands of sweat where I've never felt them before, I'm losing him. Then thank the Lord his brake lights are on again and I see him drawing up at another set of lights and they're on red, red, red, stay red, and I'm yelling inside, please God, whoever you are, if you do nothing else for me in my stupid miserable life, keep them on red. Twenty-five yards, twenty yards, fifteen yards, ten, seven, five, now it's feet, twelve feet, ten feet, eight feet, and now the lights are on red and amber and he edges forward.

And then I look and see I'm still holding the banana.

I hurl it. It hits his rear passenger window with a bang. And it causes him to look round and swerve into the left turning, half on and half off the pavement, and brake. I run up to the passenger door and he leans over and winds down the window.

'What in God's name do you think you're doing?'

For a few seconds I can't speak. Sweat is pouring from my face and I'm panting. The half-starved bloodhound desperate for the last bone in the abattoir.

'You going to Romaldkirk?' I eventually churn out.

'Romaldkirk House.'

'Not Romaldkirk village?

'No. A house. About a mile away. Why?' He sees my despair. 'What's the matter? Was it the village you wanted?'

'Bit further than that. About … about eight miles beyond Middleton.' And then the lucidity disintegrates into complete and desperate submission. 'I need your help … I so need your help.'

He takes a deep breath. 'Tell me what you can afford.'

*

He's shaken my hand and told me his name's Fraser, and he's charging me no more than what the fare would be from Barnard Castle to base camp, in other words, the fare I'd budgeted for. He tells me this won't be the first time he's gone the extra mile in every sense. The other drivers all know he undercuts them and they hate him for it but he says it won't change him. 'If you stop loving people, you might as well jump off the cliff edge right now,' he says. I feel as though instead of driving a taxi he ought to be standing in a pulpit, announcing the next hymn is number 431 and on Saturday it's the St Bridget's Over 70's Club Annual Trip To Margate.

He's picked up and dropped his pre-arranged job swiftly enough, and now that it's just us two again he's asking lots about me and I'm kind of sorry that we are just passing strangers. As far as Barnard Castle the scenery's homely and unremarkable, presenting no obvious challenges even for the novice walker. Then it all changes. We pass round the edge of Middleton-in-Teesdale and now Darlington feels like another part of the country altogether as we strike out into moorland, the only buildings consisting of isolated farms and barns, where every ruined outhouse and crumbling sheepfold is a reminder of how hard folk who work this land have to toil for every penny. And although I told myself not to think about it, I realise I could quite possibly be walking all the way back along here, and I think I'm about to wet myself. It occurred to me that hitching back might be a possibility but the M25 this is not and I've only counted three cars since we left Middleton-in-Teesdale. The ground rises steeply to the right, the hillsides no longer cosy green, lush fields tumbling into tree-shaded brooks and streams, but disapproving grey, tolerating rather than welcoming the tufts of grass and heather that dot the stark, scarred waves of rock and stones and boulders. Last night's modest fall of snow that McMurdo mentioned evidently hasn't travelled to these parts, as there's no trace of it even on the highest tops, but it's clear the next consignment of white stuff won't be long coming; the sky is now mostly white, and the sun is becoming weaker with every passing minute. Fraser seems to sense my anxiety. 'You don't need to worry,' he says. 'There's no way we'll be getting any snow till after dark. The clarity up there will be perfect. You don't want it too bright. This is the best weather you could ever ask for.' Just occasionally the sun disappears altogether and each time it does I feel my heartbeat quicken, and the screams from the sensationalist press begin to pound my eardrums. But Fraser continues to calm and reassure, and he's slowing down and applying the indicator and we've reached the border. It has all the hallmarks of military ownership and control: severe metal signs, posts, flagpoles and notice boards crammed with small print doubtless consisting of byelaws contravention of which will lead to perpetrators being shot on sight. And on every side, precipitous walls of grey create a sullen and malevolent guard, defying anyone to call this landscape beautiful or noble.

Fraser turns the car round in readiness for his return trip. I give him the fare we've agreed then reach down to the footwell and pick up my backpack.

'That looks heavy,' Fraser observes.

'I'll be okay.'

'Why make life tough for yourself?' He reaches out his left hand and pulls one of the zips of the pack. 'Tell you what. Chuck all the stuff you don't need and I'll bin it. Or I can send it on. If you want.'

I look out and the sun's disappeared again. 'Er ... no. It's okay ... really ... I'll be okay...'

'Don't be ridiculous. I mean it.'

'Honestly, I'm fine.'

'Come on. Must be some rubbish in there you don't need. Open it up. Not leaving till you do.'

So I open it. On top is the bargain bunch of bananas which has doubled the weight of the rucksack contents in one easy lesson. I need those. I dip into my backpack again and produce the debris of my Tibshelf excesses, the newly moustachio-ed Cheeseley's guide to Gragareth, and a mud-encrusted sock about to open its very own wildlife park and Gorgonzola factory. It can all go in the bin as far as I'm concerned. Then, having chucked them down in the footwell, I plunge my hand into the backpack once more. This time I find myself gripping the free paper that I never got round to reading and have even less urge to read now.

It doesn't seem to want to break free from the rest of the contents of the backpack. It goes head-to-head with the bunch of bananas. It's a solid bunch of bananas which isn't going to give up that easily. There's a rip and as I remove the newspaper from the backpack, the front page is torn to shreds, leaving the story on page three exposed to view.

I'm about to throw it into the footwell with the other stuff. Then I happen to read the headline.

DEATH CRASH HORROR VICTIMS NAMED

And I read on.

The driver and passenger of a vehicle which crashed on the Chichester bypass, killing both, have been named.

Paul Faraday, aged 45, of Nottingham, had been clocked speeding during a routine police check on Sunday 7th December. He attempted to evade the police but during the subsequent chase his Mercedes careered off the road and smashed into the side of a petrol station, killing him and his child passenger instantly.

.

19

Birks Crag(n) – Any summit which, on reaching it, you think is the one you're aiming for but isn't

Crianlarich(adj) – Having unknowingly scaled what is a **Birks Crag**, how you feel when, having boasted in the pub that evening that you reached it and how you reached it, it's made clear to you that you didn't

I just freeze and let the paper drop down into the footwell.

'What's wrong?' he asks.

'It's … it's … no, it's nothing.'

'Do you want to tell me?'

'No, honestly, it's … it's nothing, no.'

'Looks like a bit more than nothing to me, Michael.'

I bend down and pick up the paper then thrust it into his lap, placing my forefinger on the report. 'My daughter. My adopted daughter. He's killed her.'

He looks down at the report, then turns to me. 'The child passenger was your daughter?'

'Mmm.'

'And you didn't know?'

'Nothing. Nothing.' I take the paper from his lap and throw it to the floor. 'This monster, this … this callous monster, Faraday, he stole my wife and daughter from me, I never knew where they were, cut me off from them altogether, he's subjected my wife to this vile, sustained domestic abuse and he's come down to tell me she's dead, only what he doesn't say is that he's murdered her, and all the while my little girl's sitting outside in the passenger seat and he won't let me see her, won't let me talk to her, just like I don't exist, I've just been airbrushed from her life, and now he's … he's killed himself and he's killed her, killed my only child …' And now the power of speech vanishes, my emotions robbing me of further coherence, further sense, further anything, and I just sit there, my head wrapped in my hands.

Then I hear the roar of the car engine.

'What's happening?'

'I'm driving you back to Darlington.'

'Sorry?'

'I said I'm driving you back to Darlington. It's all right, I'm hardly going to charge you. I'll put you on the next train home. If you need help with that, we'll sort it out.'

He starts to manoeuvre out of the layby.

'Wait.'

He stops again.

'Eh?'

'I ... I don't want to go back.'

'I think you do. I think you need to go back. There's ... there's ...'

'There's what?'

'Stuff. Stuff you need to ... need to sort out. She's your daughter, Michael.'

'What's going to happen this evening? Tonight? That can't wait till tomorrow morning?'

'Michael, that's hardly the point. You've lost your daughter. You need to stop. Put life aside. Forget the world. It's what people do.'

'I'm not ready to go back yet. To do all that yet.'

'You're in shock.' Now he begins to move away. 'Come on. Soon get you back to Darlington. Get you on the train before it closes in.'

'I want to get out. I want to do the walk.'

'Trust me. You don't.'

'Yes I do.' I reach out with my right hand and yank the handbrake up. We skid to a halt.

He yells. 'You moron, you stupid stupid moron, what the hell ... !' He turns to face me and this time there's wrath as well as fear in his eyes. Then the wrath and the fear give way to a look of pity. 'I'm sorry. I'm sorry. I'm sorry.' He sighs and mops his brow and suddenly I'm the one feeling sorry for him.

He wraps both his hands round my right hand. We must stay there like that in silence for about five minutes. He's the one who breaks the spell. 'Michael, this just isn't ... isn't right. You need to get home. That's what's right. Surely you must see that.'

'Who's to say what's right and what isn't?' The lawyer in me springs up once more. Counsel for the defence daring the court to think the unthinkable. 'Do you know what Louise, my wife, said about me? She said I had no beliefs, no imagination, no adventure at all. She told me I was a loser. She told me Katie thought I was a loser. They were spot on. If I get up this mountain, it'll prove I've changed, that I'm someone. And I can go back and tell them that I wasn't such a loser after all.' I hear myself laughing. 'My God, it's ridiculous. You don't talk to dead people, I've never believed in all that ... but ... but if I don't do it, I'll always be that loser. I know I've got to do all the stuff you say. But I've got a lifetime to

224

do that, for God's sake. I just want to do this right here, right now.' I look straight into his eyes. 'Do you see?'

He frowns. 'I don't know, I really don't. I think I ... you ... it's ...' Out of his depth. He's used to banal conversation with his fares, the weather, the state of the traffic, next week's holiday in Fuerteventura, and I've bowled him an unplayable ball. Easier to dodge it, hope for a gentler delivery next time, fall back on bland practicalities. 'You ... you've got to be sensible, and look after yourself. Surely that's got to come first. This isn't Oxford Street. It's harsh, hostile. If you don't come with me now, you're going to have to find your own way back. I've got pick-ups all afternoon. I mean, I can try and cancel them, but ...'

'It's fine. I'll ... I'll be okay.'

'I really hate leaving you like this.'

'Like I said. It's fine.' And a moment later I'm spilling out of the car and slamming the door and walking off along the road towards the boundary paraphernalia. I'm done with the kindness and the pity and the charity. I can just about cope with me. But that is all.

*

The footpath isn't properly signed. In fact to begin with there's a fence to climb over and I feel as though I'm trespassing. I doubt it'll prove to be the toughest obstacle I have to face this afternoon. At least the weather's holding. There's no more grey cloud in the sky than what I saw in Darlington, and the sun's still trying to find a way through the columns of white but it's cold, a cold that bites and stings and hurts.

I trudge uphill through rough grass beside a stone wall, with only the merest apology for a path in places. The so-called path then drops down, and it's exasperating, maddening, infuriating to be losing some of the precious height we've gained. I shake my fist at the laughing, unforgiving heavens. Then I grit my teeth. Just do this, Mike, just get up to the top of this mountain, and after you've done it you can go back home. Go home and start doing all that stuff people do that you're supposed to do. I arrive at another crossing fence which presents me with another gymnastic exercise. I lose my stone wall, but I do have an adjoining fence which the route guide I've downloaded tells me will be my "crutch" for much of the rest of the way. Should the weather deteriorate significantly it could be a lifesaver. And looking ahead, I can see the unmistakable summit of Mickle Fell. I feel a new sense of purpose and belief and my pace quickens.

There's another climb, then another wretched descent, and a sign indicating the point at which the path enters the army firing range. I kind of expected to see a barrier, an observation turret, a couple of soldiers and a rapacious German Shepherd, but there's nothing. It's as if on this Saturday afternoon so close to Christmas, the need for military personnel to fill stockings and populate festive dinner tables outweighs the risks associated with unauthorised entry to the restricted area. One thing which has frightened the life out of me since I got the go-ahead from the authorities is the possibility of being turned away by some officious sentry because the permit's been invalidated by a spelling error in line 673 of the terms and conditions. Now I'm wondering if getting the permit was even necessary and I'm wishing there was someone there because the solitude and the silence are crushing me. I cross a beck, using a footbridge provided, then return to the fence and keep walking beside it. The going is reasonably easy for a time, but I know it can't last and it doesn't. There are further becks to cross, and then a succession of peat troughs, or hags as they're known. As the route guide says, "better to take a long way round than risk injury." There's no path as such; I just have to make sure the fence remains within sight I come to another beck, wider this time without the luxury of a footbridge. I take a deep breath and splash through fast-flowing chocolate brown water, and the reward for my successful fording is what feels like a vertical climb beside the fence. I've walked about two miles and I've reached what the guide calls a key moment on the hike, a point called Hanging Seal where another fence comes in from the left and there's a sharp right turn. "Mickle Fell is now that much closer," my description confirms. "You can start to feel you really will make it."

I look up and see the summit challenging me to take it on, but there's so much climbing to come and the thought of how exhausted I'll feel when I get even near the top seems to place a hundredweight of chewing gum on the soles of each of my boots. I tear open my backpack and force down two bananas and the Mars Bars. I've no appetite for them, and I wonder if they're going to come straight back up, but I need fuel; my petrol gauge is already showing a pump sign flashing on and off. The rigours of the journey from Sussex to this point haven't just caught up, they've encircled me and are strangling me. And I look up at the sky and I don't like what I see. There's been a subtle increase in the strength of the wind which is surging down from the north-east, the sun has given up trying to find a way through the white cloud, and the white itself has now acquired a thin cloak of light grey. The wind comes in bursts, sometimes shouting, sometimes moaning its anger and resentment at my audacity in putting off my grieving and mourning. I check my watch and it's well past one thirty and getting back to the road later than four fifteen isn't an option.

226

Now comes another descent, and it's a steep one. Clinging to the fence I veer one way, then another, and I'm fed up with the taxi-ing and I just want to take off. At last I'm heading northwards towards the side of the fell. I look around at the lifeless, featureless landscape, a rolling void of random heather, grass and peat, tortured by the wind and the rain, uncompromising in its savage unformed starkness. Such raw masculinity in the surroundings had thrilled me back in May with Natalie. I feel no thrill this afternoon, more a grudging respect for its majesty and deep awareness of my total vulnerability.

The fence remains a staunch ally and I find myself feeling a connection with the poor beggars who constructed it. Whether it was for landowners or the military or for idiots like me, who knows, but I owe them, God knows I owe them. "The going looks easier than it is," my description tells me, and it really does feel like a case of two steps forward, one back, as I claw my way across what feels like the biggest cold bath sponge in the world. Water splashes around and into my boots, while the clumps of long tufty grass and peat hags line up to provide a sequence of obstructions that would test the patience of someone actually doing this for enjoyment. The only company is the occasional grouse, not that their legendary "Go back" call would inspire anyone for the fight. Ahead, the fence rises in a straight line; at least the way forward is clear but the gradient just starts to get ridiculous and before long I find I'm needing my hands to assist me. The description recommends that walkers stop frequently to get their breath back "and admire the views which are opening up to the south." I am stopping every third or fourth step, not out of choice but out of cold necessity, and breathing comes easier as a result, but the last thing I feel I want to do is look back and enjoy the view. This isn't about seeking an aesthetic experience or even replicating the feelings of wonder I experienced on Yes Tor or on my way down to Scarth Gap. It's a struggle to prove I'm more than what my late wife and late daughter really thought I was. And as I collapse to the ground for the sixth time in fifty yards, and feel the tears spraying my cheeks, I realise just how right the girls were about me. A better man, any man, would have learnt years ago to face such obstacles as these and crush them under his feet. These are the tears of a loser.

Surely there can't be more. But there is more. The fence veers to the right and the gradient intensifies. It's like holding onto the edge of the world; I feel if I let go, I could easily just roll back down, not just to the start, but beyond the start, into the depths of a bottomless abyss. After yet another stop, and another collapse, and tears of frustration, I reach a crossing fence and a stile in the middle. Again there's no signpost but the existence of a stile suggests someone's walked this way before, so over I go, and I'm on the summit plateau and I can dare to believe the worst is over.

There's still a bit to do. I now have to turn half-right and make my way across the plateau; soon there's a green path which in the context of all that's gone before feels like the royal red carpet, and suddenly I'm not just walking, I'm marching to the Mickle Fell summit cairn with a flourish of invisible trumpets. And as I approach the cairn the views open up in all directions and although my eyes are still smarting from my tears I permit myself a gasp. Before me is the whole of the Mickle ridge opening out dramatically to the east, the Cow Green Reservoir to the north, the golf ball summit on Dun Fell to the north-west, and a banquet of moorland, valley and mountain scenery to the south. The grey cloak is getting greyer and even this early in the afternoon I can sense that darkness just can't wait to take hold, but as I walk up to the summit cairn and stand there and just stare out, I can say, Katie, Louise, yes, Isabel as well, I did it, I really really did it..

I munch two more bananas then extract my phone and I point it anywhere and everywhere, taking photo after photo. Then having got every view and every angle I can think of, I stand and stare once more.

And as I stand, I become aware that I'm not alone. Fifty yards away, seated against one of the summit boulders and sporting a bright orange coat, is another walker.

Traditional walkers' etiquette would suggest that I go and say hi. Not that I give a damn for walkers' etiquette right now. But my yearning for reassurance that there's somebody besides me left in the world, or in the universe even, leads me to stride over to greet them and congratulate them for having got up here, and offer to accompany them back to base.

And as I approach, the walker looks up.

It can't be. It's either someone who looks like her or it's her ghost or I'm simply imagining the whole thing.

But as I see this walker rising and tottering towards me, with glowing orange cheeks, lime-green eyes and jungle blonde hair, the scepticism melts away.

228

20

Vellan Drang(n) – accumulation of pieces of peel-off part of blister bandages found at the bottom of a rucksack during annual clear-out of same

There's a vacant look in her eyes as though she in her turn can't be sure it really is me. Then she runs up and throws her arms around me and kisses me again and again on the lips and the cheeks, then she holds me closer and kisses me again. Then she releases her grip and takes my hand, and we're standing there, together, not saying a word, looking out to the vastness and the savagery of the moors and the mountains and the valleys beneath the steel of the sky.

I'm the first one to break the silence. 'How long have you been up here?'

'About two and a half hours.'

'Waiting for me?'

'What do you think.' She doesn't smile as she says it. It's as if I should have expected to find her here all along. 'I didn't see how else I'd find you. I tried to phone. But I couldn't get hold of you. Not even a voicemail.'

'So how did you know I'd be here?'

'I rang Steve,' she says. 'He said he'd been trying to get hold of you as well. Then he remembered you were doing this today.'

'I nearly bottled it. Might not have made it.'

'I knew you'd make it.' A blast of wind sends a quiver through her hair. She tightens her grasp on my hand. 'I couldn't have waited much longer. I'm way behind as it is. Need to make a move. I've a lift at four.'

'Toby?'

She shakes her head. 'A friend. Rachel. I'm spending a few days with her in her house in York. She'd arranged to meet some old uni friends in Durham today, drove me out here.' She looks down. 'You don't need to ask. I'm not with Toby any more.'

'I'm sorry.'

I expect her to fold me in her arms again but she removes her arm from me and points to her watch. 'We should start walking back.'

'Can't we just wait up here a bit longer.'

She doesn't reply for a moment, and just smiles. But there's an uneasiness in her eyes. 'We need to go,' she says. 'Concentrate on getting off the fell in the daylight. We'll talk more when we're safe.'

'Please. Just a second.'

We stay there for perhaps three or four more minutes. I need so much longer. I need the time she's had, and the same again: time to absorb every detail of this terrifying pageant of harsh hills and rich heather and peaks and valleys, a landscape of aggression and harshness with an eye to the everlasting, a landscape that laughs at the pettiness of human worries and concerns. It's too much for three or four years, never mind minutes.

And now without another word she's beginning to walk across the plateau in the direction I've taken, and I find myself lagging in her wake. I have to run to catch her up. We cross the stile and begin the almost vertical plunge, and she guides me down with the expert touch of an Everest sherpa. She indicates the optimum way round obstacles. She holds my hand to help me tackle the most obstructive and aggressive peat accumulations. She reassures me that despite the ever-darkening skies, we'll be well away from the fell before the snow starts again. We're walking at twice, maybe three times the pace with which I made my ascent. The light's now declining and self-preservation has come in unnoticed and taken hold. At least the wind's helping, an angry predator turned reluctant friend. And as it carries me forward I'm beginning to see a way through, and a way back. I may have a hundred light years to travel but with Natalie's support and love these are my first blundering, hesitant steps.

And at last we're back at that footbridge over that first beck. It feels no distance from there out of the military range and I know we're winning. We stride on with increasing speed. 'We're back on schedule,' she says. 'We can stop for a couple of secs if you want.'

She throws me a reassuring smile and slips her rucksack off her back. She drops it to the floor and indicates a raised tuft of grass and we sit down. I'm facing back towards the summit of Mickle Fell, wondering how I've managed to get up there, asking myself if I really did. And then I glance at her and she's looking straight into my eyes.

'I love you so much,' I tell her.

She kisses me on the cheek. 'Thank you, Mike.'

'I really do.'

We sit there and sit there while the wind grumbles around us but the wind's the only answer I'm getting.

'I so need to know you'll love me back. So need to.' I try to kiss her lips but she turns her head to stop me.

'Mike, I really want to say it …'

'But.'

The wind is now constant.

'Mike, there's something you need to know. The reason Toby left me.'

I take a deep breath and stiffen. 'Tell me.'

She points down towards her stomach. 'He never wanted our child.'

*

And as we move on she explains. Was all going so well for them. Loved Canada, the people, the cities, the scenery, loved everything. Knew they were good together and would be staying together, not married but happy as they were, long-term partners. And only a couple of weeks in, late September time, she'd told him she wanted a child, wanted to be a mum. They'd discussed children before and he wasn't that keen. But by now she was getting worried if they left it much longer she'd be too late. The upshot was she won him round.

'I told him his life wouldn't really change after baby was born,' she goes on. 'He could still go off walking if he wanted. I wasn't going to tether him to our front door handle. I loved him, wanted him so much I was prepared to do more than my fair share. To be honest, neither of us believed it would happen anytime soon. Then very quickly I started getting all the signs and symptoms, and yes, the tests confirmed it. Found out early November. About five and a half weeks gone. It was the best feeling ever.'

She removes a bar of Kendal Mint Cake from the side pocket of her backpack, breaks off a piece and passes it to me

'How did he take it?' I ask.

'He was thrilled. At the time. He suggested we went away for the weekend to celebrate. A final bit of outdoor adventure with some mountain climbing before it got too much for me. I'd never done any proper climbing before, I was that scared, but he kept going on, it's not difficult, that I'd be okay. Saturday was fine, decent weather, easy climbs, so on Sunday he said, let's do something a bit more advanced. It was sunny, but there'd been a big storm in the night and the rock was slippery. Shouldn't have risked it but he insisted. And we came to this step and I lost my footing and tumbled over. God, it was one hell of a crash. My first thought was the baby. Thought I'd lost it, I really had. I wasn't hurt myself, just shaken but I said to Toby I wanted to get straight to hospital to get checked over.'

I bite off a piece of the mint cake and feel the bombs of flavour explode in my mouth. 'Sounds sensible.'

'Not to him. He got all funny about it. Didn't lose his temper. He never did. I almost wish he had done, might have cleared the air, but he didn't. Just sulked, and avoided eye contact. Kept on about how we might not get to do this climb again, how much he'd looked forward to it, how the weather was perfect for it, how much we'd spent on the hotel for nothing.

And I asked him what was more important, that or our unborn child, and he just clammed up.'

'So what did they say? Was the baby damaged?'

Her pace seems to quicken with every step. 'Doctors couldn't find anything wrong. But they were very cautious, very non-committal. Baby was so tiny and they couldn't rule out complications later. Or rather wouldn't. I think they were just covering their backs. But because they didn't pronounce baby A1 there and then, it really freaked Toby out. He never said a single word on the way home. And when we got back I kind of lost it with him, told him he was behaving like a baby himself. Then he came out with it. He said he didn't want the baby, he wanted me to get rid of it, and maybe this was Nature's way of saying it wasn't the right time for us. I knew what was going through his mind, the worst case, complications, hospitals, tests, deformities. He saw his walking and climbing schedules ruined. Said he kept on getting these visions of being cooped up at home with a small child and resentful of not being able to walk. It was late. I went up to bed, told him we'd talk again when he'd calmed down. Hoped he'd have sorted out his head next morning. Then when I got up next morning he'd gone.'

She breaks off another piece of the mint cake and slides it into her mouth, then replaces the rest of the bar in the side pocket. The cold is now weighing on my cheeks and round my neck and it's an effort to look into her eyes, but I don't need to, I can feel her tears and her anguish.

'He left me a note to say he needed time. I'd never felt so lonely, so scared. I didn't know where he was, anything. After a couple of days he came back. We muddled along for a week or so but that's all it was, muddling, both of us tiptoeing round it. Couldn't even look one another in the eye. Then one morning over breakfast he said he'd thought about it and said either I got rid of baby or he got rid of me. And when I said I couldn't agree to terminate he said he wanted me to leave. I phoned mum and dad and came more or less straight home. Stayed down in Cornwall with them. I'd not been back long and he rang. I thought he was going to say sorry, beg for me to come back. Then in the next breath he said he was seeing someone else. Someone who ... who ...' And now she's sobbing. '...Who wasn't going to suffocate him like our sick baby would do.'

'He didn't mean it.'

'He meant it, Mike. Trust me, he meant it. I've never cried so much in my life.'

'What about the baby? Is it okay?'

'My doctor thinks so, yes. Not that that's ever going to be enough for Toby. I thought long and hard about whether I should actually terminate.

Thought that might get him back. But then I thought, what if I never got another chance ... I'm ... I'm not going to terminate, Mike. I want the baby.'

'So where are you going to go? How will you manage?'

'I don't know, Mike. I just don't know.' She sighs. 'It's got more complicated.'

'How?'

'Not long after moving to Canada with Toby, I got a bit of casual reporting work. Freelance, very informal, pocket money really. Not sure whether I should have been declaring it. All very casual. But I loved it. Really loved it. And this girl I was doing the work for, Elaine, rang me a few days ago, says she wants me to do a lot more. She's talking about a proper contract, everything. She's having a house party over Christmas and she's invited me over to spend Christmas and New Year there then stay on and work for her. Possibly permanently.'

'Will they let you? Permanently, I mean?'

'I don't know. I've got to look into it. Not really had time to let it sink in. But even just Christmas in Canada would be brilliant. And if that doesn't work out, and I end up coming back to England, Elaine's invited me to go over and stay with her next May and do a bit of travelling. A last fling before baby arrives.'

'When are you flying back for Christmas?'

'Day after tomorrow,' she says. 'I travel to Heathrow tomorrow afternoon, booked on a flight first thing Monday. The thing is ... is ...'

'What?'

'I've ... I've not decided whether I want to go yet.'

'You've booked your flight and you've not decided.'

'I wanted to ... to check first.' I see her turning towards me but she avoids my eye. 'Check whether, you know, you and I, whether there was something ... something there ... between us ...'

'Nat ...'

'I knew I was taking a bit of a risk coming up here today,' she says, feeling her stomach. 'I knew you might reject me. I knew even if you still loved me you might not be able to cope with all this. I couldn't blame you if you weren't interested in being a stepdad and decided you couldn't take that on. You've got your own adopted daughter, I know you've got difficulties with her, but ...'

'My daughter's dead.'

'I'm sorry?'

'Katie's dead.'

I hear the scrape of her boot on the ground as she applies the brakes.

*

I turn to look at her and now she's the one whose mouth opens and who gazes out to space in shocked silence.

'How ... how did she die?' she stammers.

I tell her how. 'And it's all my fault. All my stupid stupid fault.'

'What do you mean?'

'I was the duff parent, wasn't I, the one who stands by and lets my daughter go, leaves her at the mercy of this monster, this evil despicable monster who deliberately takes his own life even if he knows he's going to kill her too ...'

'You can't be sure of that.'

'He knew what he was doing. I'm certain.'

'This was never your fault.' She wraps me in her arms. 'Never your fault.'

'It's all my fault. I tell him I was phoning the police. He sees them. Bang. And as for Louise, that was my fault, God rest her ... whatever ...'

'She's not died as well?'

I just nod.

She bursts into tears. She wails. Begs me to tell her it's not true. And now she's not only draping her arms round me, she's rolling her tear-stained cheeks round and round my shoulders and my chest. Everything is why. 'Why didn't you tell me before? Why did you just let me go on? Why didn't you tell me? Why didn't you say something? Anything?'

'Never the right time. Never the right words.' Now we're both howling in each other's arms.

She struggles free. 'Mike, I know this is hard. But we need to be moving. Need to get back to the road.' A more determined expression seems to sweep over her face. She shines the torch along the direction we're headed in. 'When we're back Rachel can pick us both up and you'll stay with us tonight. Not just tonight. As long as you need. I'll put my plans on hold. Elaine will understand. We can talk and talk and talk. That is if you want to. Or you can sit and weep and I'll just sit and listen and be there for you just as long as you need. Just ... just keep walking.'

'It's fine. I'll be okay.'

'It's not fine.' She starts to move then seems to check herself. 'Look,' she says. 'I'm there for you, I always will be there for you. Whatever happens, you're mine, I'm yours. Okay?'

'Okay.'

And she kisses me.

234

*

We're on the move again. There's an almost frightening urgency in Natalie's pace. She's now walking ahead, the squelch of her boots on the soggy heather becoming louder with each step. I'm struggling to catch up and as I try and make up some ground I stumble and I'm crashing to the floor. I don't think I'm hurt, it's shock more than anything, but the shock causes me to cry out and the next moment Natalie's there beside me.

'Get up,' she says. There's an edge in her voice I last heard when she was telling me I had to go to Bristol. It stings me into rising to my feet. 'Come on. We're running out of light. We've got work to do.' And she starts walking. 'Stay with me.'

We walk in silence for a few minutes.

'Remember when it was me getting you off a mountain?' I ask.

'Uh?'

'Pen-y-fan. After you fell flat on your face.'

If anything her pace seems to increase. She glances at her watch. 'God, this is going to be tight. Keep walking. Just … just keep walking.'

A blast of wind threatens to lift my head off my shoulders. I know I can trust Natalie. But looking up and seeing how the sky and hillsides have dissolved into a uniform mouldy grey I feel tension in my muscles and tension in my heart. I need to defuse it. Introduce the mundane, the everyday, the ordinary, the life going on out there, outside the prison walls of snow that are waiting to encircle us. I pick a detail at random.

'Can you remember the name of the place we stayed the night after Pen-y-fan?' I ask her. 'When I told you about Isabel?'

'Hold on a sec.' She stops, unzips her backpack and produces a torch. She switches the torch on and the sharp beam of light it produces seems to accentuate the deep greyness around us. Then she zips up her backpack, shoulders it again and we're moving from nought to sixty in three seconds. 'That's it, Mike. Just keep going. Stay with me. Okay.'

'Well?'

'Well what?'

'Where we stayed.'

'I don't know. Marlborough maybe?'

'It wasn't Marlborough. We stopped there next morning.'

'If you say so, Mike. Don't know.'

It's coming back. Detail, lots of detail, lost in the frantic demands of my Bristol schedule, Louise's return and Natalie being wrenched from my grasp. 'That's right. We had elevenses in Marlborough. Talking about the hills we still had to climb. For Toby's book. You said you thought they were all in England. Then we saw the box of maps. All of them northern Scotland and Western Isles.'

'Mike, we need to keep walking. Save the chat for later.'

'Hang on.' I slow down and rearrange the pieces in my mind. 'When you saw the maps, you said there was just one on the list for Scotland but it wasn't nearly that far north.'

'Mike, can we talk about this later.' And by the light of her torch I can see her moving away and walking ahead, twice as fast as before.

I catch up with her. 'Only we've not been to Scotland. Have we.' I turn to face her.

'No. No, we haven't.' She doesn't look at me.

'Then why wasn't it on your to-do list Steve gave me?'

'I ... I don't know. Perhaps he ... he ... I ... look, Mike, we'll talk later. Okay.'

I place my hand on her arm and force her to stop. 'You've done it, haven't you.'

'Done what?'

'The walk. The Scottish walk. Whatever it was. Climbed it. Bagged it. Crossed it off. Without telling me.'

'Mike, we need to keep going.' She tries to struggle free.

'You did it with Toby. Didn't you. And that's why you never told me.'

'I ... I can't ...'

'Yes or no?'

'Mike, stop it.'

'I'm stopping all right.' Again she tries to break free but I pull more tightly and she stops. Now I find myself gripping both of her arms.

'Mike, we've got to be back at four. We've still a bit to go.'

'Rachel can wait, this can't.'

'Mike, don't do this. You've bigger worries than that.'

'Yes or no?'

In the light of the torch I can see her turning towards me. Her face has lost its determination and focus and I can see submissiveness, trepidation, fear. 'I'm not going to lie to you, Mike.'

'What haven't you told me.'

'Where do I start,' she moans. 'Where the hell do I ... look, Mike, can we just get back and I'll tell you. I really will. Tell you everything later.'

I shake my head. 'Now.'

She steadies herself and sighs. 'Okay. This is what happened. I'm at work one day and I get this phone call. From Toby. He said he'd found out people thought he was dead. He told me he was coming straight home. I picked him up from the airport next day.'

236

'When?'

'Just after you moved to Bristol. Late June.'

*

I feel as though I've been hurled onto the roof of the Paris-Bordeaux express. 'No. Please God, Nat. Please.'

She looks at her watch and shines the torch on it. 'Look, we've got to get down there. We're going to be late. And once that snow starts ...'

I tighten my grip on her arms. The wind's now screeching and I can hear the rattle of the nearby wire fence. 'Go on.'

'When he'd got back and told me everything, Stella, all that, he asked me if I still wanted to go to Edinburgh. You know. The birthday weekend I told you about. At first I said no way. Told him he had a cheek to ask. I said I'd moved on, had a new bloke. He said, fine, but he was going to go anyway as he was going to bag that missing Scottish one. Ben Lawers it was called. And I told him that the publishers had asked me to take over the project because we all thought he was dead and he said, great, in that case let's do it together, we'll just go up as good mates. And that's what it was like. We went up, and ... and ... I'm sorry, Mike. I am so sorry ...'

Again she makes as if to move but I shake my head. 'Tell me.'

She puts her arms round me. 'We made a long weekend of it. Drove up there in my car, stayed the night in Edinburgh, separate rooms, went on to the mountains next morning, bagged Ben Lawers, back to Edinburgh, we had dinner together, then a few drinks to celebrate what we'd done, next thing we ... Mike, honestly, it was tearing me to pieces. I couldn't stop thinking about you, and how you'd feel, and it scared me, scared me that you'd ask how I'd managed to climb the missing Scottish peak, scared you'd find out everything, but I realised I couldn't stop loving Toby, and I ...' She grinds to a halt.

'So what happened when you came back? Did he go or did he stay? '

'He stayed, yes, he stayed. Not every night. He was away a lot, trying to find work. Which as you know he got. Yes, he stayed with me.'

'Lived, you mean. Man and wife. Come on, Natalie, just tell me the worst. I mean, what do you care, eh.'

'Mike, don't be like that.'

'Like that?' My train of grief and shock smashes head-on into a juggernaut of raw fury. 'You watched me. Watched the sheer joy wash over me when you came down to Bristol and we had that weekend together. Watched me melt with love whenever I set eyes on you. As good as told me you'd be there for me to help me love Katie. Told me you loved me. Taught me to

237

reach out for something better. The best days of my life. So much love. So much trust. And all the time, all that time, you were sharing your bed with Bear ruddy Grylls!'

'No. Not all the time.'

'You never stopped loving him, did you. Never stopped making love to him all those weeks. No wonder you'd changed so much when you came to see me. No wonder you'd become so confident that day we walked on Dartmoor. And there you were, happy to let me believe, that time I saw him, that he'd walked off the plane five minutes before.'

'I never said he had. You never asked.'

'You should have told me anyway. Told me as soon as he came back. Didn't you owe me that?'

'Mike, for God's sake.' Now she does manage to break free and starts to walk on down the hill towards the road.

I just stand there.

'Mike, come on, for goodness sake.'

'I'm going nowhere.'

'Don't be ridiculous.'

'Just go, please.'

The last traces of daylight have been sucked away but in the light of her torch, I can see her standing there, a fragile tree, stripped of its leaves, shaking and swaying in the wind.

'Mike, you're in shock,' she says. 'But the important thing right now is your safety. Getting you back to civilisation in one piece. Please.'

'And what if I don't want to go back?'

'What do you mean?'

'What if I just stay?'

'Mike, that's not an option.'

There's a sudden gust of wind which almost blows me off my feet.

'Who says. Who says it isn't an option.'

'Mike, you're scaring me.'

'Just go. Just leave me.' Flames are now playing all around my body, flames of anger, of hatred, of emptiness.

'You don't mean that.'

'I do mean it,' I tell her. 'I don't want you. I don't want you in my life any more. I want you to leave me. Just go, go to Canada, your new job, your child, whatever. Leave me.'

'Mike, you realise if I leave you now, you're on your own. You'll have to manage, get yourself home, on your own.'

'Suits me. I got out here on my own, didn't I.'

'I don't even know if you can get a signal round here.'

'Fine. In that case I'm carrying this around for nothing.' I take my phone from my pocket and hurl it into the darkness.

She shrieks. 'My God, Mike. What the hell did you do that for?'

'No reason.'

Now by the light of her torch I see her walking towards me. On her face I see a smile, not a smile of love, but a smile of desperation and fear and loneliness.

'Mike, I know you're devastated,' she says. 'I can't begin to think what's going on in your mind. But I just need you to understand. Yes, he came back sooner than I led you to believe. But put yourself in my position. If you can. I loved him, really loved him. He was everything to me. I told you, didn't I, if he walked back into my life, I'd forgive him anything. But no, I really honestly thought he was dead. I learned to love you. So what the hell am I supposed to do when he comes back into my life? I mean, what would you do?'

I just look at her.

'Relationships aren't like broken plates, Mike. You don't just chuck them in the bin, start again with another one and forget the contents of the bin. That's not how love works. I loved him. I loved you. I couldn't help it. There's no law that says you can't love two people at once. That's how it was for me. But it's different now. He's history, he isn't ever going to be part of my future.'

'Isn't he.'

Panic is now written on every last corner of her face. 'He's got a new partner, and even if he hadn't, he'd never have had me back unless I terminated which I'm not going to. He and I are through, Mike, and I may have loved him, and may still love him but it's love that's never going anywhere and … and … I'm not explaining this well, but … just … look, just come with me, we can go back with Rachel, we'll go to Cornwall and start again and walk together, along the cliffs, across the moors, anywhere, and talk together as much as we need and as long as we need and …'

'Shut up! Just shut up!'

'Mike.'

'Shut up and get out of my life. Leave me.'

'I can't leave you.'

'Yes, you can. It's my decision. My responsibility. Not yours. Go. Now.'

*

And then there's silence, broken only by another gust of wind which blows her jungle blonde hair across her tear-stained face.

Inch by inch she turns away from me and begins walking on down the hill towards the road. And through the groaning, grumbling north-easterly I hear her steady sobbing and watch the wavering of her torch, the last drop of light in a dark world that's darkening still.

*

It's dark. It's dark dark, black dark, dark black dark. It's not four o'clock, it's half past midnight and it's only the hands of my watch that don't seem to be aware. I remember something from our religious studies lessons at school about darkness that might be felt. The one that came after the plague of locusts, or was it the fire and hail or the flies and lice. It's not just a case of feeling the darkness. The darkness has smothered me and submerged me, and I look out, and there's nothing, nothing, nothing. As a child I once screamed our house down when a babysitter switched off the landing light by mistake and robbed me of that horizontal stick of yellow under my bedroom door. But the darkness then was the most iridescent explosion of luminosity compared with what I'm in the middle of now. I can't even make out shapes. I guess there are hills rising up on both sides of the path, but nobody could tell where they stop and the sky starts.

The wind seems to have eased and it isn't as cold. Then I feel little flecks of something brushing my hair and my arms, frozen insects with no eyes and flying without wings. I've no torch, and to begin with I can't make out if it's rain or snow but as the flecks begin to smash against my cheeks with ever increasing speed and intensity, I'm just waiting for someone to come and shove a carrot in the middle of my face and on the count of three there'll be Aled Jones walking in the air.

I just stand there.

I've a choice. I can lie down in a pool of peat, make myself reasonably comfortable, finish my bananas, wait to freeze over and then allow my lifeless body to be used as a human boardwalk, of some good at least to those coming after me. The alternative is to blunder on, hope I make it to the road, and flag down the next vehicle to go past. Which given the current conditions could be any time between Christmas Eve and the second Sunday after Pentecost.

I can't decide. So I keep standing there. After standing there for a few moments I decide to forge on. But I've not moved more than a couple of steps when I stumble against a piece of loose rock and crash to the ground. For a few minutes I can't move. Then I begin to feel stiff, and twinges of cramp assail my left calf, and the pains become more violent and I yell and curse and all the time I feel the fragments of wintry precipitation descending with greater ferocity across my nose and my lips.

If this is the fates' way of telling me this is where I succumb, I want to do so without agony. I'd like a slow, peaceful disappearance. But a disappearance into what. Into a world of harps and incense where Louise's bruise-free arms reach out to greet me and forgive all my sins and things left undone that it was just too much trouble to get done, forgive my not loving enough and giving enough, and wipe out all our hate and resentment and stupidity, or into a godless void that's wider and deeper and higher than the sum of all imaginings, as meaningless as life itself. Whichever it is, I just want it soon.

I manage to ease the rucksack off my back and reach inside for the remaining bananas. I demolish them in under a minute. That's the quick and easy bit. Then it starts to get longer and harder. The pains have eased but the stiffness is spreading and the cold is getting inside every last piece of protective fabric and as the invasion proceeds it's clear it won't be satisfied with anything short of unconditional surrender. I close my eyes as if hoping this will accelerate the process. I start to speculate. I try to anticipate the agony I'll have to suffer before I lose touch with reality, hoping the hope of the stupid that when it actually hits me I won't feel it at all, that instead I'll lapse into a hallucinatory state in which I'm receiving a foot massage from a mystic entity attired in waterproof crimson robes dotted with Velcro fasteners, zips, pockets and hoods, bearing more than a passing resemblance to Jodie Carteret …

'Michael.'

It's a man's voice.

Push off. Leave me to rot in peace.

'Michael.'

I open my eyes and I see a torch playing possibly fifty yards from me. In its light I can see a bright yellow jacket.

'Michael.'

I hate he knows my name. I don't want him to care. I don't want anyone to care. It's Natalie's doing, it must be Natalie's doing. She cares too much. Despite all I've said to her she won't let me just die and I hate her for it and I love her for it.

'Michael.'

Go away, please. Let this be my call, my own way to the exit doors. I crawl forward and make contact with what feels like a bush. It may afford camouflage, it may not. But as I crane my head round I can still see that torchlight, and it seems to be getting closer … .

'Michael.'

No more, please, no more.

'Daddy!'

A girl's voice.

I hadn't expected the hallucinations so soon. I certainly hadn't expected them to be so cruel.

'Daddy! Daddy!' Twice as loud.

No, please God. I shut my eyes and cover my ears.

'Daddy! Daddy!'

'Go away. Just go away.' The exasperation of an addled and crazed mind bursting into flames of hysteria.

'Over here.' The man's voice again.

I open my eyes and put my hands down. And in the torchlight I can see two figures. On the left, the torchbearer himself, a tall greying bearded man with glasses. And on the right …

'Daddy! My daddy!'

She's smiling and then she's laughing as she's never smiled and never laughed at me before and it's real, she's real, it's happening, it's my daughter, it's my Katie, and she's alive, alive, alive, alive, alive …

I jump to my feet and from nowhere I find I can run, I can jump, I can fly, and in a moment I'm enveloped in her arms.

'I thought you were dead, sweetheart. I thought I'd lost you. I read that you were dead. Killed with Paul in his car.' Now locked in embrace, we gaze into each other's eyes.

'I wasn't in Paul's car.'

'Who was it then? Who was killed?'

'Pamela,' she says. 'His daughter. He was taking her home to Hayling Island. He was coming back to fetch me after. Why did you think it was me?'

'The jacket. The red one, with the …'

'With the white dots. I grew out of it. Paul gave it to her.'

'So what are you doing here? How did you find me?'

It's now the bearded man who speaks.

'The newspaper article, of course. You in the photo with Jodie Carteret. Mentioned you'd be up here today. Nobody knew where you were. We tried your house, neighbour said you'd moved out for good. The thing in the paper was our only real hope. We'd planned to drive up today, got snowed in this morning, only made it a short while ago. We were about to give up. Assumed you'd come and gone. Then a woman came by, told us where you were.'

'And … who are you?'

'I'm Paul's dad.' He extends his hand to me. 'Eric Faraday.' Now he points the torch in the direction they've come. 'Come on. Time we were getting back. Try and beat the snow.'

We begin walking together, Katie and I hand in hand, Eric behind us lighting the way ahead. And in that yellow light I see the snowflakes, multiplying with each step we take, playing above her head, teasing and dancing and cavorting and lingering and in that moment she's Isabel, just as she was when she first came into the world, new, and perfect.

The moment gives way to harsh practicality, that of getting ourselves down to the road without injury, fearful that this night of enchantment might yet be ruined by a slip or slide or smash. They say the last part of the walk's the hardest. I read once that at the end of the day's tramp there's always a tendency to think you're a lot nearer the finish than you actually are. By the light of Eric's torch I can see what looks like a vehicle passing by on the road, and I guess it's probably only a hundred yards. If it were a golf hole I doubt Tiger in his prime would need to swing his wedge back more than six inches to propel the ball to the flag. But now it seems as though it should need two full blasts with a driver. The accumulation of snow, an ever-thickening Axminster, conceals the loose stones and rocks and puddles which form mini cascades and rivulets as they're crunched under the weight of my boots. Perhaps it's my sojourn beneath the bush, but I still feel unsteady and keep stumbling and it's Katie, in her pink wellies, who has to steady her dad. Eric's torchlight doesn't always provide the best indicator of what lurks on the ground beneath, but it's the only light we've got. There's apprehension in my steps, and there's fear too in my heart, fear that I may be all this perfect little girl has got and that may still be nowhere near enough; that the answer to her emotional needs, needs springing from not one, not two, but now three such destructive relationships, may be a million miles beyond my capacity to provide. So many questions, so many doubts, and I feel a spasm of fear in my heart for the cold reality that's poised to descend on me once this honeymoon period is past.

At last we negotiate the fence at the bottom of the path and we hit the road, that precious strip of metal, itself now being submerged by winter's latest leg-spinner. I'm back where Fraser left me and there's a car, just where Fraser was parked.

We walk towards the car and the torch is shining straight onto the bonnet, separated from me by a constant, incessant swirl of fresh, new, frolicking snowflakes. Katie lets go of my hand to brush the snow from her face and tighten her gloves. And in that moment there's a mighty, furious gust of wind, a gust which seems to have sprung from nowhere, a freak shot of Arctic air amidst the whirlings and groanings of the north-easterlies. It causes me to stumble on the slippery surface and I'm swept off my feet. A moment later, I'm sprawled across the snow-covered ground.

I'm not hurt but I'm shaken and I'm shaking. I need to get up and not risk destroying myself, now that I've a future just a short walk and car journey away. I put my hand out and it's met by another hand.

But as I look up, just like on that Norfolk station platform what seems like a century ago, it's not my daughter.

For a moment I'm mesmerised, I'm overwhelmed, my body a sculpture of stone. Then my eyes fill with tears and I'm kissing her frozen lips and gazing into her lime green eyes and brushing the little globes of ice from her jungle blonde hair.

EPILOGUE

Towthorpe(n) – On nearing the end of a hot tiring day's walk and seeing a sign giving the number of miles separating you from your destination, wishing that you'd been kept in blissful ignorance

We've left the best walk till last, our fourth of this weekend. At Natalie's suggestion we climbed up to Halnaker Windmill yesterday morning, and after a pub lunch in Halnaker village Katie requested we went up onto the Trundle, although I think she just likes the name. It's hard to tell which of these two summits provides the best view to Chichester Cathedral, Chichester Harbour, Portsmouth with its Spinnaker Tower, and the Isle of Wight. On exceptionally clear days you can see the Seven Sisters, some fifty miles away, from the Trundle, but you can't from Halnaker, so I suppose that gives the Trundle the edge. I love them both: firm clear paths, minimal pain, maximum reward. They're good for Natalie too. She's seven months gone now, but the walks are still manageable for her. She just has to take things that more slowly. Then this morning we strolled on the beach at Selsey, the southernmost point of Sussex, hurling pebbles into the sea, playing hide and seek with the incoming tide and sipping hot chocolate from a beach-side burger van. Its owner's an opportunistic Pole who told us the only English he knew on coming to Sussex was "Thank you" and "I love you." What else do you need. We've come home and Natalie's cooked us roast beef and Yorkshire pud while I've produced a more successful than feared apple crumble and custard. Too much exercise after a heavy meal isn't the best idea so we've decided upon a stroll along the Centurion Way for our final exercise of the day. It's part of a stretch of disused railway just north of Chichester which has been converted into a footpath. It offers a mixture of woodland and open walking, and the open sections provide views towards the South Downs and the nearby nature reserve. Straddling the path's surface is thick grass carpeted with riots of cow parsley around which skulk buttercups and bluebells. It's been a mild winter on the whole, and everything's early this year. Each hawthorn bush sports milky white flowers and throws its own delicate fragrance across the path, daring its neighbour to provide a better one. As we enter an area of woodland the rays of the early May sunshine cut through the branches of the horse chestnuts, their young rich green leaves complemented by pillars of elegant purple blossom. I've always been wary of woodland walking because the trees deprive you of landmarks but our path is straight and well signed and only a genius would get lost. Its surface is so smooth you can walk it in Converses, as we have been, and as it's an old railway there's a sense of walking on history and connecting with our past. I think that part's rather been lost on Katie, who's been yanking bluebells and daisies from the ground as though they're the last ones left on the planet. For her school science project she says. Then she owns up that she's just joking and presents me with a bouquet and gives me a kiss and I ask myself, how in God's name could I ever not have loved her.

Natalie and I have walked arm in arm, Natalie every so often running a protective hand over her bump and me at last remembering, having gone blank this morning, the manner of the Gunners' FA Cup exit in 1963. The Nerdalympics are less than a month away and Natalie's told me under no circumstances am I to let that berk win again. No prisoners are to be taken. And I've been thinking ahead to my chat with the building society tomorrow. Things are looking up on the financial side: I'm getting more consultancy work than I did, and I'm now taking on court and police station duty rota cases. On top of that, the walking book I completed for Toby appears this month and when it does I'll be paid a fairly generous advance. But the building society still need a longer-term plan and with some help from Natalie I think I have one. It's that kind of walk, where every problem which seemed insuperable at the start seems manageable by the end of it. I remember a guy I went to uni with saying that nobody ever comes back from a long walk a worse person than he was before he went. At the time I thought he was either drunk or on something illegal and dangerous. But maybe he'd just walked the Centurion Way on the second Sunday in May.

It's not far from the end of the Centurion Way to our house and I open a four-pack of egg custards which we gorge in front of the Sky footie. It's the only sport I've watched this weekend so the girls don't begrudge it. After it's over Natalie and I hang out the washing and she helps me dismantle a curtain which Katie has somehow managed to decorate with a mixture of Morrisons mayonnaise and Lidl tomato ketchup. Then Natalie sits down and I bring her the material I've prepared for the chapter on charity walking in Steve's new book. I've asked if she'll read it over for me. I've checked it and double-checked it but she still finds six typos and three grammatical howlers in the first dozen lines. Then while Katie stays in the front room Natalie and I open a bottle of Liebfraumilch and sit on the patio and drink to families and happiness and love.

We finish our second glass each and Natalie looks at her watch and says she wants an early night as she's got to get up at three thirty for the taxi to the airport.

I kiss Natalie goodnight and come downstairs. My phone bleeps and it's a text from Gavin inviting me to go walking with him one weekend in July and I tell him I'll have to talk to Katie first. Then I go into the kitchen and there's at least nine meals' worth of washing and wiping to do and it's too much trouble to even put the pans in soak. But it'll get done. Before, it was never going to get done.

Katie doesn't like talking about the before so we don't. I'm no nearer finding the truth about Paul. Maybe I will one day but for now Katie's wishes and feelings must come first. She's settled back at her old school better than her teachers thought possible and to mess with her head again would be unthinkable and unforgivable. There's stuff I have managed to do. I've gone to see where Louise's ashes are laid to rest and I've put out one or two feelers about the circumstances of her death but I've been given no evidence to suggest they were suspicious. My initial enquiries of the coroner's office and the police have drawn a complete blank. But then again Paul was a clever man. Eric's not been a lot of help and I've still no idea how much he knows. He took it upon himself to clear out his son's house in Nottinghamshire, which I've still never seen nor want to see now, and came down not long after Christmas with the rest of Louise's effects. Most of them ended up at the charity shop. Not the stilettos of course – Katie just can't wait till her feet are big enough – nor the important things like the framed picture of Isabel and the photo albums. But we don't need all her old clothes and books to remind us of those pre-isn't days. I still have the orange jug and I've reprinted that picture off my phone. I had it enlarged and it's in a frame all by itself. It sits next to Isabel. Each night I look at them both and allow myself a few tears. Sometimes more than a few. I'd never cried for Isabel before, not after the first few days anyway, when Louise was alive. Now I do. I just hope Katie hasn't seen.

I'm looking at the pictures now. Katie comes up and looks at them with me and I put my arms round her and for the twentieth time that day I tell her I love her and she tells me she loves me. 'Bedtime, sweetheart. School tomorrow.'

'Can we just play the new game?'

The new game. I think back to Louise's full-blooded enthusiasm for the new game, whether it was a home-made one or charity shop one or car boot sale one or birthday or Christmas one. She, the games MA. Me, still swotting for my games GCSE's. But the point is, I am swotting. Showing my love by swotting. Gavin was right. To love is to give, really give, and to love that act of giving, and to love what comes back.

Katie doesn't wait for an answer. She takes me by the hand and leads me into the front room and sits me down. On the floor is a large piece of stiff paper on which are drawn circles, squares and triangles, some with numbers in, some with letters in, some without anything in, and on top a quantity of fake banknotes and coins, a collection of miniature houses and toy cars dating back to the 1970's, a variety of counters and pieces of card, and silver balls which have been recycled from a bagatelle set mum gave us when she and dad moved north. We go through the object of the game and the rules. You start off with two silver balls and two pieces of card, which can be of any colour except blue. The idea is to work our way round the board with the aid of the circles, squares and triangles, and to end up with a house and a car and a job while still having at least some money to spend … It makes Katie's previous offering, the one I saw at Paul's house just before she and Louise did their disappearing act, a model of simplicity. But the level of complexity of this new creation is matched by the love that has gone into creating it, the joy of unveiling it, and the delicious anticipation of the fun and laughter of trying it out.

Katie turns to me and kisses my cheek and smiles. 'Looks like a great game, Daddy. How long did it take you to make it?'

THE END